THE NINE MODERN DAY MUSES (AND A BODYGUARD) 10 GUIDES TO CREATIVE INSPIRATION

THIRD EDITION
(LOTS OF NEW GOODIES)

BY JILL BADONSKY

THE NINE
MODERN DAY MUSES
(and a Bodyguard)

THIRD EDITION
ADDED SECTIONS FOR NEW APPLICATIONS:
CREATIVE AGELESSNESS
CURES FOR PERFECTIONISM
MARKETING YOUR BUSINESS WITH MUSE WISDOM
AND
YOGA AND CREATIVITY

JILL BADONSKY
MUSE CHANNELER

RENEGADE MUSES PUBLISHING HOUSE
SAN DIEGO, CALIFORNIA

Renegade Muses Publishing House, San Diego, California.

Illustrations and Cover Design by Jill Baldwin Badonsky
Book layout design by Paula Verdu

Grateful acknowledgment is made for permission to reprint the following:
An excerpt from STAND STILL LIKE THE HUMMINGBIRD, copyright © 1962 by Henry
Miller. Reprinted by permission of New Directions Publishing Corp.

An excerpt from A RETURN TO LOVE by Marianne Williamson, copyright © 1992 by
Marianne Williamson. Reprinted by permission of HarperCollins Publishers Inc.

JUST DO IT™ is a registered trademark of Nike

LIBRARY OF CONGRESS CATALOGING-IN-PUBLICATION DATA
Badonsky, Jill Baldwin.
The nine modern day muses (and a bodyguard) : 10 guides to creative inspiration for artists,
writers, lovers, and other mortals wanting to live a dazzling existence / Jill Baldwin Badonsky.
p.   cm.

ISBN-978-0-615-31484-6
PCN 200101345

1. Creative ability. 2. Self-actualization (Psychology). I. Title.
BF411 .B27 2003
153.3'5—dc21   2002027159

Printed in the United States of America.

Dedicated to
My Mom
My very first Muse

When you are convinced
that all the exits are blocked,
either you take to believing in miracles
or you stand still like the hummingbird.

The miracle is that the honey is always there,
right under your nose,
only you were too busy searching
elsewhere to realize it.

The worst is not death but being blind,
blind to the fact that everything
about life is in the nature of the miraculous.
—Henry Miller, novelist

CONTENTS
PREFACE: ix

PART ONE:
STUFF IN THE FRONT

The Emergence of the Modern Day Muses...15
Welcome to the Mystery...19
The Mystery of Creativity...21
Entering the Garden of the Illustrious Muses...23
Muse Map...24
Pretrip Preparations to Make the Journey a Little Richer...25
How to Propel Forward by Using the Truth of Your Dream...29
Equipment Assembly for the Journey...33
A Muse Primer...37

PART TWO:
THE ILLUSTRIOUS GARDEN OF THE AMAZING MUSES
(and a bodyguard)

Arnold: The Bodyguard...47
Aha-phrodite: Muse of Paying Attention, Passion, and Possibilities...61
Albert: Muse of Imagination and Innovation...75
Bea Silly: Muse of Play, Laughter, and Dance...99
Muse Song: Muse of Nurturing, Encouragement, and Good Company...119
Spills: Muse of Practice, Process, and Imperfection...139
Audacity: Muse of Courage and Uninhibited Uniqueness...157
Lull: Muse of Pause, Diversion, and Gratitude...173
Shadow: Muse of the Dark Side...191
Marge: Muse of Okay-Now-Let's-Get-Started...207
What Muse Are You?...225

PART THREE:

Stuff in the Back...229
New Applications for the Modern Day Muses...233
Creative Agelessness...235
Cures for Perfectionism...245
Marketing Inspiration for the Muses...249
Yoga and Creativity...253

BIBLIOGRAPHY

ACKNOWLEDGEMENTS

Thanks to Randy Herman, Paula Verdu, Chris Dunmire, Mambo and Sappho, Rae Warde, Janet Whitehead, Reba Spencer, Jacob Glass, Ron Kofron, all Kaizen-Muse Creativity Coaches and Modern Day Muse Facilitators, the readers of The monthly Muse Flash, wherever that Spirit of Creativity comes from, and all of the people who understand my weird sense of humor.

PREFACE

The age of miracles is here.
—Thomas Carlyle, Scottish essayist, historian

 ## ANOTHER FINE MYTH

On a warm, still day in the reverie of a café near the ocean, I sat sipping a latte as the bougainvillea felt inspired to throw purple petals on my writing notebook. I was recuperating from a job chosen by my fears, not my heart. Once again, I had ignored my creative passions due to something silly...like security. (phhhffff!)

Recently, I had started paying attention to my odd reactions to the jobs that led me away from the genuine creative expression I believe I was meant to share during my stay on the planet. When I take a job simply for financial security and disregard the skills that bring me joy—writing, teaching, art, or performance—I basically become a complete moron. I become incapable of anything but a series of blunders. It is as if I intentionally sabotage myself so that I can't work in such situations. I think this is the message: I'M SUPPOSED TO BE USING MY CREATIVE TALENTS ...(pronounce capped words in a loud voice, thank you).

My last job took me so far off my path of creative expression (into, of all things, middle management, ahhhhh!) that the spell of stupidity I fell under made the need for public flogging the only acceptable outcome I was creating. I was constantly losing little things—like entire mailing lists, keys, and paychecks. I would regularly trip over furniture, computer equipment, and the occasional client. My shoulder pads would end up on the outside of my dress by the day's end (it was the early 90s so, yeah, shoulder pads)... a sure sign one is in the wrong place. Obviously, I was not really there...mentally, spiritually or effectively. I was a blockhead masquerading so as to fit into a round slot.

Reaching my threshold of humiliation, I finally took the leap out of the job, without any support waiting for me (at least in the form that I had been accustomed to), and looked up into the fluff of the clouds and asked, "HELLO?...JUST WHAT IS IT THAT I'M SUPPOSED TO DO?...I KNOW IT HAS SOMETHING TO DO WITH CREATIVITY, BUT COULD YOU GET A LITTLE MORE SPECIFIC?" I could use a miracle at that point. I knew what was next had to be something creative because my soul was pestering me regularly to release my inner creative-related rumbles. What I soon found out was that all sorts of people seem to be experiencing just about the same thing. Maybe you're one of them. While musing about what truly motivated me, I realized that it was my twentieth anniversary of being a creative junkie. I was obsessed with the creative process and had applied this obsession to writing and performing plays, writing columns, telling stories with multimedia, painting mixed media, drawing cartoons, joining an improvisational comedy troupe, developing marketing plans across the country in a one of a kind way, public speaking in unpredictably irreverent ways. I was deepening my passion for teaching and coaching people on how to find and follow their creative passion mainly because I believed it could be done in a way that inspires people despite their human tendencies. "I think it's time to write a book," I thought. "If only I could get over the resistance to starting, the fear that it will be no good, the possibility that there are already enough books on the subject, the responsibility it implies, and the feeling that I do not know what I am doing (i.e., if only I could use what I am teaching)."

I looked up from my latte's snowy foam to see nine Muses sidling up to my table with expressions of suppressed laughter, and the kind of raised eyebrows that foretell impending surprise. These Muses, however, were not of ancient Greece. They were a new and improved, updated variety—colorful, hip, full of chutzpah—and they had a Bodyguard with them. They pulled chairs up to my table and stared directly into my bewilderment. Well, eight of them did. One of them refused to sit because she was inventing a new mambo.

Another one, who introduced herself as Aha-phrodite, seemed to be the spokes-muse. She informed me that it was time for the mortal public to learn about the Modern Day Muses. "It is especially important now," she explained, "when so many mortals are unfulfilled because they have abandoned the expression of their creative gifts and inclinations and gotten stuck into places of unfulfilling routine." So, a more relevant and savvy breed of Muses was now required to meet the challenge of inspiring ideas, follow-through, and fulfillment for these misguided modern mortals. And here they were...in all their glory, at my table in the sun.

They introduced themselves one at a time: Aha-phrodite, Muse of Paying Attention and Possibilities; Albert, Muse of Imagination and New Thinking; Bea Silly, Muse of Childlike Play; Spills the Imp, Muse of Practice, Process, and Imperfection; Audacity, Muse of Courage and Uninhibited Uniqueness; Lull, Muse of Pause, Diversion, and Gratitude; Shadow, Muse of the Gifts of the Dark Side; Muse Song, Muse of Encouragement, Nurturing, and Good Company; Marge, Muse of Okay-Now-Let's-Just-Get-Started; and the Bodyguard, who protects us from blocks, fears, and abandonment. (I called the Bodyguard, Arnold in the first and second issue, but now you get to conjure up your own bodyguard image).

I admit, I was bemused by their presence and a little afraid they would want me to buy them all coffee and bagels. Existing on savings and newly developing freelance work (since the allure of working for someone else was beyond resuscitation), I was a bit prudent with expenditures. Marge, the Muse of Okay-Now-Let's-Just-Get-Started, assured me that, yes, indeed, they did want coffee, but to worry about income when an experience of such flow and fascination was about to be unveiled was just plain silly. The Muses were here to inspire a book that would not only introduce them to the masses of individuals interested in giving voice to the soul's creative authenticity, but would also provide practical exercises to make these concepts absorbable and effective. So I bought them all double mocha cappuccinos and a variety of scones. Except for Bea Silly—she wanted a cupcake with a small rotating flowerpot on top. Do they make those yet?

THE REALITY

All nine new Muses were there...in the spirit of my imagination. I started toying with the idea of turning creative concepts into personas of Muses just for the fun of it, or perhaps because I was spending too much time alone. Anyway, I was telling one of my friends, Jennifer, about the Muses and she got excited. She was in the middle of creating her own business and was tickled by how my Muses could help her. Coming up against an obstacle or a stumbling block, she would call me up and ask me which Muse could help:

"Who will help me create a clever price sheet to display my services?" I told her about Albert. "Who will get me to a place where I don't fear what people think when I make public presentations?" Audacity fit the bill. "Who will help focus me when I seem to do everything except the thing I'm supposed to do?" That would be Marge. "I'm not enjoying doing my work right now." Bea Silly and Lull then helped her out. "How do I deal with these voices inside my head that are ridiculing me and trying to sabotage everything I'm doing?" Muse Song would soothe the savage voices, and the Bodyguard would defend and reinforce her moves forward.

Jennifer would call me back, enthusiastic from success, talking about the Muses as if I had dispatched them to her home like doctors making house calls. The Muses, of course, were only concepts to ignite her own strengths. They just made it clear what energy she could draw upon from *inside herself.* And pretending that they were actual entities made it fun and enticing when leads to motivation. Fun and play are what we engage in as children to lure us to the experiences that successfully serve us as adults. Hello! Let's get wise and use fun as adults to make the validating human experience of creativity more accessible.

Creativity gives us the optimal experience of what Mihaly Csikzentimihalyi has described as a state in which creative energy flows freely and effortlessly. He writes, "The process of discovery involved in creating something new appears to be one of the most enjoyable activities any human can be involved in." He explains that creativity is a central source of meaning in our lives. We bring something new, needed, or novel into existence and experience in the process a timeless flowing, a release from stress and of peak experiences.

Abraham Maslow describes self-actualization as a person's need to be, and do, that which the person was "born to do." When we feel something missing in our life, many times it is because we are not expressing that which we were born to share.

My mission in life is to deepen my own creativity and teach others to do the same. When I discover something that works, I have such an urgency to let others know what it is in an irreverent, entertaining and inspiring fashion, that I cannot dispute that I'm am supposed to be doing this. It's my passion. I'd do it for free if I could live off of oxygen alone.

If there is something that can make creativity fun and easier, hey, I'm for it! The Muses say this book will help.

you
are
here

My Toast To You...
"Here's To The Unfolding of Your Brilliance!"

THE NINE
MODERN DAY MUSES
(and a Bodyguard)

PART ONE

STUFF IN THE FRONT

It is as if the Milky Way entered upon some cosmic dance.
—Sir Charles Scott Sherrington,
author of The Integrative Action of the Nervous System

Each one of us has a fire in our heart for something.
It's our goal in life to find it and to keep it lit.
—Mary Lou Retton, Olympic gymnast

THE EMERGENCE OF THE MODERN DAY MUSES

THE EMERGENCE OF THE MODERN DAY MUSES

Artist (n.)—Someone who chooses to share the call of their soul through the expression of artistic passions, the selection of thoughts that create joy, and the activation of authentic approaches to living life. Someone who is not afraid to be his or her true self with others.
~Muse-kipedia

French Riviera, two in the afternoon. The nine Greek Muses, once beacons of creative inspiration, were lolling in the sun getting fat from pear tarts and chocolate éclairs. They sipped on the concoction of champagne and Tang they had invented that morning.

They invent things like that almost every day. They are, after all, a creative bunch, so why not? They are the Muses. The mythical girls from ancient Greece with the ability to inspire song, art, verse, and...spanakopita. They give the i's dots. Yes, the i's of every i-dea... they provide inspiration, intuition, innovation, ingenuity, intrigue, interesting, invaluable qualities of waxing authentic, extraordinary, and other applicable i words that I may have forgotten like...maybe: incredible. They entice possibility. They tango with the peculiar, dangle with participles, and dare mortals to "climb every mountain and follow every star," to "carry moonbeams home in a jar."

Those Muses ...

They were in the middle of an extended sabbatical on the French Riviera, a rest place away from the think-tank towers of Mount Olympus. They were on an off-ramp from the inspiration-operated superhighway of creative vibes that rides into the magic kingdom of the mortal mind. They were removed from their duty to engage the mortal mind in one of the top five most enjoyable pursuits of the short human life...creativity (in league with other favorites such as romance, altruism, eating, and line dancing).

Okay, to tell you the truth, it really wasn't an extended vacation...let's get rid of the euphemistic cover-up. They were laid off in the Mount Olympus downsizing that happened May of last year. A survey taken by Hercules indicated that demand for their services had been in a critical decline since the invention of TV, the advent of the Internet, and the amplification of the mortals' preoccupation with other various addictions: swerving intentions, deliberate avoidance, Gummi Bears, hallucinogenics, numbing agents of the rich and famous, street drugs of the roaming desperate, anesthetic indulgences of talking endlessly about nothing, Wild Turkey shooters, withdrawal from pursuits of passion, denial, denial of denial, persecutory delusions, immobilized good intentions, frozen interventions, abandoned renovations, Tootsie Pops, free-floating anxiety, enigmatic pain in the fifth vertebra, incessant cleaning of kitchen counters, allergies to wheat, dairy, and tabby cats, and a hypnotic trance toward reality TV and social networking traps. And, to top it all off, modern mortals want things to be quick and easy. Creativity is a divinely installed feature of ever new joy, but it simply cannot be categorized as "quick and easy."

The Muses were actually getting tired of the French Riviera and were ready to get back to what they loved the best...inspiring mortals to blessed creative expressions of innovative solutions and delectable realities. The heck with the layoff—being the resourceful beings they were, the Muses knew they could get their posts back. They were just taking a necessary creative lull, enjoying a pastry binge, and relishing the opportunity to appreciate the quality of the light in Provence. But things would have to be different.

So they discussed their reemergence over papaya smoothies. And as their conversation progressed, the Muses became a little unsettled. The fact was, mortals had become just plain hard to reach; they were distracted, overwhelmed, and had difficulty focusing. Many were not even listening. They were giving bad excuses about why they were not engaging in the spirited acts of creativity.

Yet the Muses were eager and unfettered, mostly being the love the word, "unfettered." The Muses love nothing better than to solve creatively an unsettling, perplexing, and fetter-prone problem. And this was a big one. So they began by reviewing the facts. You see, every mortal is given the ability to dance with the Universal Spirit of Creative Expression. Every mortal. Every, every, every mortal, even the ones who whine, "Who me?...Oh, no, no...I'm not creative in the least bit." EVERYONE IS CREATIVE. The thoughts we think create the feelings we feel which create the actions we take. We have a choice. The palette of thoughts is filled with a gigantic selection of perspectives, attitudes, and angles. We create lists, plans, gardens, events, children, drama, healing. We create strategies, conspiracies, responses, vacations, solutions, and sauces for asparagus.

Every mortal has some way to be a creative beacon—a lightbulb for the circuitry of the soul. Whether it be to make luscious variations of portobello spaghetti sauce, to write a ditty about falling stars for the girl at the wi-fi cafe, to invent a fugue in D, a duet in E, and a ballad in Biloxi, to dance wild new steps to silly old songs, to smile radiantly from the heart, or to create awe in the studio audience of the mind, of life, of the effervescent magic of the soul—every mortal has a creative light just waiting to shine brighter. To be creative is, yes, to do art. It has also been identified as one of the top qualities of an effective manager and the edge a successful entrepreneur has on competitors. It is an inner beauty that radiates on the outside no matter what age you are. Creative expression is the beacon your soul mate will detect to find you. It is the key to relationships that flourish, and the means through which parenting becomes joyous. It is the tool that takes a mundane reality and makes it extraordinary. Creative problem solving is the answer to life's most challenging dilemmas. If you choose to be creative, life is a fulfilling journey where wonder awaits every twist of thought and turn of attitude.

All mortals have at their fingertips the great joy that comes from the delight in what they create. They have the colossal kick of a time-defying flow of present-moment bliss, the kind that comes when they engage...in creating.

But they watch TV instead. So...

Those Muses came up with a variety of ideas to redirect mortals to their magnificence. Their favorite was to reinvent themselves as Modern Day Muse Equivalents. Yes! That's it. They would become updated, savvy Muses geared to combat the modern mortals' hardcore avoidance strategies. They would drop their old names, domains, and constraints and invent new ones. As they mused at their moxie, the Muses contemplated the big human truth: MORTALS MUST DO WHAT THEY ARE HERE TO CREATIVELY DO OR THEY WILL BECOME CRANKY.

The Muses decided this makeover would have to happen in order to stamp out irritability, surliness, and most of all, lost potential. So they did reinvent themselves.

Now, they are ever so eager to reveal the newly concocted modern secrets of creative inspiration. They especially want to share the new creative blockbusters: the bypasses to the grandeur of the mind, in concert with the heart, emerging through the hands and touching every soul that stands close. Dare to venture further; "you were only waiting for this moment to arrive."

My name is Jill. I channel Muses. For the last eleven years I have faithfully tuned in to the six o'clock Muse report bandwidth and frequency line. I have frantically taken down the daily Muse flashes. I have condensed the best parts into this book so I can share with you all the "Muse fit to print." There was a lot of undecipherable chatter, hysterical laughter, and mumbled musings that I didn't include, but I have notes if you want to see them.

So let's begin. Let's excavate our dreams.

Sarah Ban Breathnach, author of Simple Abundance, says, "If we're unsure of our passions, we must continue excavating until we rediscover them, for if we don't find outward expression to our passions in little ways every day, we will eventually experience the spontaneous combustion of our souls."

And this can be very, very messy. I wouldn't know where to start cleaning up a combusted soul, would you?

"Got five minutes?
Start an Idea!"

WELCOME TO THE MYSTERY

JUST SAY YES TO THE WORLD INSIDE OF AN IDEA.
—AHA-PHRODITE, MUSE

The Muses announced that in their new, updated, modern forms they would be hanging out in a metaphor. Since they are somewhat metaphorical themselves, we shouldn't be expecting to see them at Starbucks or Denny's. They chose the metaphor of a garden, specifically, the Amazing Garden of the Illustrious Muses. (Obviously, they feel very good about themselves - something mortals also need for creative success.) Come on in!

To get into a metaphor you must open your mind a bit and don a childlike awareness with a twist of imagination. Walk down your garden's path in a spirit of exploration and wonder. Pay attention to the experience beyond the intellect—the one within your spirit. Listen to the reawakening of an enchanting loom of the possible. Surrender to the deep knowing of your heart. Seize the miracle of your dream. And weave the tapestry of your experience with passion and authenticity.

Follow your heart by complying with the signposts of your intuition. Intuition will amplify your courage, as Joseph Campbell says, "to leave behind the life you planned, in order to find the life that is awaiting you." As you walk down the garden's path, a Spirit, whose only purpose it is to lift you beyond your limitations to the dreams that await you, will guide you. Feel the charge of Spirit's optimism, compassion, and faith in you. Now be ready to experience the reverie and awe that comes from entering the realm of a mysterious process. And begin to simply trust. Trust.

Trust the process of the subtle push toward art and creative expression from inside you—it is the gentle call of your heart and renewed search for soul.
~Donald William Mathews, author of Beginning the Way of the Arts

THE
MYSTERY
OF
CREATIVITY

THE MYSTERY
OF CREATIVITY

The most beautiful experience we can have is the mysterious: It is the fundamental emotion which stands at the cradle of true art and true science. He to whom this emotion is a stranger, who can no longer pause to wonder and stand rapt in awe, is as good as dead: His eyes are closed.
—Albert Einstein, Swiss-German-American physicist

Creativity is a puzzle and a paradox. Artists, writers, scientists, rarely know how their original ideas arise so there may never be a scientific theory of creativity. The apparent unpredictability of creativity defies any scientific explanation or prescribed formula. Divine inspiration? Romantic intuition? Innovative insight? The Muses explain that because creativity arises from the spirit, the mind may not have the comprehension or even the words to explain where it arises. Ideas arise beyond the intellect, through intuition's dosey-doh with the subconscious.

Therefore we must look to the heart and the soul for our spring of creation. How do we do that?

*The world of reality has limits;
the world of the imagination is boundless.*
—Jean-Jacques Rousseau, French philosopher, author

First we must give ourselves permission to go beyond our fears. Some of us miss out on a life of creative joy because we blindly listen to our fears and live a life based on their illusion. We fear inadequacy, we fear we will lose people or gain responsibility. We fear giving up comfortable routines, wasting time and resources, looking foolish. Money worries prevent us from pursuing that which does not ensure an income. We fear giving up a lifestyle filled with material objects for a life filled with creative expression, authenticity, and pure joy. Starting the creative process is hard work with no guarantees that we will succeed in the classic sense of financial success or artistic masterpieces. Attachment to the way things need to be is rarely is ever a winning formula.

How come such a process of joy brings up so many fears? The answer could be because creativity is the ultimate growth process; fear can be simply an affirmation that growth is happening. When we are unattached to the results of our creative journey, we can move through the fear and find rewards greater than the purpose that initially drew us to the journey. We may think we want to write a book or act or sing, but what we find if we stay on the path is a deeper experience of how to live life and love ourselves. The skills we obtain by saying yes to the creative process are skills we can use in all areas of our lives: flexibility, intuition, risk-taking, confidence, playfulness, open-mindedness, resourcefulness, acceptance, to name only a few. But these skills will only come with patience, willingness, and participation in the process despite the insecurities and fears that will arise. So embracing these higher qualities of humankind—patience, perseverance, compassion, acceptance—grant us the reward of living the deepest possible experience of life. Those willing to live life deeply will embark on the journey. You other people can stop reading here.

If we want to grow past our insecurities and into our magnificence, the creative experience is just what our soul ordered. Overcoming each obstacle of creativity gifts us with a little more depth of living. This is a guarantee. Plus, something inside the preciousness of our being steadfastly lures us to our creative expression. To discard it only leaves us feeling unsettled. That inner knowing has its reasons for alerting us:

- We were born with an affinity toward a particular creative talent that allows us to share with others something unique about ourselves.

- We have something that is uniquely our own to say, depict, or demonstrate, and thus we contribute variation, interest, and new dimension to the world.

- There is an audience for our art, no matter what form it takes. Finding what channel of expression is uniquely ours, gives us creative flow and flight, if we do not compare ourselves with what and how others have chosen to express themselves. If we are working with who we truly are in our own way, comparison becomes unimportant.

- The process of creativity produces optimal conditions for being alive. As we create, our minds and bodies are their most energetic, stay vital, and even heal.

- Our self-esteem rises, our confidence deepens, our coping skills are strengthened, and life becomes easier and more enjoyable.

- Creativity is a spiritual outlet, and while being creative we can feel the divine working through us. We impart to the world our deepest gifts.

Creativity Tip:
"Turn off the phone during your sacred creative time."

ENTERING THE GARDEN
OF
THE ILLUSTRIOUS MUSES

Enter the Garden and pass a still and peaceful pool. Take a moment to gaze into its waters to see your reflection. Although it is a mystery, there are conditions that make creativity more attainable. Let your reflection register this knowledge with a brightened confidence. Light shines through you, making the reflection possible.

This is your first faith-filled step in the process: simply wearing an expression of confidence. Start as small as this one expression. Validate your optimism with an indisputable countenance indicating that you have faith in the weaving of your life's dreams. Each tiny step like this one leads to another, and another and another, and the gradual accumulating result will astound you. You may think you need a grand vision with great sweeps of action. But you simply need lots of little, little, little acts true to your intention. As long as you stay on your path without straying due to fear, all you need to do is take tiny steps and have patience. Those who veer off their path because the risk seems too much find themselves in unfulfilling jobs and unsatisfactory ways of living. They are not being true to themselves. They are probably not someone with whom you would want to take a long road trip.

Are you being true to yourself? If not, this is a good time to start. As you meet the Muses, translate their purposes to best meet your needs. They are eliciting your own energy, so design them to serve your own uniquely divine splendor.

> To live with an open heart means that pain is no stranger,
> but wonder will be a constant companion.
> —David Oldfield

Creativity is something we can carry with us all our lives. And as we do, it breathes mirth, play, and intoxicating discovery into the everyday possibilities of our malleable existences. It makes a connection to others that is all about the extraordinary. Many people go through life with their music still inside them. This is your chance to let your soul sing.

PRETRIP PREPARATIONS TO MAKE THE JOURNEY A LITTLE RICHER

If you fear that your creativity has been buried under all of the day-to-day responsibilities or completely lost, be assured that you can rediscover your creative potential. Increasing your creativity is truly possible.
Whatever your current creative experience is, you can achieve far more than you ever dreamed or imagined.
—Beth Flynn, leader of Knock Your Socks Off Creativity

YOUR CREATIVE PASSION

Preconceived ideas about what it takes to be creative can be a hindrance to expanding our creativity. No matter what our creative experience has been, we have the ability to bring into existence greater dreams than we can imagine. Living life creatively does not necessarily mean we write, paint, draw, compose symphonies, invent contraptions, or the like. On this journey, our creative passion refers either to our chosen artistic outlet or to our desire to live our life artfully. The second case can mean that we wish to be a vehicle of creative expression. We want to live life authentically, being ourselves without effort, and using our predestined talents in whatever way makes sense to us as individuals. Additionally, we may have a talent that we have not yet tapped that is waiting to be discovered. Imagine that. Oh, boy, oh, boy.

We create our existence by the thoughts we choose… QUESTION YOUR THOUGHTS if you are not doing something that brings you joy. The Muses all have contributed thoughts they think will help you realize that your dream is not only possible…it's happening as you read this book. Keep reading.

When you plug yourself into the dream you were meant to cultivate, it is as if you have just realigned your existence. It's sort of chiropractic. You have clicked into the patterns of a life meant for you. You can move forward now with the natural grace of who you are. You will feel that you literally fit into a groove specially made for your authentic reality. Conditions arise to gently prod you forward. It is still not always easy so do not let occasion obstacles throw you… stay true to your core intention, take breaks, have a papaya smoothie.

There are two kinds of talent, man-made talent and God-given talent.
With man-made talent you have to work very hard. With God-given talent,
you just touch it up once in a while.
—Pearl Bailey, singer, actress

AN EXERCISE WHERE YOU GET TO CIRCLE THINGS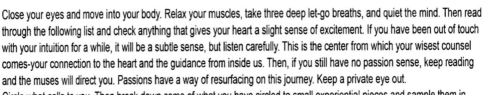

Close your eyes and move into your body. Relax your muscles, take three deep let-go breaths, and quiet the mind. Then read through the following list and check anything that gives your heart a slight sense of excitement. If you have been out of touch with your intuition for a while, it will be a subtle sense, but listen carefully. This is the center from which your wisest counsel comes-your connection to the heart and the guidance from inside us. Then, if you still have no passion sense, keep reading and the muses will direct you. Passions have a way of resurfacing on this journey. Keep a private eye out.

Circle what calls to you. Then break down some of what you have circled to small experiential pieces and sample them in abbreviated form to see where they take you.

Authentically Expressing Who You Are in Your Daily
Approach to Your Life
Finding a Satisfying Creative Outlet
Art
Painting
Collage
Drawing
Multimedia
Sculpture
Ceramics
Jewelry Making
Beading
Music
Dance
Writing
Performance Art
Theater
Art Appreciation
Other Arts or Crafts
Hobbies
Filmmaking
Public Speaking
Returning to a Creative Outlet You Had Earlier in Your
Life
Coming Up with Ideas About Anything
Increasing Your Intuition
Meditation
Solitude
Your Relationship with Yourself

Your Relationship with a Partner
Your Relationship to Any Others
Volunteer Work
Event Planning
Creating Winning Attitudes
In Making Everyday Life a Little More Festive and
Enjoyable
In Relationship to Your Environment
Decorating
Making Sacred Spaces
Gardening
Organizing
Your Work:
Your Attitude Toward Work
New Ideas to Improve Your Work
Follow Through with Ideas You've Had in
Marketing What You Do
In Team Building
In Finding Joy in Your Job
Sports
Cooking
Baking
Socializing
Vacations and Traveling
Family Outings and Get-Togethers
Being Silly
Other _____

CHILDHOOD PRIVATE-EYE WORK

Childhood Detective
Work

When we were little, we naturally gravitated toward the talent we were supposed to share with the world. We guilelessly engaged in it with no inhibitions. What we were drawn toward when we were little has huge clues and significance for our life as an adult. Do not make the mistake of thinking that all children are drawn toward the same thing. There are as many dreams, dispositions, and personalities as there are children.

As children we partook in activities that delighted us without the expectations, conventions, and judgments that lead us in a less authentic direction. The things you played with, how you played, what games you chose to play—these give you information about your inclinations in the present. Revisiting childhood memories can give you some clues about where to focus creative energy if you have lost your connection with your true self.

Go back to your childhood and Quick List in your journal all of the things you wished to be and what kinds of things you liked to do. What were the qualities of things you gravitated toward? Were they solitary, with one other person, or with groups? Did you get along easily with other kids? What talents did the people around you tell you they noticed about you? What did you do that inspired compliments from others? Were you dramatic, imaginative, scientific, logical, whimsical, social, or independent? Did you enjoy reading or did you prefer to be active? Were you musical? What kinds of arts and crafts did you like to do on your own, in school, or in summer camp? Did you like the movies? Sports? Can you remember what filled your little body with excitement? Be like a detective to your own childhood and uncover who you were before the world tried to make you uniformly consistent with the status quo. Then with each piece of information you have rediscovered, find the clues to the passion waiting for your attention now. Free-associate what pursuits could be related to what you loved as a child. You may not be able to remember everything right away, but opening to this listing experience oils the memory centers, and little by little more may come back to you than you think is possible.

Though it may not now be feasible to be an astronaut, the qualities of being an astronaut—adventurousness, curiosity, and bravery—can be applied to other pursuits. If you once wished to be an actress, you can toy with public speaking or take on roles—whether they are theatrical, dynamic, or challenging—or you can actually audition for a play. Do not assume it is too late for many of your childhood wishes. In the second half of life, there is an opportunity to take dreams that have been shelved, and return to them, sometimes with more freedom.

Studies show that we were born with the personality, the disposition, and even the body type related to the talent that we are here to express. This is a compelling argument for plugging into our creative destiny. Listen to it.

PRESENT-DAY-PASSION INVESTIGATIVE REPORTING

Walk through a bookstore and see what sections beckon you over to them. Whom do you admire in the world? What creative outlets intrigue you? Where do you go and what do you see that ignites a fire of excitement in your deepest being? What about you do people compliment? Pay attention to these things. What are the qualities of books and movies you like? Humor, irreverence, romance, mystery, classic? They are the directional signs to passions waiting for you.

You might as well set the miracle in motion. Use the space below to answer the Childhood Private-Eye Work and Present-Day-Passion Investigative Reporting questions above:

"Are You Still Paying Attention?"

HOW TO PROPEL FORWARD BY USING THE TRUTH OF YOUR DREAM

A dream is the bearer of a new possibility,
the enlarged horizon, the great hope.
—Howard Thurman, U.S. educator, theologian

🏃 Declare what dream you wish to weave into your life.

🏃 Imagine, with all your senses, what your experience will be on every level.

🏃 Notice if any fears emerge during the declaration of this dream and write them down.

🏃 Where do those fears reside in your body?

🏃 The simple awareness of the fears will help you move through them.

🏃 Thank your fears for sharing, and move on.

🏃 Write down what the "essences" of the dream will be when it has come true.

🏃 Notice what "essences" about your dream are already in your present existence.

🏃 Invite yourself to fill with joy and an effortless sense of gratitude for what you have.

🏃 Stay true to your dream and watch it *continue* to unfold.

🏃 Pay attention to what qualities you would like to experience during the journey and hold them as your anchor: Lightness? Inner peace? Mischievousness? Irreverence? Mirth?

🏃 Mortals can do that… when you begin to stray from those feelings, reboot, realign, sit up straight. Your existence is now a celebration of realizing your creative potential.

"EAU DE NOW": THE ESSENCE OF YOUR DREAM

The mental and visceral acknowledgement of the "essence" of a dream validates the dream's existence. Our dreams are coming true as we speak.. Are you able to recognize that parts of your dream are already happening? Look close at what is happening in your life right now, and you will discover that some of it is related to that which you desire but have decided that if it's not in full wish-form that its manifestation is still far in the future. Here is an example in my own life.

MY DREAM, GENERALLY SPEAKING

My intention is to expand my own creativity and creatively inspire people with my inherent talents, humor, and fun-instigating skills. To find prosperity in many different forms the pursuit of my dream. To be gracefully, peacefully, compassionately and creatively awake almost every day. To experience a sense of inner peace, joy, humor, and appreciation for the entertainment value of simply being alive. Sharing these things with special people with whom I feel a connection.

ESSENCES OF THAT DREAM

Essences: Acknowledgement, expression, connection, inner peace, love, joy, security, fun, and connection.

AWARENESS AHA

When I look closely at my life, I see that many of the essences of my dream are happening right now. My dream IS already happening. It is a journey and although I have a vision for how I want it to look, if I'm not attached to that vision I am in full experiential mode and the world brings treasures beyond what I envisioned. I need to actively acknowledge what's already here or my ego-mind will default to wanting more and feeling like I do not have enough. This prevents what happens to many people who have instant fame or those who work hard but are never satisfied.

Unless I can recognize what parts of my dream are manifesting themselves already, I will not be able to FEEL or appreciate the experience when my dream even if it is fully realized. My dream may manifest in the exact finished form that I requested, but unless I am paying attention, my ego will fall back on the automatic mortal condition of discontent, of just wanting more. Acknowledging "dream pieces" as they present themselves is the pathway to contentment. Actually, it creates contentment in the moment that is AS important as the realization of any held vision.

Before I "got' this on a visceral level, I had a vision of my dream that was always in the future—like a mirage. I sure hoped it would come true. I did not realize that so many elements of my dream already exist in the present. I am no longer chasing an image that never gets closer. Likewise, acknowledging what pieces of my dream are already present <u>attracts more</u>.. Overlooking what is already in my environment will repel that which I am seeking.

Here is the continuing truth:

- Continue the journey with willingness, and self-love.
- Trust that you will be led to more miracles than you can presently imagine.
- Trust and feel that trust in your body even if it's just for 15 seconds at a time.
- Leave behind your expectations—the journey rarely looks like what we expect.
- Setting up expectations will only cloud the direction that manifests according to the order of the moment's divinity for your dream.
- Honor intuitive detours (unless the intuitive detours are really you avoiding the hard part of the journey)
- Follow through on things that energize you—pay attention to what works. Let intuition and common sense be your compasses.
- Surrender to new plans that surface according to the response you have gotten from your efforts.
- Relish the process by fully experiencing it with all your senses.
- Hydrate.
- Now It's Your Turn

Name your creative dream concisely here or in your journal or sketch pad:

Just for fun, take a moment to expand that dream to something five times greater, moving beyond your former limitations. Now what does it look like?

Name the essences of your original dream and recognize even the smallest part of those essences that are already occurring. Express gratitude. Express gratitude again. Skip around the room. Then continue on the illustrious path of your dream taking <u>very tiny steps</u>, knowing they will build in momentum and if your process is filled with joy, miracles can happen.

Starting any kind of heart-driven action toward your dream will result in the presence of energy and teeming miracles to direct and support you. Your role is to stay the course and not be redirected by fear of any kind. Take a break now and then but know that fear is normal in the creative process, as it is in life. Simply nod at it, acknowledge its looming existence, and then choose trust, belief, confidence, and inspiration. If you find yourself low on fuel, gas up with joy, trust, supportive individuals, and continued practice, patience, and progress forward. Your association with the Muses will steer you toward what you need. Just believe. Breathe and geez, lighten up a bit.

Equipment Assembly for the Journey

"Get Ready...
Get Set
Go Get Creative!"

EQUIPMENT ASSEMBLY FOR THE JOURNEY

When you come to the edge of your reality as you presently know it, and step off into the darkness, faith is knowing that there will either be ground just below your feet or that you shall sprout wings and fly.

—Someone Wise

❀ **Joy:** Joy is the greatest magnet of all. When it's the core value you have during any journey you will attract to you all that you need. If joy seems difficult at this stage, begin where you are and move in the direction of joy, even if it's just 5% at a time. Bring back joy-filled memories and toy with applying that feel, both in mind and body, to the present moment.

❂ **Trust**: Trust is infinitely more powerful in the manifestation of creative power than fear. You may have to start small if trust is foreign but when you build trust you magnetize dreams—maybe not exactly like your initial vision but possibly in a form more consistent to your true nature. Dream manifestation is not instant, but if you stay true to the course, manifestation is certain. Fear leads to talking yourself out of perseverance. It derails you from the miracles that are waiting for you. The development of trust and confidence leads to a thousand rewarded adventures. Trust is born of the heart and spirit; fear is born of the faltering mind. I know I keep saying this, but that's just cause it works: TRUST. Surrender to the process. And if it's not easy have patience and practice.

◎ **Patience**: Patience is an endangered species in modern times. Our fast-food, microwave, drive-through society reinforces immediate gratification. Impatience is a detriment to the creative process and to living an artful life. Most growth processes do not happen quickly. Creative change takes time, compassion, and perseverance. This process is designed to let you evolve into a better person—patience is part of the package you win. If you presently feel short on patience, build it. Be aware and compassionate toward your impatience. Decide on a new intention called patience. Breathe during frustrations, put the problem down for a bit—but always come back to it, and stay with it a little longer each time. In your patience you are gifted with the beauty of grace. Be honest with yourself about your impatience. If you falsely convince yourself you are patient, but the evidence shows you that give up quickly, admit your impatience and practice the alternative. Throughout this book, patience is a thread that makes the weaving of dreams possible. If you're not patient at first, just keep practicing.

✿ **Focus**: Focus takes practice. When the mind is all over the place—worrying about this, planning that, judging everyone and you—it is not focusing. You cannot control your mind all the time, but you can redirect it. The creative process requires focus. When you are in an undivided but softly focus about on the next step in your journey, ideas will come to you spontaneously. They are like a reward for paying attention. The focus is on what is in the present. The more you attempt to focus, the more disciplined the mind will become. Yoga practices can help with focus; the simple shift of the mind onto breathing and body gives the mind practice for concentrating. Redirect an unfocused mind with compassion and acceptance. Start small and build. Repeat.

✬ **Creative Foreplay**: Playing around in your mind with thoughts of your creative endeavor will increase your commitment to your dream and will summon up inspiration and discipline. Imagine the joy in the process and the results of your endeavor. Think about the discovery and flow of the process - mistakes that can turn into inspired new directions. Act "as if" you are fully engaged in the process and notice how this can set fire to your motivation.

✳ **Confidence**: A key ingredient to creativity. With disciplined practice, the power of confidence comes alive. Be willing to accept whatever successful or unsuccessful consequence may come from your journey. The process will reward you with so much personal and spiritual growth that you may find that the benefits reaped by experiencing the process outweigh what you previously thought would bring you happiness. Confidence is one of the most powerful forms of fuel you can have for achieving your potential. Again, if it's not there in all its glory now, practice it, act as if you have it, imagine having just 5% more each time you think about your endeavor.

ESSENTiAL ACTioNS

Nurturing: Care for yourself with grand gestures of pampering. If you think you have mastered nurturing yourself, consider that you may have mastered it at a minimum. You can make room for much more. Muse Song will tell you more, but it is important that you know this from the beginning of the journey. As you honor your creative magnificence by honoring yourself as a delicate instrument, the universe will honor you by creating all that you need to succeed creatively.*

*****Okay, listen. I asterisked this one because it is vital and I'm thinking it may not have registered on your first glance because you may just be looking at the words and not really reading them. I thought that this little asterisk here would increase the probability that you will know that the Muses are serious here and you should pay attention.

Our programming around self-nurturing is sadly deficient. We need to undo the guilt, unproductive feelings and perceived selfishness that have become attached to it. If you do not feel completely pampered and worthwhile, why would you feel you had something worthwhile to share with the world? I can't fully explain it, I can just tell you I've seen it enough times to believe it. I've seen it in my own life a jaw-dropping number of times. Treat yourself to the goodness and pleasures of life. Don't hold back—then watch the creative magic happen.

Breathing: An inhale is an inspiration, an exhale is an expression. Later on the Muses will suggest some ways to use the breath...it is the pathway from the mind's constant tirade and useless chatter to the flow and fruits of the present moment. Breathe delightfully as you journey through the creative process, and let the breath intoxicate you with the magic of the present moment.

Journal Writing or Sketching: Journal writing is a powerful part of the Muse journey. Writing integrates your experiences on a level deeper than just thinking. At times you will be given the choice to write, draw, paint or even move and dance to the exercise. Have a journal and/or sketch pad ready to use. Writers, be willing to experiment with drawing, painting, and dance to create new pathways for ideas.

"I write to create fabric in a world that often appears back and white. I write to discover. I write as a witness to what I imagine. I write because I believe it can create a path in darkness. I write because it is dangerous, a bloody risk, like love, to form the words, to say the words, to touch the source, to be touched, to reveal how vulnerable we are, how transient." ~Terry Tempet Williams

Appreciation, and Daily Credit Report: Write regularly a list of what you are glad you did, what you're glad that happened, what feels like abundance to you. These are simple, but powerful magnetizers.

A Daily Creativity Routine: Create a routine at preferably the same time each day. Make it only five to fifteen minutes. Routine implies an automatic response without the power struggle the term discipline can bring up. Making your creative endeavors into a habit is the surest way to ensure that you will keep the journey going. The Muse Marge will tell you more, but since she's the last Muse on the garden path, she wants you to know this rule right at the beginning. You can achieve any creative dream you want by starting for five to fifteen minutes a day. Make it anything from writing, to doodling, to free dancing, to free-associating, to meditating. Initially it does not have to be goal-directed. Choose one of the Brainstorm activities you see in each Muse section and use it in your daily routine.

Quotes: The Muses have collected many quotes from mortals who have beautifully verbalized their concepts. Some of these quotes will move you to a greater understanding...some you will connect with on a heart level...some will not do a thing for you. Be aware of the feelings you feel when you read them. If one resonates with your heart, highlight it or copy it to a place where you can frequently be reminded of its power.

You connect with quotes because they stir your soul, and soul-stirring is paramount to healthy creative changes. Quotes are soul medicine. If you saw them as often as you see the billboards or store signs in your environment, they would dramatically change your belief system, which would, in turn, dramatically change your life, which would, in turn, be dramatically excellent. Flow chart, please! Many of the quotes are from people who have encountered and overcome challenges—so drink in their wisdom. Make their wisdom your own.

Solitude: Willingness to spend time alone is also indispensable to the creative process. Write it on your calendar. Tell others you have a doctor's appointment. To expand creatively we must be willing to be intimate with ourselves, to release external distractions and to listen to our inner voice. As we get to know who we are without other people, we find our unique voice and know who this self is that wants to be expressed.

Whew, now that we have all that stuff out of the way, it is time to meet the Muses.

"Mileage May Vary.
Not available in any store.
Side Effects may include peak experiences,
break dancing, and a youthful stride."

A Muse Primer

The Muses of classical Greece were the daughters of Zeus, king of the gods, and Mnemosyne, goddess of memory. Their mission was to inspire mortals to creative art, writing, theater, and science. They met with major obstacles when they kept using the same old devices with the modern mortal. Distraction, avoidance techniques, and fears rendered the Muses ineffective. They have had to upgrade their approach, personalities, focus, and mode of transportation to get the attention and cooperation of the modern mortal.

Greek mythology tells us there were nine Muses, each a custodian of a different art. The keepers of the sciences were Clio and Urania; they were the Muses of history and astronomy, respectively. Terpsichore was the Muse of dance. Calliope was the eldest of the Muses. Her name meant "sweet voice," and she was the Muse of heroic and epic poetry. She said to be able to play any instrument. Erato, whose name was similar to that of the love god, Eros, was the Muse of love poetry. Her symbol was the lyre. Euterpe's symbol was the flute, and she was the goddess of instrumental music and lyric poetry. Her name comes from the Greek euterpein, meaning "to please well." Her sister Polyhymnia was called on by singers. Her name was a combination of the words for "many" and "hymns" and she was the muse of vocal music. Melpomene was the muse of tragedy, while Thalia was the muse of comedy. Their names come from the words melpein, "to sing" (ancient Greek tragedies were usually sung), and thallein, "to flourish."

Table for Timesaving Convenience:

Name	Meaning	Domain	Symbols
Polyhymnia	She of Many Hymns Sacred	Poetry	Pensive Look
Calliope	The Fair-Voiced	Epic Poetry	Writing Tablet
Clio	The Proclaimer	History	Scroll
Erato	The Lovely Love	Poetry	Lyre
Euterpe	The Giver of Pleasure	Music	Flute
Melpomene	The Songstress	Tragedy	Tragic Mask
Terpsichore	The Whirler	Dancing	Dancing with Lyre
Thalia	The Flourishing	Comedy	Comic Mask
Urania	The Heavenly Astronomy	Astronomy	Celestial Globe

MODERN DAY MUSE TABLE

FROM THE NINE MODERN DAY MUSES (AND A BODYGUARD) BY JILL BADONSKY

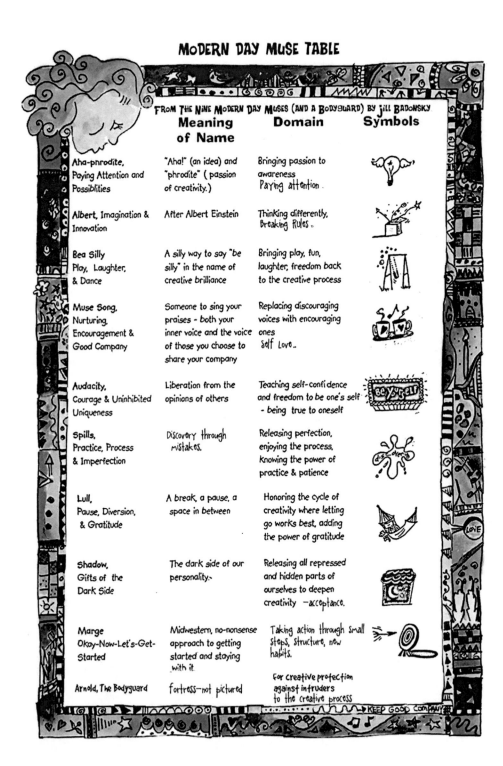

	Meaning of Name	Domain	Symbols
Aha-phrodite, Paying Attention and Possiblities	"Aha!" (an idea) and "phrodite" (passion of creativity.)	Bringing passion to awareness Paying attention .	
Albert, Imagination & Innovation	After Albert Einstein	Thinking differently, Breaking Rules .	
Bea Silly Play, Laughter, & Dance	A silly way to say "be silly" in the name of creative brilliance	Bringing play, fun, laughter, freedom back to the creative process	
Muse Song, Nurturing, Encouragement & Good Company	Someone to sing your praises - both your inner voice and the voice of those you choose to share your company	Replacing discouraging voices with encouraging ones Self Love..	
Audacity, Courage & Uninhibited Uniqueness	Liberation from the opinions of others	Teaching self-confidence and freedom to be one's self - being true to oneself	
Spills, Practice, Process & Imperfection	Discovery through mistakes.	Releasing perfection, enjoying the process, knowing the power of practice & patience	
Lull, Pause, Diversion, & Gratitude	A break, a pause, a space in between	Honoring the cycle of creativity where letting go works best, adding the power of gratitude	
Shadow, Gifts of the Dark Side	The dark side of our personality.-	Releasing all repressed and hidden parts of ourselves to deepen creativity —acceptance.	
Marge Okay-Now-Let's-Get-Started	Midwestern, no-nonsense approach to getting started and staying with it.	Taking action through small steps, structure, new habits.	
Arnold, The Bodyguard	fortress—not pictured	For creative protection against intruders to the creative process	

MUSE SOLUTIONS...
MORE IN EACH CHAPTER AND FOR YOU PERFECTIONISTS SEE STUFF IN THE BACK

CHALLENGE → MUSE ↓	DIFFICULTY STARTING	DIFFICULTY FOCUSING	DIFFICULTY FINDING TIME	FEAR OF WASTING TIME AND RESOURCES	DIFFICULTY DEFINING YOUR PASSION
Aha-phrodite, Paying Attention and Possibilities	pay attention to what worked in the past, to remembering the bliss of being in the process, to the next tiny weeny step, to thoughts of creative joy	pay attention to your soul's intention. remind yourself of your passion, pay attention 5 minutes at a time and build your focus muscle	Pay attention to how you're spending your time, to the moments where you can be asking small questions that increase your desire to get started and make time. Notice whether this is an avoidance strategy.	pay attention to the process where creativity is its own reward. pay attention to the doors that open when you are simply in the process	Pay attention to asking small questions that do not need an immediate answer— What energizes me? Pay attention to action and the accompanying feeling.
Albert, Imagination and Innovation	You're not the only one. Reframe starting.. make it an adventure OR do it with wild abandon. try on a persona who is someone who you imagine starts things. Add a quality of curiosity to your approach.	use your imagination to summon any scenario that draws your attention in.. imagine the "Focus Olympics." Again, bring to mind someone who DOES focus and borrow their persona.	Did Einstein have difficulty finding time? Ok.. I'm being a smart ass. Change your thinking to "I have plenty of time." Begin to believe it... it works. Think about small moments and their possibilities.	You REALLY need to change your thinking on this. We repeat Creativity is it's own reward. In the process you are gifted with what makes you a better person.	Change your thinking to — I am on my way to discovering my passion. I'm am curious about how it will be presented to me. I get to find my passion!
Bea Silly, Play, Laughter, and Movement	Ask— What would make this fun? How can I play with starting? Allow yourself to play without pressure or expectations. Make an I GET TO list instead of an I HAVE TO list.	Got difficulty focusing? SO WHAT. DO IT ANYWAY. Make it fun to increase your desire to focus. Reward your child-like spirit for focusing. Hula Hoop around the house as a focusing ritual.	Make finding time a contest. Have a chart where you give yourself stickers every time you find time. Be like a stubborn child and demand your time. Keep that inner child-like spirit happy by finding time to play.	Got Fear? SO WHAT DO IT ANYWAY! If you have a creative call, ya really need to follow it or you might explode or turn into a cockroach.	Remember what you loved to do when you were a kid. in that information is passion. Pretend you are a Passion Detective.. foil the mystery.

CHALLENGE → MUSE ↓	DIFFICULTY STARTING	DIFFICULTY FOCUSING	DIFFICULTY FINDING TIME	FEAR OF WASTING TIME AND RESOURCES	DIFFICULTY DEFINING YOUR PASSION
Muse Song Nurturing, Encouragement, Good Company	Try a little kindness. Do you have anyone in your life that inspires you gently re: starting? Bring them to mind. Say kind things to yourself, it works better than harshness in the long run. Consider what worked in the past.	Muse Song is going to be rather consistent with saying— be on your own side with compassion, acceptance, and gentle but firm nudges that come from love not pressure or judgment.	Rather than making this a big issue, try the strategy of gently making time. Sometimes there's more room for gentleness than pressure.	Again, kindly reframe from such a pressured approach to your creative work. Think of all you are gifted with in the process, proceed with appreciation for what will surely be discovered.	Ask others about how they discovered their passions. Reach out for ideas from others. Who is expressing their passion, and how does that inspire you?
Spills Practice, Process, Imperfections	Lower your expectations! Give yourself permission to do stuff badly at the start... for fun and lowered pressure.. IT WORKS! Assign a quality you choose to experience in the process like wonder, joy, ease or mischievousness.	Try focusing imperfectly.. it might be less pressure. Or give yourself credit for ANY focusing you ARE doing, even if it's not as much as you thought it should be. Practice focusing.. develop the muscle.	Practice finding time... your discovery of it doesn't have to look the same everyday although that often helps. Fall in love with the process SO MUCH that you find that you MUST make time.. that works best for me.	This is often a fear of a perfectionist mentality. Having rigid expectations for the creative process is a set-up for disappointment. Opening to the discovery possible in the process, is... as we have said above— It's own reward.	You don't even have to be perfect about defining your passion. Experiment with different things.. notice which PROCESS you enjoy the most. Be light about your wonderings.
Audacity Courage and Uninhibited Uniqueness	Start with courageous, ruthless and wild abandon. Be an audacious, outrageous Starting Maniac. OR.. use a tiny amount more of courage than before & see what happens.	Focus with courageous, ruthless and wild abandon! Don't be afraid to repeat yourself. Pretend you are Super Focuser! Inspire the world with your starting power. Be courageous enough to say no to distractions.	Courageously.. ruthlessly FIND THE TIME. I believe you CAN.. I've seen the most busy people on the planet with 17 kids and 5 jobs find the time.. so can you. It's not a good excuse! Sorry.. see Muse Song for compassion.. Audacity is ruthless... etc.	Trust, believe and get over it.. No time spent in the creative process is wasted. You become more interesting, alive, magnetic, inspired, love-worthy, sublime, authentic — when you're IN the process. It's it's own reward.	Act as IF you are passionate! Keep practicing Acting As IF You are passionate and all of a sudden.. guess what?

CHALLENGE → / MUSE ↓	DIFFICULTY STARTING	DIFFICULTY FOCUSING	DIFFICULTY FINDING TIME	FEAR OF WASTING TIME AND RESOURCES	DIFFICULTY DEFINING YOUR PASSION
Lull Pause Diversion Gratitude	Unless it's an avoidance strategy, expose yourself to things that inspire you. Let go of the pressure. Take stock of how you HAVE started in the past.	Unless it's avoidance strategy, take a break.	No help here from Lull except to daydream about finding the time.. maybe an answer will bubble up.	Take stock of what gifts, qualities, experiences you gained other than what you were going for in your past processes.	Expose yourself to all different things, even things you didn't think you were passionate about.
The Shadow Gifts of the Dark Side	Sometimes clogged up emotions overwhelm us.. Make a list, explore in writing emotions that need some attention. Then ask yourself — What do I want to do?	Emotions can also affect our ability to focus. What needs some attention? Where can you let go of your story? How can you channel your angst into your art?	Use the energy of your more powerful emotions to create the power to find the time. Anger can be channeled into making time! If not now.. when!!!?	What's the worst that can happen? Is that true? Are you in control of your fears or are they in control of you? Is it time to trust?	Allow your dark side to write to you about what might be blocking your passion awareness. Be passionate about channeling emotions into creativity.
Marge Okay— Let's—Get— Started	Marge is the expert here. Read her whole chapter. Break it down to tiny steps! Find structure, get a buddy or a coach, take a class, build a habit.	Don't wait until you FEEL like focusing.. or you'll get nothing done. Just do it over and over, without giving up, a little at a time — it'll become a habit.	Get a coach, set up Parallel Universe Time, take a class. Find moments in between activities. Just 5 minutes can get the momentum going.	Oh ... for Goodness sake, get over that one, sweetie. Okay? If ya have a creative call, ya gotta follow it.	What does your common sense tell ya? Reach out for help. Just begin something, see what happens.

CHALLENGE → / MUSE ↓	COMPARING SELF WITH OTHERS	LOW SELF CONFIDENCE	FEAR OF GIVING UP A COMFORTABLE RUT	SELF SABOTAGE	DIFFICULTY FINISHING THINGS
Aha-phrodite, Paying Attention and Possibilities	Pay attention to yourself. Pay attention to your uniqueness and to what You've done already. Pay attention to messages that shift you OUT of comparison	Pay attention to how your confidence increases when you keep going. Pay attention to where you're getting it right.	Pay attention to the fact that this is a lower level comfort. Comfort from a higher purpose is being engaged in your creative passions.	Pay attention to how you sabotage yourself and practice making it more comfortable to choose a different action or thought.	Pay attention to what worked in the past, to the feeling of finishing things, to practice being okay with the feeling of success.
Albert, Imagination and Innovation	Make up your own rules. Imagine what you would be like if you didn't compare yourself.	Try on an attitude, persona, or emotion of healthy self-confidence and see how that feels. Make up the rules as you go.	Be different.. make your comfortable routine a colossal adventure of creative brilliance.	Replace your comfort with disappointing yourself with a comfort with being happy with what you do. Mind sculpt then employ. new actions.	Use the persona and energy of someone who finishes things. Think differently about finishing things. What would make it easier?
Bea Silly, Play, Laughter, and Movement	Be like a little kid and be proud of YOU. See what others are doing and say— I'M GOING TO DO IT MY OWN WAY!	Be like a little kid and have uninhibited self confidence. Plunge into action and know that action begets self confidence.	Play with a new comfortable routine.. one filled with the fun of your creative process and the child-like wonder of creation.	Talk kindly to the child inside and instead of being disappointed in all he or she does, be understanding and encouraging.	If you've had a hard time with this in the past... SO WHAT! FINISH THINGS ANYWAY. Make the ending fun. Create a fun ritual and reward around finishing.

CHALLENGE → MUSE ↓	COMPARING SELF WITH OTHERS	LOW SELF CONFIDENCE	FEAR OF GIVING UP A COMFORTABLE RUT	SELF SABOTAGE	DIFFICULTY FINISHING THINGS
Muse Song Nurturing, Encouragement, Good Company	Imagine the voice of a nurturing, benevolent spirit telling You how wonderful You are. Just accept 5% more of that at a time.	Practice saying encouraging things to Yourself like You can Do this.. and the more You DO it the more confidence You'll feel. Be on Your own side.	Gently but firmly give Yourself permission to give up ruts that don't serve Your higher purpose. But allow play and relaxation.	Practice treating Yourself like You would a good friend. Practice kinder messages and giving yourself permission NOT to sabotage Yourself.	Love Yourself just the way You are and then finish things.. knowing this is a kind of self-love too.
Spills Practice, Process, Imperfections	Practice telling Yourself there's no need or good in comparing Yourself to others unless it's to inspire further action. But You don't have to be perfect about this either.	Love the process, practice is the key to self confidence. PRACTICE.. PRACTICE and be patient.. but then Practice.	Seduce Yourself away from Your rut with the amazing and rewarding process of creativity. But again, no perfection is required here.	Make sure Your expectations are reasonable. Unrealistic expectations is a sure way to sabotage Yourself. Perfection not required.	Know when to let go. Give Yourself permission to be close enough, to finish things imperfectly, let go and move on. It's a great feeling to finish things.
Audacity Courage and Uninhibited Uniqueness	STOP IT! You are a wondrous, incredible light. Shine in Your own unique way.. no one can shine like You do. Trust.. believe.	Act as If You have self confidence over and over.. and guess what happens?	Use Your audacity to tell Your TV and the Internet that You have a date with Your creative time.. GET BIG and FORMIDABLE about it.	Trust that You have the power and the courage to move through self-sabotage.	Be audacious and just finish things.. IF NOT NOW... WHEN?

CHALLENGE → MUSE ↓	COMPARING SELF WITH OTHERS	LOW SELF CONFIDENCE	FEAR OF GIVING UP A COMFORTABLE RUT	SELF SABOTAGE	DIFFICULTY FINISHING THINGS
Lull Pause Diversion Gratitude	Take stock of who you uniquely are and where you've excelled in the past. Divert your attention from them to the wonder of YOU.	Take stock of who you uniquely are.. where you've excelled in the past. Feeling grateful feeds self-confidence.	Expose yourself to OTHER comfortable routines... ones that serve you.	Expose yourself to what you've been successful with in the past.	Take a break and see if your energy is renewed but don't forget to come back. Expose yourself to something that restores you. Take stock of all you have finished
The Shadow Gifts of the Dark Side	Comparison is the ego's way of thwarting your progress. Fuel up with emotions that serve your own beauty and uniqueness.	Be aware and compassionate about it and then go talk to Audacity.	Be aware and compassionate about it and then go talk with Marge.	Make a list of where you sabotaged yourself in the past, and where you might sabotage yourself today. Use that awareness as the power to choose something different.	Use the energy of your more powerful emotions to fuel your conviction. Give up your story about not finishing things and rewrite it.
Marge Okay— Let's-Get-Started	That's just not good common sense. Those people have their own path.. You'll get to where you're supposed to go if you take small steps.	Low self-confidence has no place in the creative process. Just keep "doing" and your confidence will soar.	Make your comfortable routine one that honors your higher purpose not your sloth purpose. Start one tiny step at a time, repeat, repeat.	Keep practicing saying encouraging things to yourself and do small actions you are proud of.. over and over.	Read my chapter. Structure, coaching, parallel universe time, classes, conviction, stamina, fortitude, will!

PART TWO
THE ILLUSTRIOUS GARDEN
OF THE AMAZING MUSES
(and the Bodyguard)

PRioR To gARDEN joURNEy EMBARKMENT

Come now and take flight into the incredible journey of the creative process. You may be embarking upon the journey because your soul is saying, "Excuse me, I have something I want to share!" Or perhaps it is your heart that exclaims, "A life artfully lived? I'd love to be that!" And, as is the reality of the creative process, you are feeling . . . well, sort of alone.

However, the urge is still strong to be creative. So how do you start the dream with all the scary things lurking out there to stop you? You consider the scope of your fear, but advance forward anyhow, realizing that being true to dreams is essential to the fabric of your happiness. You weave on.

All of a sudden, you see someone else doing exactly what it is you want to do, only they are further along in the process. You get slimed with an attack of envy. Yuk, the green stuff stains the best of your intentions. Mustering up more courage, you say, "That's okay, I'm still going to do it."

Then you start to express a little of yourself in some creative medium, and this loud voice that seems to be coming right from inside your own head says, "YOU'VE GOT TO BE KIDDING, WHAT DO YOU THINK YOU ARE DOING? YOU CAN'T DO THAT. YOU'RE NOT GOOD ENOUGH. YOU'LL LOOK LIKE A FOOL!" Or maybe someone close to you glances at what you are doing and gives you a look like "That is NOT a good idea."

Okay, okay, then there is this one: You fear that if you try to rise to your true potential, it would mean you would have to take on too much...responsibility. Ahhhhhwwwww! That one may not even be in your conscious awareness, it just steers you away from advancing.

yoU ARE BEiNg TAKEN CARE OF

Regardless of what you are saying or not saying, the Muses have assigned you a Bodyguard. "A Bodyguard?" Yes, a Bodyguard, to protect you from all of these adversaries of the creative process—the traitors to your unfolding as a creative possibility in self-realized splendor. Your Bodyguard will be with you throughout the journey, so the Muses want you to meet him now. Use his powers as your own.

"What would it be like
to be on your own side?"

THE BODYGUARD

If your heart is in your dream,
no goal is too extreme.
—Ned Washington

SUMMON THE BODYGUARD:

 Anytime you are feeling creatively discouraged or fearful.
When you need to be reminded that you have an inner strength that can overcome any odds.
To unleash your best defense: your arsenal of passion and desire for your creative dream.

BOTTOM LINE

The Bodyguard persona mobilizes fantasy and mirth to instantly call upon a tangible image of protection. An image of a bodyguard can be easier to employ than the abstract qualities of bravado, patience, or will. This energy empowers us not to give our power away to others. When our passion and commitment to the expression of our talents comes from a source inside that's unaffected by anything external, no worldly fear or discouragement will stop us from bringing them into fruition. We are always protected if we remember our connection to our creative source. We replace feelings of fear, discouragement, disregard, disillusionment, and frustration with peace and determination. And just reading this above paragraph every now and then can snap you out of any flailing, weak place so…REMEMBER TO DO THAT.

THE BODYGUARD SELECTION

The Muses know that the modern mortal is subjected to all different kinds of attacks of discouragement. Many obstructive and scary intruders emerge as we walk down the garden path to our creative awes, kind of like the scene from The Wizard of Oz where the flying monkeys from the special-effects department at MGM are buzzing Dorothy and her threesome.

Mortals need valiant protection against these forces. The Muses themselves are not in the business of protection. They are in the business of inspiring gestures of progressing ahead. They are too creatively focused to keep a lookout for intruders, and they don't work out at the gym. So they proposed the Bodyguard Act, which stipulates that Mortals Will Be Supplied with a Full-fledged Bodyguard for the Thwarting of any Evil Force That Prevents the Expression of Creative Magnificence. The bill passed the Mount Olympus congress and the populace gasped with awe (the gesture was very controversial). But, the Muses didn't care. They are of the creative bent—avant-garde invention is their forte. They are passionate about their cause and focused for action. So ultimately the Mount Olympians dismissed the eccentricity of the Muses saying, "Oh, well, I guess they can add bodyguards and stuff like that. They're artists, and artists break rules."

The Muses encourage you to come up with an image, a gesture, a statement that helps you embody the body. Ideas: Arnold Schwarzenegger [as his movie characters], Zena the warrior goddess, Iron Man, any formidable character- real or imagined. Or standing up straight and puffing in a threatening manner, wearing a special totem that you endow with the powers of strength, eating your spinach, etc. - These can work.

YOUR BODYGUARD ENERGY

Nothing and no one makes sure that the creative side of your existence is honored except you and your connection to the truth of your creative spirit. This is both ironic and understandable. You are born with a creative destiny. Fulfilling that destiny places you in a process of both the highest human potential and highest mortal fulfillment. But it's kind of frightening. So you have to prove your commitment to, and enlightenment about creativity by overcoming the odds of being discouraged. A little help wouldn't hurt.

The image you come up with of a Bodyguard in and of itself becomes a protective Spirit. Coming up with an image or gesture gives you something to call upon when you come face-to-face with those forces that stop you from finding and acknowledging creative fulfillment. It reminds you that you have power inside you and that to give that power away to others by putting their opinions ahead of your own is a crime of unnecessary defeat. Imagine having on your side the formidable attitude, intimidating physique, and unwavering intention of a strong movie hero. Imagine this figure on your side standing in front of anything that comes in your way. He or she stops it, or them, long enough for you to get refueled by the particular Muse you need for the reinforcement of confidence, perseverance, passion, or whatever power seems to be missing. Place the bodyguard between you and both your internal and external predators. And hey, REMEMBER TO DO THIS.

We need to make the world safe for creativity and intuition, for it's creativity and intuition that will make the world safe for us.
—Edgar Mitchell, Apollo astronaut

THE BODYGUARD'S PROTECTION TECHNIQUES

The most powerful defense against quitting or discouragement is your strength of your passionate desire. In other words, PASSION. If you want to answer your creative call badly enough, desire opens up your reservoirs of passion. Desire can create a creative flow so forceful that it washes away anything that stands in your way. Fueling this reservoir includes visualizing the dream coming true but it also includes setting an intention to tether yourself to the process with lightness, joy, and some defining aspect of yourself. For me that defining aspect includes playfulness, inspiration, and irreverence. See the results of the process completed and feel the rewards of letting the divine power of creativity express through you. This mind-set of strong desire is the first avenue that the Bodyguard you explore. If that doesn't work, here are some other suggestions.

THE ANCHOR

Another of the Bodyguard's most powerful tools is the anchor. This is the use of some thought or activity that you can access when you feel discouraged. It is a touchstone of strength. It is something that we can breathe in, in order to defend against discouragement. The anchor serves to prime and center us for the miracles awaiting our discovery. Mostly it takes the part of our mind that torments us and replaces it with the thought or the feeling we need in order to continue full speed ahead. Or if you're not in full speed mode, even hobbling along is better than discouragement.

Anchors can be thoughts of people who empower us, music that soothes or inspires us, memories of situations that have empowered us, focusing on the nurturing nature of breathing and releasing our plight with the exhale, the visualization of turning our discouragement or discomfort over to a higher power or a loving angel, quotes or affirmations that replace our negative thoughts or hurt feelings and pull us back to power. Anchors can be actual people who stand in your court when you need support. Conjure up these images and thoughts, or call your designated real-life bodyguard when you need your fears and discouragement thwarted.

QUOTES THAT SERVE AS ANCHORS

Damn the torpedoes—full speed ahead!
—David Glasgow Farragut, naval admiral

What people think of me is none of my business.
—Terry Cole Whittaker, author, spiritual leader

An invasion of armies can be resisted, but not an idea whose time has come.
—Victor Hugo, writer

Success seems to be largely a matter of hanging on
after others have let go.
—William Feather, author

Great spirits have always encountered violent
opposition from mediocre minds.
—Albert Einstein, Swiss-German-American physicist

The HELL I won't!
- I just stuck this in here cuz I like it.

This, too, shall pass.
—Anonymous, someone very well adjusted

So what, I'll do it anyway.
—Bea Silly, the Muse

SELF-TALK THAT SERVE AS ANCHORS

- Through fear I find courage.
- I do not allow life's obstacles to impede my progress. Instead of being defeated by them, I look for ways that will take me over them.
- I am so passionate about my dreams that nothing can stop me. I set the course and per-severe—not ever giving up, ever.
- Fear is an affirmation of my growth. I am fully willing to be myself and work through the fear.
- If the door of opportunity closes, I will go through the window.

QUESTIONS TO ASK YOURSELF TO ACTIVATE BODYGUARD POWERS:

- What anchor empowers me to protect and stay committed to my creative process?
- What does it feel like to use this anchor?
- How can I remember to use it?
- What does passionate commitment look like and feel like to me?
- What example of someone else's success can I remember to empower commitment toward my own?
- Can I remember that I can be imperfect at activating my Bodyguard Powers and still succeed …brilliantly?
  What can I say to myself to empower my strength?
  What's a memory from my past that validates that I can do this too?
  What would I do if I felt just 15% more courage?
  What if I just didn't listen to doubting voices and skeptical detractors?
- How can I apply anger to creative action?
- Suggestions:
  Make a shield with anchors, images, quotes and role models on it.. hang it.
  Stand, close your eyes, and let your body take on the power of your intentions: to be strong in the face of the detractors.

THE BRUSH-OFF

This is the Bodyguard's simple but incredibly effective, time-tested technique to release either your own negative thoughts as they arise, or the discouraging comments of oth-ers. Here is how it works: Upon catching yourself thinking a negative or antagonizing thought, or being "accosted" by someone else's derailing comment or facial expression of criticism, simply take your hands and physically brush the thought or comment off your body as if you were getting rid of dirt or bugs. Try it right now. The physical action combined with the intention to remove negative energy somehow works better than just the thought of trying to ignore or to get over the situation. (Works with people who cut you off on the highway, too.) REMEMBER TO DO THIS. Remembering to do things you know that work puts you ahead of 85% of the population.

CREATIVITY OFFENDERS

The Bodyguard's energy is a solid stock of your belief in yourself. He, she, or whatever will protect you from these antagonists to the creative process:

- Discouragement in any form
  - Wet blankets
  - The desire to quit
  - Envy of others
- Others envying and neglecting you
  - Jealousy from you and of you
    - Unworthy criticism
  - Disheartening criticism
- Ridicule, mockery, shaming, and really weird looks from people
  - Rationalizations about not having enough time
- Thoughts about what we think we should be doing instead of creativity
  - Partners who don't respect your creative needs, space, and time
    - Your guilt about taking your creative space and time
      - Unfounded self-doubt
    - Gravitation toward TV reruns
  - Checking the e-mail every fifteen minutes
  - Veers left when your creativity is on the right
    - Fright, terror, heebie-jeebies
  - Superficial socializing as an avoidance strategy
    - Fear of responsibility
- Distractions of telephones, visiting friends, and demanding pets
  - Money concerns
  - Giving your power away
  - And the pull of oblivion

THE BODYGUARD'S REINFORCEMENTS TO THWART CREATIVE ENEMIES

Keyed to above offenders. Be advised: the Bodyguard is tougher than the Muses. Some ruthlessness may be employed to keep you loyal to your creative call.

DISCOURAGEMENT IN ANY FORM

When you are discouraged to the point of wanting to quit, stymie that desire with focused action instead. Use compassion and self-love. Start really small until you can let the passionate flow lift and carry you. Keep going forward. Realize the power of practice, patience, and perseverance. You're allowed to feel discouraged, you're not allowed to stop unless it's for a brief break.

JEALOUSY AND ENVY

When feeling jealousy and envy, identify what these emotions are telling you about what you are neglecting in your life. Start that action with patience. Or if that does not apply, engage in a creative activity that reinforces the magnificence of your gifts. Know that jealousy and envy CAN be an affirmation that you have the same energy as those you are observing - begin in gentle, small steps to use it YOUR way. Also use the brush-off technique. Brush jealousy off your body and soul. Get back to who you are as an amazing mortal and what others are doing will not even matter.

CRITICISM

When you receive unworthy or disheartening criticism from people who may be jealous of you, or who are just unconscious of what they are saying, take your power back. Love them from afar but free them from your life. Do not give your power to others. Be conscious when you do give your power away. You need that power in your court to keep you going. Once you hand your power over to the opinions of others, you are at the mercy of an unconquerable force. If you have been deeply true to your creativity, you will have both admirers and critics. If you subscribe to the opinions of others, you will be on an out-of-control roller coaster. With each display of your staying power you will become stronger and more self-confident. Strength and self-confidence are the ingredients of your creative freedom. See the Muse Audacity. If the criticism is helpful, you will have an intuitive hit that this is so, and gently consider what it's about.

RIDICULE, MOCKERY, SHAMING, AND REALLY WEIRD LOOKS FROM PEOPLE

If you are ridiculed, mocked, or shamed, same as above: Take your power back and consider the source. Brush it off and choose to use the ill feelings that this type of crime has caused you to fuel more action. Not that you have to prove yourself to people who are not your supporters, but allowing them to mobilize the powerful energy of anger inside you can serve your efforts for creative dream manifestation. Make an inventory of the people you are hanging with...Get new ones if you need to, life is short.

NO TIME

Rationalizations about time restraints: Recognize anything that stops you from your creative work as the excuse it is. Creativity is not meant for your spare time. Creative moments are possible every day, and when you take them, you act in your divine interest. When you learn that creativity can happen first in your mind and then in five to fifteen-minute time-slots, time will never be an excuse for you again. Even just five minutes a day will get you further than no minutes because you think you need to do an hour at a time and don't get to it. Assess where you are spending your time now. Admit if you are addicted to TV, the Internet or other distractions and find some structure as in classes, creativity coaching or parallel universe time. Set a timer when you're on the Internet., one that's in another room so you have to get up to turn it off.

Also realize creativity is not just about sitting and doing something. Creative thought is a precursor to creative action. When you simply spend time when you are on-hold, waiting for something to upload, stuck in traffic, thinking about your next small step in your creative passion - you are engaged in a valid part of the creative process that is often overlooked by our productivity oriented society. (see Marge for more ideas).

THOUGHTS ABOUT WHAT WE THINK WE SHOULD BE DOING INSTEAD OF CREATIVITY

Hoodwinked by shoulds. If you "should" be doing everything but your creativity, redefine your values, they are not in line with your higher purpose. If the shoulds are leading you to your creative work, be easy on yourself. Half of our shoulds are born out of unnecessary pressures. Evaluate them, then let your compassionate heart advise you, not your inner critic.

PARTNERS WHO DON'T RESPECT YOUR CREATIVE NEEDS, SPACE, AND TIME

First evaluate if this is truly a problem or an easy out for you avoiding your creative work.

Explain to partners who demand your attention how important your creative time and space are to them as well as to you. Tell them that you are more human and kind, and less of a snarling, fang-endowed lunatic, when you can spend time in the creative passions that are calling to you. Healthy relationships are born of respect for each others values. Read that five times if it did not sink in the first time. A creative call is important.

Other ideas: Get a baby-sitter. Create activities for the offending parties; encourage them to work at the same time you do on something creative or something they enjoy. Parallel activities like this can add to the depth of a relationship and more discipline to both of your pursuits.

Bargain, deal, and compromise to get time and space for your creativity: Your creative time and space are necessary for you to grow into the best "you" possible for everyone involved in your life. A small amount of time each day will not kill those who depend on you, and your example frees them to consider and participate in their own process. Share as much of the process as you can with them. Dedicate your finished results, or the process, to them, and include them by asking for ideas. Make creative things for them once in a while, and tell them they are one of your inspirations (if indeed they are). Let them know how important they are. You know deep inside when you really need to be setting boundaries...and some of you, who's values are being dramatically compromised know deep inside that some of those relationships need to be released.

guilT ABouT TAKiNg youR CREATiVE SPACE AND TiME

"Guilt is the ego's orgasm." Marianne Williamson

Guilt and worry are the most wasted use of time and energy ever invented. Worry is usually always worse than the actual results even when your most dreaded worry comes true. Figure out what message guilt is giving you, learn from it, then let it go. If what you are learning is that taking time for yourself is not right, you have downloaded the wrong lesson plan. We were intended to express our creativity. Be creative about finding how to do that without guilt. If your creativity is coming from your heart, the world needs it. Period.

UNFouNDED SElF_DouBT

Patience, practice, and taking small steps amend self-doubt. Defend yourself against your untrained mind. The mind is only an enemy when it torments you with fear's imagination. The trained mind can be your cheerleader. The truth is you can get good at what you want to get good at and no one can stop you but yourself. Make a truce. Sign an accord. Share a hot fudge sundae. Audacity, Spills the Imp, and Muse Song are also enlisted to solve this major offender to creative action.

gRaViTATiON TowaRD TV RERuNS

(and Other TV, Too)

This is one or a combination of the following: a habit, an avoidance strategy, weak will, or proof of having no life. In moderation it can be periodic mindless relaxation, but moderation is not the two to three hours a day that many mortals believe it is. Most TV is often an enemy to the creative process. This is the Bodyguard's feeling because he or she is programmed for disciplined self-actualization. Reruns play no role in that quest, and most TV shows suck your brains out anyway. The Bodyguard is rather graphic, sorry.

CHECKiNg THE E_MAiL EVERY FiVE MiNuTES

Chronic e-mail and social networking checking is the electronic addiction distraction of the twenty-first century. It can negatively affect your productivity if it's not controlled. Come up with a structure: Three times a day (once is best) is a good maximum number of checkings, or reward yourself by checking after a certain amount of productivity on other work. Or read e-mails when you feel like it, but answer them two times a day, because replies most often take the most time. On certain days allow yourself to check e-mail as much as you like. After all, it is like getting mail several times a day, which is pretty neat from your artist child's point of view. If you are too strict with the childlike curiosity it brings up, resistance to productivity will be the result. But know that the creative warrior is disciplined. Have a role-model of a disciplined individual and bring that individual to mind when you're feeling weak.

I have a time limit I allow myself. It makes it a game to get all my social e-mail out of the way in 15 minutes, then get back to my work. (most of the time).

VEERING LEFT WHEN YOUR CREATIVITY IS ON THE RIGHT

U-turn and go right.
Fear, Terror, Heebie-jeebies
Write down your fears. Determine which are irrational. Tell them.. "Thanks for sharing and then plow ahead." See Audacity and Marge.

FEAR OF RESPONSIBILITY

Fear of responsibility can sometimes sabotage you subconsciously. Beneath the veneer of "Go team" may be the dread of the increased responsibility that comes with success. Is it hard enough being an adult without something extra like creativity? Get over it. You were meant to be divinely creative, and sometimes that means responsibility. The triumphs will lighten the weight you may perceive responsibility to be. Practice pairing the feeling of success with the feeling of lightness and relaxation; if that doesn't compute just try it 15% more or for 10 seconds at a time in frequent intervals.

Take it slow so you do not undermine yourself when the pressure sets in. Ask for support. Take breaks. Endow the process with lightness - it does NOT have to be increased pressure. Know that the growing ability to be responsible for creative causes is a highly spiritual transformation. The high you get from the accumulating progress you make as the process unfolds is completely worth the responsibility it takes to get there. You will hear angels sing your triumph when you pursue and bring your dreams to fruition.

DISTRACTIONS OF TELEPHONES, VISITING FRIENDS, AND DEMANDING PETS

These distractions just indicate a need for a little more focus, discipline, and commitment. All great works of creativity require devotion, so get used to that truth. Once you are in the creative flow, those distractions will lose interest for you. Unplug the phone. Place a DO NOT DISTURB sign on your door. Save social encounters as much as possible for after a session of creative work. When you do not give in to distractions, you will earn a self-respect that will feel like a badge of invincible confidence. It will serve you in every other endeavor including the noncreative ones. And again, deciding that the process will be joy-filled, not pressure filled will enhance your devotion.

Money Concerns

The money does follow when you follow your heart. Your step-by-step plan of five to fifteen minutes a day will begin your dream, and as it catches on, money matters take care of themselves. Keep your job to support your passion until you can and want to release it. Devise your escape plan for a few minutes as daily as possible. The spiritual abundance you fill with will attract prosperity. Here's another place where the triad of trust-intuition-common sense can make you bigger than your fears. It needs to make sense. Make sure you gravitate that which is in alignment with your joy, not someone else's formula for success.

Neediness, fear and manipulation repel abundance. Showing up with joy, grace and passion attracts prosperity. It's a law - enforce it.

Self-Sabotage

Sometimes if you are not finishing a project or not even starting it, if opportunities arise and you pass them up for no good reason...you are in self-sabotage. The Shadow Muse talks about how mortals sabotage because shame subconsciously convinces them they are not deserving or they may have "disappointment" software from having parents who were never satisfied. Be observant of unrealistic expectations. Mortals sabotage themselves by having so much on their plate that it's overwhelming and thus, triggers avoidance. Or they don't do well in any of it - another from of sabotage.

Then there's screwed-up permission. This is permission mortals somehow adopt that prevents them from reaching their goal. Permission such as "I have permission not to write a book." Or "I have permission not to make money doing something I love." Mortals pick this up from some influence in their environment, most often a parent or a teacher who questioned their skills or put them down. They adopt this permission not to succeed to stay loyal to parents in a somewhat twisted fashion.

The Bodyguard's powerful weapon in this case is also extremely simple: Proclaim out loud or even put it in writing whatever permission it is that you need to begin to act: "I give myself permission to succeed." "I give myself permission to pursue doing the things I love." "I give myself permission to finish this book (art piece, class, show, etc.)." It may seem awkward because subconsciously you haven't been giving yourself this permission before. Proclaim it and you may begin to feel a certain pull toward your passion as well as a freedom. Proclaim it more than once if you need to...proclaim it regularly. That's what I did to get this book written. Get permission from your higher self to feel comfortable engaging in your creative call, not from the lower self to engage in distractions like endless TV.

MORTAL EXAMPLES

These mortals could have been thwarted by public opinion. Instead they protected their dream by staying with their dream despite the odds. The Bodyguard guards against giving up.

- ❀ Dr. Seuss's first book was rejected forty-five times.
- ❀ JFK finished last in his Ivy League college.
- ❀ Charles Schulz was rejected by Disney.
- ❀ Buckminster Fuller, inventor of the geodesic dome, was expelled twice from Harvard.
- ❀ Jack Nicholson Marilyn Monroe, John Travolta and many more actors who became superstars were told they couldn't act.
- ❀ Abraham Lincoln: Failed in business—age twenty-two.
  Ran for the legislature and was defeated—age twenty-three.
  Again failed in business—age twenty-four.
  Elected to legislature—age twenty-five.
  Sweetheart died—age twenty-six.
  Had a nervous breakdown—age twenty-seven.
  Defeated for Speaker—age twenty-nine.
  Defeated for Congress—age thirty-four.
  Elected to Congress—age thirty-seven.
  Defeated for Congress—age thirty-nine.
  Defeated for Senate—age forty-six. Defeated for vice president—age forty-seven.
  Defeated for Senate—age forty-nine.
  Elected president of the United States—age fifty-one.

HISTORICAL KILLER PHRASES THAT DIDN'T WORK

These killer statements were aimed at people who were protected by the passion they had for their personal creative journey.

As to Bell's talking telegraph, it only creates interest in scientific circles; its commercial values will be limited.
—Elisha Gray, inventor, 1876

What use could the company make of an electric toy?
—Western Union, rejecting the right to Alexander Graham Bell's telephone, 1878

Heavier-than-air flying machines are impossible.
—Lord Kelvin, Royal Society president, 1895

No mere machine will replace a reliable and honest clerk.
—President of Remington Arms Company
rejecting patent rights for the typewriter, 1897

Television won't be able to hold on to any market it captures after the first six months.
People will soon get tired of staring at a plywood box every night.
—Darryl F. Zanuck, head of 20th Century-Fox, 1946

The automobile is only a novelty—a fad.
—Michigan Savings Bank president about investing in Ford Motor Company

I'm sorry, Mr. Kipling, but you just don't know how to use the English language.
—Publisher rejecting Rudyard Kipling, 1889

In the beginning the universe was created. This has made a lot of people very angry and
has been widely regarded as a bad move.
—Douglas Adams, English novelist

Stay committed to your heart's journey. Remain bold. Know that you are not alone. Call upon your inner strength. Surpass your own expectations. Boogie.

ENTER THE GARDEN

A Muse is there to greet you at the garden's entrance. See before you a goddess of light... bulbs. She leads you to the garden gate. Looking over the gate and into the garden, your awareness shifts vividly into the present moment. She summons you to walk through the gate and you cannot refuse because you sense there is something you need to know for the weaving of your creative dreams. Through this gate you see flashes of insight, the pure, uncut rapture of creative enlightenment. The moment is alive—there are new possibilities. Her light-bulbs are the whimsical beacons of new ideas. You follow their glow and feel a little...lighter.

The Muse has turned off interruptions from the noisy voice of worry. Preoc-cupations of future and past, the distraction of rehearsed conversation, guilt or regrets, judgment or self-criticism, are muted. The mind then opens like the curtains of a movie screen. You realize you have the ability to connect to the mind's fleeting electric-ity, which creates stories, rhymes, rhythms, insights, and visions including one of you as a freely expressed agent of the creative spirit.

The world is a smorgasbord of ideas waiting for your selection. Driving becomes a time where ideas billboard your attention. Taking a bath becomes a reservoir of bubbling ideas. As you work in the kitchen, new ideas spontaneously brew. These amazing flashes awaken you. They open the senses right here and now making the creative process possible...mak-ing the theater of the mind a blessing within your reach.

ADMIT ONE, YOU HAVE THE TICKET...
ENTER THE GARDEN.

*"Ask Small Questions to program your
subconscious for AHA moments!"*

AHA-PHRODITE:
MUSE OF PAYING ATTENTION, PASSION, AND POSSIBILITIES

If I have ever made any valuable discoveries,
it has been owing more to patient attention, than any other talent.
—Isaac Newton, mathematician

SUMMON AHA-PHRODITE

- ◎ To reawaken your passion for creativity.
- ◎ To use the power of attention paying for your creativity.
- ◎ To invite you to capture and savor your inspiration.

BOTTOM LINE

If we pay attention to the present moment, we will discover that inspiration is not elusive or out of reach. An unfathomable amount of inspiration is already right in front of us. Creative electricity is everywhere, and we when we connect to the voltage of our awareness, anything in our environment can become a conductor of new ideas. Everything from the way the grass blows to the music of a child's laughter can become the art of our lives and the substance of artistic expression. In this consciousness, the passion for the creative process is irresistible.

Paying attention is (1) feeling awake and alive to the beauty in the manifestation of spirit; (2) being fully conscious as a gentle witness in all of life's offerings; (3) noticing when we have been presented with a rare and wonderful inspiration, insight, opportunity, notion, sensation, or gift.

THE SELECTION OF AHA-PHRODITE

So the nine Greek Muses were sitting around chattering in the Muse brainstorm chamber. As they began the selection process, lightning flashed from the electricity of their ideas. "What New Muse Transformations Do We Need to Make in Order to Jump-Start the Creatively Destined Modern Day Mortal Mind?" That was the question the Muses wrote on their Muse Dry Erase Brainstorm Board. (They wrote it in dazzlediphead, a popular Muse color).

They decided that the first Muse named should be representative of both the Muses in ancient Greek mythology and the newly upgraded Modern Day Muses. Polyhymnia (she of many hymns) exclaimed, "Aha!" and the rest of them agreed. Thus, Aha-phrodite was named.

Aha-phrodite's name was inspired from Aphrodite, goddess of love and beauty and well-known daughter of Zeus and Hera. The "Aha" portion of the name was gleaned, of course, from the "Aha!" discovery of a new idea. It was then combined with the old Greek name stem phrodite, from Aphrodite, making the new name a combination of both old and new, and of passion and discovery. This, they believed, was not only politically correct but rather clever as well.

YOUR AHA-PHRODITE ENERGY

Aha-phrodite energy is about paying attention. When mortals use this energy, they awaken to the recognition of an idea's presence and are thus able to consider its possibilities. They also begin to become aware of their thinking and choose those thoughts which exalt the creative process and tell the rest to "Go on now, get!" Mortals feel blessedly alive when an idea unpredictably makes itself known because it summons the expression of their unique originality. It is a nudge from their creative Spirit and a prompt to touch the world by sharing their singular uniqueness with others.

WHY PAY ATTENTION?

Paying attention is the source of great creative connections as well as the acknowledgments of gifts that come our way in the form of creative opportunities, careers, relationships, so we see, hear, feel, sense, that creative inspiration is everywhere all the time.

What is this thing called inspiration? It is anything or anyone that gives you that rising passion in your heart to create something, to feel something, to sing something. It is what makes you breathe deeply and love life if for only one moment.
—Tony Branch, columnist for "Artist's Inspiration," Suite 101

One of Aha-phrodite's favorite roles is to remind people about the love relationship we can have with the creative process. The union results in freeing our imprisoned splendor, sharing with the world our splendid remarkableness. Ah, the gift of an idea can be so sublime, so delightful. As English poet and religious leader Gerard Manley Hopkins reflects, "I want the one rapture of an inspiration." When we imagine looking through the portal of life with loving eyes, inspiration becomes daily awe and life has more color.

THE MAGIC OF PAYING ATTENTION

Aha-phrodite says loudly in the key of "yes": "Wake up to the present moment! In the moment, a glorious profusion of sensation, emotion, and stirring thoughts translate themselves into the form of a luring inspiration. You have the freedom to weave these inspirations into dreams, into art, into a reality you can step into with celebration. Why would you pass this up? What's that all about?"

Let's pause from our automatic routine to honor the appearance of an inspiration. If we are stuck on automatic pilot, ideas will be like wallpaper: unnoticed and two-dimensional. When we begin to recognize their presence, the windows open up and in fly possibilities, heralded by trumpets and dressed in Technicolor© discoveries. To invite more ideas, ask small questions. Here are some examples from Aha-phrodite herself:

- ❀ Where will I find inspiration today?
- ❀ What in this moment is imbibed with emotion, amazing, amusement?
- ❀ Who will say something or what will reveal itself today that will inspire in me a new idea?

Creative people have extensive idea-capturing skills. They know when and where good ideas occur to them, and they stand ready to preserve them. If we are not paying attention, we will miss the idea and the subsequent possibility for the joy that a new idea brings. It is important to capture ideas as they occur since ideas are fleeting. Aha-phrodite's main plea to you is this: "When an idea arrives, write it down!"

THE MECHANICS OF PAYING ATTENTION

The aim of life is to live, and to live means to be aware,
joyously, drunkenly, serenely, divinely aware.
—Henry Miller, novelist

Aha-phrodite wanted to be scholarly and share with us some dictionary definitions of attention from the Word-Weaver, Webster. Then she added her own comments for creative consideration.

ATTENTioN

Webster   "mental concentration and readiness"

Aha-phrodite "It's like reverse paranoia: knowing that something good is out to reveal itself to you and being hyper alert to what it is."

Webster: "care or consideration"

Aha-phrodite: "Please be considerate of the vast amount of inspiration in the vicinity of your soul's reach. Be fully conscious, as a gentle witness in all of life's offerings. Turn down the worry, the judgment, the constant commentary and open yourself to receiving"

Unless we learn to open up to each moment and squarely face what it presents to us, our life simply hurtles toward its certain conclusion. To be able to inhabit emotional/feeling time, we need to expand our moment, to wedge it open so we can step inside, linger without fidgeting, and experience what's going on within it.
—Stephen Rechtschaffen, M.D., cofounder of Omega Institute, author

TiME ShiFTiNG: CREATiNG MoRE TiME To ENJoY YouR LiFE PAYiNG ATTENTioN To OPENiNGS

When mortals embrace a creative path, opportunities, people, events, gifts, classes, avenues, signs, signals, and insights often begin to appear to support and inspire the valiant progression. If mortals are not open to these possibilities, if they are not *paying attention,* the opportunities float by like leaves falling from a tree—landing in a pile of lost chances and neglected blessings. See them . . . they are there. Catch them, follow, and watch your world branch out into new vistas. (Esoteric note: Press your lost chances flat in a book and write poetry about them… they made come alive again).

WHAT PAYiNG ATTENTioN iS NoT

When we are caught up in mind's default function of worry, preoccupation with the past, projection of the future, judgment, commentary, comparison, never-enough-dom, we are not present enough to see just what exactly is real in the moment.

If we are eating a sumptuous banana split but are thinking about the stock market, we have missed out on one of life's important fringe benefits—the delight of food. Our taste buds are registering pleasure, but if the mind does not acknowledge it, it might as well not have happened. And who wants to consume all those calories without the benefits? If your cat is racing through your living room in that crazy way cats do when they have monster drills, or if your child has just said one of those endearing things that children say and you are thinking of what how George wrong was in yesterday's staff meeting—you have just sacrificed a joy that makes up the sacred moments of our journey through life.

AHA-PHRODITE'S ENERGY DETECTOR

One way of paying attention is to notice what energizes you. Begin to be a keen observer of your energy meter. What seems to make you feel more awake? What perks your ears up? What makes you stop the autopilot daily routine and open your eyes to the event, the activity, the means for self-expression that has energized you? This is a divining rod leading you to where you will excel the most. That energy will help hurtle you past the obstacle that may come up for you in the process.

If you have difficulty paying attention to one of your ideas, narrow them down to the top three - like judges from a reality talent show might do. Have them audition for your attention, and chose based on the energy of your intuition. Three is a good number to work on at once versus seventeen or 389.

The energy that summons your attention will flower into ideas, intuition, and innovation. It actually is one of those things that make incredible sense, but because we may have lost a sense of who we are, we ignore it. Why would we spend time in those things that don't energize us? Those things that energize us give us fuel to follow through with them.

MOMENTS OF DELIGHT

When you are filled full with moments of delight you are "fulfilled." It is in the moment that we are fulfilled—not in some imaginary place in the future. Pay attention and you will see how easy it is to make a creative shift and fill with the extraordinary abundance of the ordinary. Joy happens.

Joy is what happens when we allow ourselves to recognize how good things are.
—Marianne Williamson, lecturer, author

MORTALS WHO WERE INSPIRED BY AHA-PHRODITE

As you walk on the garden path, you hear the voices of mortals who reflect the sentiments of Aha-phrodite. As you hear these words, you begin to the feel the passion of creativity, and spirit-lifted attention antennas open your awareness to the inspiration around you.

Any great work of art . . . revives and readapts time and space, and the measure of its success is the extent to which it makes you an inhabitant of that world—the extent to which it invites you in and lets you breathe its strange, special air.
—Leonard Bernstein, composer, conductor

I think the one lesson I have learned is that there is no substitute for paying attention.
—Diane Sawyer, broadcast journalist

Life is denied by lack of attention, whether it be to cleaning windows or trying to write a masterpiece.
—Nadia Boulanger, French conductor, educator

Today a new sun rises for me: everything lives, everything is animated, everything speaks to me of my passion, everything invites me to cherish.
—Anne de Lenclos, fifteenth-century French beauty and wit

The days are long enough for those who use them.
—Leonardo da Vinci, Italian painter, sculptor, architect, engineer

Only one thing has to change for us to know happiness in our lives: where we focus our attention.
—Greg Anderson, basketball player

Ideas are the mightiest influence on earth. One great thought breathed into a man may regenerate him.
—William E. Channing, moralist, author, clergyman

I dwell in Possibility—A fairer House than Prose—
More numerous of Windows—Superior—for Doors.
—Emily Dickinson, poet

MUSE PROFILE OF AHA-PHRODITE

SYMBOL

A lightbulb with wings symbolizes an idea taking flight. Aha-phrodite turns on by enlightening awareness and shifting attention to this idea's capacity to bring something new into existence.

HOBBIES

Aha-phrodite spends her time experimenting with various attention-getting devices, sandwich boards, neon signs, spotlights, searchlights, bells and whistles.

CAR

Aha-phrodite drives one of those newfangled electric cars.

True passion is intoxicating and invigorating, soothing and sensuous, magical and mystical. I just thought you should know what you're in for.
—Tazo tea bag: "Passion"

RITUAL TO SUMMON AHA-PHRODITE

Materials to summon Aha-phrodite: a white candle, your favorite incense, a lightbulb, and your journal or sketchbook.

To summon Aha-phrodite: Light the candle and the incense. Fill a page of your sketchbook or journal with a drawing of a lightbulb. Freely write ideas that come to mind about artfully living a life, or about your specific creative passion. Don't worry about making sense, just fit random thoughts inside the bulb to ignite your brilliance. Or color the lightbulb with designs and shapes using crayons, colored pencils, markers, watercolors, or oil pastels. Coloring within a contained spaced can center us giving us practice paying attention to one thing at a time.

Under the lightbulb write: "I honor Aha-phrodite's presence in my life by having notepads, journals, sketchpads, or tape-recording devices ready wherever I am, in order to catch inspiration's possibilities." Sign your name with light and love. Say one of the affirmations or ask one of the questions listed below and blow out the candle. Write the affirmation or questions in your journal every day this week, or write it on a card and post it where you can see it regularly. Watch for inspiration. It will arrive with every breath.

AHA-PHRODITE AFFIRMATIONS AND SMALL QUESTIONS

🌀 I am awake in each and every moment to the inspiration that surrounds me.

🌀 I collect ideas as they come to me and cultivate their possibilities.

🌀 There are ideas waiting for my attention everywhere!

🌀 Something creative is about the happen.

🌀 How will I remember to capture each new idea that comes to me?

🌀 Where will I get inspiration today?

🌀 What's paying attention really feel like?

And there you have it. Your Aha-phrodite energy is awakened.

JOURNAL CHECK-IN

1. Take out your journal and write about where you are with your Aha-phrodite energy. What were you thinking about yourself as you read the chapter? What aspects of creativity are you passionate about? Keep going with this unfinished sentence or fill it in differently five or six time: When I pay attention…

2. Let your inner critic have its judgments and criticism about how you pick up on inspirations and see their possibilities. Writing critical thoughts on paper foils the inner critic's future effects on you. Then laugh at your inner critic and with Bodyguard energy, say, "Thanks for sharing, but I'm unthwartable…which I know is not a word but I don't care."

3. Look over the quotes by mortals who were inspired by Aha-phrodite (p. 66). Pick one, and either continue where it stops or write anything from your own life that the quote brings up for you.

4. For the next five minutes, write, draw, or paint as if you actually were "the present moment." Then write about how you felt during the five minutes. For extra credit, do the same with "inspiration." For extra, extra credit laugh maniacally at your participation with Aha-phrodite.

5. Take a few deep let-go breaths. Get comfortable, and embody your own essence of Aha-phrodite. Then, using speed-writing, regular writing, or your nondominant hand, write a letter to yourself from Aha-phrodite. Let her give you some specifics and encouragement about paying attention and the possibilities in each new day. Let her praise you for what you are doing now and let her counter the voice of the inner critic compassionately.

MUSE WALK
AHA-PHRODITE STYLE

Go out for a walk and be as mindful of the present moment as you can. Be open to inspiration without pressuring yourself. Be in a receiving mode. Walk with your palms open as if they were an open conduit for receiving the energy of inspirations and the blessings of synchronicity. Let go of any expectations. Ideas gravitate toward open places. Movement invites inspiration. Practice moving mindfulness—stay so present that inspiration cannot resist your attention. Pair walking with the asking of small questions. Believe that on your walk there may be some inspiration, in a form you do not need to know, awaiting your attention.

Everything has beauty, but not everyone sees it.
—Confucius, Chinese philosopher

BRAINSTORM

SPONTANEOUS KNOWING

Complete the unfinished sentences below as if you were already living your dream come true. For instance, you might complete the first sentence with "I am a flower shop owner," and then answer the next sentence with what a good day would look like for you in the flower shop world, and so on.

Keep your hand moving as you speed-write so you don't think too much about the answers. The less thought you give to your answers, the more real information gets through uncensored. Some surprises may surface. Give yourself about thirty seconds for each sentence, then go on to the next.

If you do not know what your passion is yet, fill in the first sentence with "I am living fully in the present moment." Pay attention to your feelings in this exercise; watch for twangs of fear or nudges of excitement. This makes your dream real, so if you feel fear, see if you can identify its source and figure out what it is telling you. Just the identification of fear can allay its effect on you. Go for it.

I am ...
A good day for me includes . . .
My latest accomplishment is . . .
When I get scared I . . .

I no longer . . .
I feel good about . . .
First thing in the morning I . . .
My next step is . . .
I get angry when . . .
It makes me laugh when . . .
One day I know I will . . .
In my free time I . . .
I hide when . . .
One thing I would like to tell the world is . . .

And now for a completely different use: For beginning and experienced artists and writers, repeat this exercise for any character you may be developing in writing, painting, theater, or other areas of art.

PREREQUISITE TO CATCHING A DREAM: FINDING THE JEWELS OF DELIGHT

Every day we are blessed with dozens of experiences capable of bringing us delight. We notice some of them with only partial awareness, allowing us to only partially partake in their pleasure. Fuller awareness of these little instances of enjoyment will give us regular jolts of appreciation. This new awareness allows our desire for always needing "more" to disappear at the same time abundance begins to fill our lives. It is a Muse-bending experience.

JEWELS OF DELIGHT

Here are some examples: the first light in the morning, seeing a jumping dolphin, unexpected humor that makes you burst with laughter, having no one sit beside you on the airplane so you can stretch out, the feel of clean sheets (especially with shaved legs), the smell of coffee, the first exciting moments of a road trip, coming home after a long trip, saying something brilliantly funny at the right time, good friends having dinner together, putting on clothes that have just come out of the dryer on a cold morning, stepping into a warm car after feeling chilled, the look of someone who appreciated your unexpected help, the day you feel better after having been sick for a while, those moments of awe while attending a great play, putting on jeans that feel looser than the last time you wore them, the bite of the first juicy nectarine of the summer, a flock of birds in flight, Sunday mornings, holding hands, running into a good friend, knowing you are about to see a great movie, a breeze, the wonder of a perfectly formed flower.

These are the ingredients of fulfillment. If you cannot connect to the delight in these simple things, you will be unprepared to feel deeply the delight in life. If you reserve all your pleasure for the mirage of a dream far in the future, you miss out on the daily grandeur that the world's wisest people tell us is what truly makes life enjoyable in the moment. That is where we are, in the moment. After listing twenty of your jewels, notice that you begin to spontaneously experience more of them because you have put activated radar for increased joy-detecting frequency.

Take out your journal and Quick List twenty jewels of delight now. Or even better, have a list on which you can regularly add more jewels. They become a mood-lifter or antidepressant when you have the blues. They regularly reinforce the splendor of your existence.

JUST SAY ❀ AWE ❀

The jewels of existence address delight—the feeling of awe is a little different. Webster the Word-Weaver defines awe as "a mixed feeling of reverence, fear, and wonder." What makes us feel awe, stirs our soul's passion and can inspire our creative expression. Poetry, plays, paintings, film, photography, and music are many times the products of what awe inspires.

We can feel awe for anything from how diamonds are made to how some people can be incredibly rude on the freeway. I feel awe for lightning, how computers work, how many people there are on earth, ants, how many sunglasses I have lost, the human body, how quickly the kitchen floor gets dirty, people who can sing on key, prayer, and the depth of the ocean. Consider how the things you feel awe for can be worked into your creative passion.

Quick List twenty things that inspire awe in you. For extra credit, pick one or more of the awe items and write from its point of view, or speed-write anything it brings up for you. Notice the creative juice that awe gives you.

YOU ARE A MOVIE

The function of art is to renew our perception.
What we are familiar with we cease to see.
A writer, for example, shakes up the familiar scene,
and, as if by magic, we see a new meaning in it.
—Anaïs Nin, author

View yourself, throughout the day, as if you are watching yourself in a movie you are shooting with your eyes. This brings you clearly into the present moment and gives you an enhanced perspective that can attract new ideas. Watch your facial expressions and your responses to your daily activities. Watch what you say to others and how you respond when they talk to you. You begin to see the things you take for granted or a new creative perspective forges new pathways for creative ideas. Many ideas for stories, screenplays, performances, and even for sculpture and painting can be inspired by this "cinematic consciousness." You are starring in the movie of your life. Is it a comedy, a drama, an adventure, a short documentary, or a commercial?

CATCHING IDEAS

Think about your daily routine. If an idea popped into your head that could make you rich and famous or could simply keep you cleverly amused, would you be able to record it:

By the bedside at 3:00 A.M. or when you got up?
In the bathroom?
In the shower, bath, or brushing your teeth, etc.?
In the kitchen?
While commuting—car, train, bus, cycling, walking, ferry, airplane?
At the office?
Out to lunch?
By the phone?
In the coffee shop?
In any kind of motion?
In meetings?
In dreams?
In inspiring lectures?
In play and experimentation?
In reading works that inspire you because of their voice?
In lyrics and music?
In quotes?
In nature?
In mistakes?
In organizing?
On a walk?
In somber waves of angst?
In movies?
In loose associations and stream-of-consciousness writing?
In dancing around in the middle of your living room?
In a greenhouse?
Running, cycling, swimming, rock climbing, hiking, walking, sex, yoga, martial arts, weight training?

"YOU MUST BE PRESENT TO WIN"

¡DEA BANK

Once you have established the habit of carrying idea-catching materials, Aha-phrodite will comply by producing even more ideas. She's good like that. As you catch all these ideas, consider starting an Idea Bank where you can deposit your notes. The Idea Bank could be a file folder, shoebox, desk drawer, or a card index box. If you are an avid journal writer, stick notes that you caught outside of journal-writing time in your journal with tape or Post-its. Other material can be added to your bank or journal such as newspaper clippings, cartoons, quotes, or helpful hints. You may also want to store your ideas in a computer database. Ideas are not limited to sitting down and thinking.

Sometimes in my journal writing, viable ideas for projects, writing, or art will spring out of my daily dribble. It is important for me to circle or highlight these ideas so I can easily find them amidst all the other writing.

WAKiNg UP To PAYiNg ATTENTioN

A good way to wake up to paying attention is to set your digital watch, your phone, your MP3 player, or your computer to go off on the hour, to remind you to be fully aware of everything around you at that moment.

> The idea is to suddenly fracture the routine consciousness that put your powers
> of observation to sleep.
> —Paul Kaufman, author of "The Creative Spirit"

Quick List of What You Have Learned From Aha-phrodite

_____

_____

_____

Where can you Pay Better Attention?

_____

_____

_____

Where are you good at paying attention?

_____

_____

_____

THE NEXT STOP IN THE GARDEN

On the path through the garden you come across a male figure. He is beside a chalkboard wildly scrawling words and pictures, lists and flow charts, doodles and hieroglyphics. He's having a good time. You have wanted to be more resourceful in your creative process, to prolifically spawn new ideas or new ways to look at things. This guy greets you and in a German accent he says:

"Your mind can be scho much greater den mediocre. Just tweet a little here, reverse a little dare, imagine schome more under dis, schimmy a vord or two into somesching new, and ve schall see new ideas zat vill set ze world on fire with newness, novelty, and miracles. Ve have definite vays of being mysteriously schpectaclar. It's all in za thinking...so just think you can think somesching new and zen vatch the fireverks."

"Look at what everyone else sees...
And THINK SOMETHING DIFFERENT!"

ALBERT:
MUSE OF IMAGINATION
AND INNOVATION

There are only two ways to live your life.
One is as though nothing is a miracle.
The other is as though everything is a miracle.
—Albert Einstein, Swiss-German-American physicist

SUMMON ALBERT WHEN

⊚ You want to expand into the joy by changing the way you think.

⊚ You want to think differently in order to cultivate creative resourcefulness.

⊚ You want to reawaken and enrich your imagination.

⊚ You want to question existing parameters and "break the rules"
in the name of creativity, innovation, and the occasional miracle.

BOTTOM LINE

We have the power to think differently about our lives as well as about creative thinking. If we look at the same thing everyone else sees and think something different, we have just become creative. When we can fluidly list a myriad of ideas, we are innovative. When we plug into that place inside that can invent a world filled with intuitive symbols and spontaneous wisdom, we are imaginative.

We can choose thoughts that change the way we feel that then change the way we act that change our destiny. Now ZAT is creativity. In choosing creative thought, we create a deeper level of existence and a continual resource of ideas, solutions, and attitudes that best reflect the unfolding of our authentic self. What we previously defined as mundane has an element of the amazing. Our lives fill with the magic and the miracles that possibility thinking can create. This is the physics of fulfillment. It's full of phyzzle.

THE SELECTION OF ALBERT

"What do mortals need next?" thought the Muses about the continuing inspirational upgrade they were executing. They thought and thought and thought, and then they decided to stop thinking because it was getting monotonous. They needed a change in thinking. They started experimenting with words, sounds, images, associations, mirrors, and fusion. And new thoughts started percolating.

Soon afterward they said, "Okay, enough already. Let's quit dawdling." They were just stalling, because stalling is an unexpected thing for a Muse to do. And that is what the next Muse is all about. Yes, he is about defying the obvious for the innovative, moving from the mundane to the magical. He is about surprises to the cerebrum. He inspires mortals to see with new eyes so that what they were used to seeing one way can be construed in a much different way.

To get into the spirit of this Muse, protocols were broken and boundaries were stretched. Thus, this Muse is a male instead of a female. And not only that, a mortal inspired the selection of this Muse in a realm where Muses usually inspire mortals. They giggled at this disobedient gesture of pure genius, and then I can't remember which one, but one of them said, "Well, we've got to throw in some surprises or else the mortal mind will stall in complacency when it could be cruising in possibility."

All this, because from the psychic telescopes in the Muse Labs, they could see that those mortals often think as if they were confined within a little box. This is ironic because outside of the little mortal think-box side marked THIS SIDE UP is a takeoff ramp to the sky. It has been there all along. Some mortals have discovered it and used its power to reinvent their thinking. After meticulous scrutiny the Muses found one such mortal. They decided that a German scientist named Albert Einstein was the perfect mortal to inspire a Muse.

So, the next Muse is named and modeled after this mortal icon of innovation, imagination, and revolutionary thinking. Albert Einstein broke the rules, revered imagination, and believed that we had a choice to live life as if it were a full-blown miracle. Thus, we have Albert the Muse.

YOUR ALBERT ENERGY

To infinity and beyond!
—Buzz Lightyear, Toy Story

Albert is the catalyst for original thinking. The use of his energy can expand a mortal's world into a new reality. When mortals allow their consciousness to move beyond what they had previously thought possible, they can relinquish old, tired, discouraging styles of thinking and shift to an unbounded existence.

Aha-phrodite beckons mortals to pay attention to what inspiration is around and inside of them. Albert's energy takes that inspiration to the next step. He encourages mortals to bypass obvious solutions for the ingenious, to continue beyond the first and find several new ideas so that a more brilliantly informed selection can be made. How exciting to think mortals can move beyond automatic "default thinking" to "possibility thinking." Possibility thinking enables mortals to be deeply alive, as well as to invent, be resourceful, solve problems easily, and forge into dazzling and brilliant new realms of expression. Exploring a new realm of expression is a promise of reaching a wider scope of mortal possibility. It makes the Muses' feet dance to think about it. Possibility thinking is a blast, but it means a shift in consciousness.

Our thinking creates our reality... What are you thinking these days?
—Albert the Muse

THINKING DIFFERENTLY ABOUT THINKING

No problem can be solved from the same consciousness that created it.
—Albert Einstein, Swiss-German-American physicist

Let's step into a new consciousness. According to studies on the potential of the human mind, we use a small percentage of our brain's true potential. And generally speaking, we do not do too badly as a species just using that much. Will you imagine that notion for the next thirty seconds? We hear these studies, but none of them ever say HOW to use more the brain's potential. Enter Albert. Can you imagine how different our lives would be if we used just thirty percent more of this magnificent organ we have?

insert IMAGINATIVE Thinking Here

SLOW DOWN: BRAIN IN USE

Studies have also shown that we think similar thoughts over and over each day. Albert defines "default thinking" as a style of thinking that disregards that there is a more original way to think. If we recorded our thoughts and played them back, they would sound sort of like a broken record spiced rarely with a few novel things and a couple of new worries at spontaneous intervals. The broken record of default thinking usually consists of a smattering of judgments, worries, self-criticisms, running commentaries, and future plans. Not to mention rehashing the past, fabricated fears with no grounding in reality, routine thinking involving buying groceries, cleaning the crumbs off the counter, and paying the bills, and maybe an occasional desire to win the lottery.

Default thinking is not to be mistaken for an even less desirable weakening of mind that Albert calls "staring obliviously at the TV as well as the Internet" (SOATTAWATI). This is a condition mortals have succumbed to when they are unable to engage in anything more difficult than operating a remote control after dealing with a complex world that leaves little energy for dreams and soul expression. What's wrong with this picture? The TV and computer screen have replaced our ability to think original thoughts...that's what.

I don't know about you, but default thinking and SOATTAWATI scare me. Let's take our brains back! There are all sorts of ways to begin using more of our brain to deepen and brighten the experience of our life. The first one is to question the existing rules.

BREAKING THE RULES

> Creativity not only involves coming up with something new,
> but also with shutting down the brain's habitual response,
> or letting go of conventional solutions.
> Kenneth Heilman, a neurologist

Albert Einstein won a Nobel Prize for his work on relativity. He broke the rules of physics that, until his time in history, were considered unchangeable. His deviation out of existing parameters proves that rules can be broken and that enormous advances in science are possible. Thus, the Muses believe his example can motivate anyone who wants to make even small advances in their creativity. The Muse Albert illustrates one of his tools of innovation, the "tool of association between two unrelated ideas." The Muse Albert associates the relativity from Einstein fame to the modern mortal's need to think differently. See the box with my attempt to illustrate what I just said.

THE MUSE ALBERT'S NEW THEORIES OF RELATIVITY

The greatest discovery of my generation is that human beings
can alter their lives by altering their attitudes of mind.
—William James, philosopher, psychologist

✳. You will enjoy life relative to how much you are inclined to think about life in a way that makes it worth enjoying.

✳ You are creative relative to whether you think you are creative or not.

✳ You use a small percentage of your brain relative to how much you can use.

✳ You will come up with new ideas when you relate two or more formerly unrelated objects, notions, images, or words. This is the foundation of innovation, humor, new products, novel concepts, and Reese's peanut butter cups.

✳ Ever-new solutions and ever-new possibilities are relatively easier to discover than you may think.

Nothing is written about how we must do art, or how we must live our lives. For the most part, we get to make up our own rules—ones according to our morals, values, religious beliefs, culture, idiosyncrasies, and experiences. When we find aspects of life or art that don't work for us, we can make our own rules based on finding new ways to live within the framework of those six things listed in the last sentence. When we do find new ways to live, we create another dimension in which to express ourselves, to live life more deeply, and to inspire others to do the same. So then, why do we insist on following the narrowly contrived rules of others?

"Let the beauty we love be what we do."
—Rumi, thirteenth-century poet

The Muse Albert is eccentric and unafraid to experiment with thought. He encourages us to break existing rules that limit new ideas—just as Albert Einstein did in his groundbreaking work on physics. If we move from automatic thinking to innovative thinking, we can start thinking differently about the way we can think. When we think we need to follow someone else's rules about creativity or art or writing or artfully living our life just because everyone else used them through centuries of time, we must question why.

NEVER STOP QUESTIONING

When teaching concepts of creativity, I attempt to illustrate what I am talking about by how I teach my class. I make it a point to add a qualifier after the instructions for an exercise to test people's ability to go beyond my instructions to their own resources. I add after the original instructions, "Or however you want to do it, there is no right or wrong, this is a *creativity* class." Participants are encouraged to break the rules so that something new has a chance to be discovered. Most students have a hard time actually following through with this instruction. Some feel absolutely liberated breaking the rules, and still others are uncomfortable with such an open structure. Our school-age training was often so rigid and geared toward following directions that we forgot to think for ourselves. Instructions are really just one or more person's point of view, so why not question them for a bit of creative growth? Why not rearrange them for our greatest creative potential? Some rules need to be followed for safety or for correct implementation of procedures, but many rules can be changed to reach beyond set parameters to discover something new. Next time you embark on a creative endeavor, look at the instructions through a different lens—see how you can change them to better accommodate *your* individual style and expression. Start with chicken salad.

> A truly happy person is one who can enjoy the scenery on a detour.
> —Anonymous

This concept of breaking rules, or revising them for our greatest creative good, is foreign to most of us. We will religiously follow instructions even if they do not meet our needs. And if they don't work for us, we think we have failed, when in fact, if we change the rules according to our identity, experiences, subculture, resources, and desires, discoveries can be made for excellence, rather than failure. We can forge into the blessed country of Originality! We do not get a grade in our daily creative expression. Einstein's questioning resulted in a Nobel Prize because existing parameters did not allow for the discovery he made. He questioned the rules and made up his own.

CURIOSITY AND WONDER

> Curiosity is one of the most permanent and certain characteristics of a vigorous intellect.
> —Samuel Johnson, English lexicographer, critic

Curiosity is an attitude that can be cultivated and expanded. Our curious attitude can find new possibilities in anything. Curiosity is a form of wonder—being in a state of wonder is being open to all there is still to learn. Being in wonder is to be in love with life. It is a return to childlike expectations, untainted by adult rigidity and cynicism.

Erich Fromm stated, "The creative attitude first requires the capacity to be puzzled. While most children still have this capacity, most adults believe they ought to know everything—that to be surprised or puzzled by anything implies ignorance." The Muse Albert believes that we should never stop questioning. When we stop questioning, we become complacent about the answers, and "dat's just about da scariest thing I can think of since the Stepford wives. Mortals will be at da mercy of becoming obsolete and zen da opportunity for creative joy will just plain be down da drain with da chicken fat."

CULTIVATING RESOURCEFULNESS

Albert has devised some ways that mortals can use their brains more efficiently. "Un zen more creative ideas come with da little effort and da lots of good time." The result: Mortals generate more ideas than they ever thought possible. Every mortal possesses Albert's power inside. He simply needs the mortal's permission to share his inspiration. In the following sections, Albert shall reawaken the center of the mortal mind, where ingenuity resides. He will help us to forge new brain pathways to make it easy for many different kinds of ideas to flow through. Dip into some trust in this process and get ready for amazing effects.

If we settle for the puddle of knowledge in which we sit, we shall never know the majesty of the sea and its endless possibilities. The ocean is our creative consciousness. Stretching the mind with novelty can let in some of the ocean mist so we can taste where the mind is capable of going. And instead of being stuck in the muck we can embark upon a new way of existing that we did not even know was possible, one of creative authenticity and daily awe. Just open your mind and say, "Awe!"

First:	Be willing to let go of your old way of thinking. Say out loud, "I am ready to let to let go of my old way of thinking." Then think about what saying that means to you. What thoughts would you let go of? What rules do you now follow that really don't make sense from an aerial view of your life?
Second:	Realize that the mind is meant for the weaving of dreams, not the nagging of noise. Take the mind under your own control—you need not be at the mercy of old patterns.
Third:	Begin to take the mind under your control instead of being at the mercy of old patterns.
Fourth:	Let your brain feast on all the different dimensions of life, of art, and of love that it can consume now that you are beginning to be where you have always wanted to be.

BRAINFEAST:
A BANQUET OF IDEA-GENERATING TECHNIQUES TO ENHANCE YOUR LIFE AND YOUR DUCK 🦆

MILKING THE ABSURD

Let your mind free-associate to an absurd degree and write down what it says. You might find the duck in the subtitle above out of place, or to you it may have some deep-thought-provoking meaning. But like a Zen koan, its purpose is to bewilder you—help you stretch out of a complacent place of thinking. If you try to figure out why it is there, literally, you actually create more openings in your mind for ideas to slide through. Feel the barriers of your mind tremble as you read the following Zen koan:

Show me your original face, before you were born.

THE PHYSICS OF NEW IDEAS

The suggestions below are ways to expand your mind so that you think in new ways and consequently come up with new directions. Let your mind stretch to understand the short definitions listed below. They are concepts of innovation that may seem foreign to logic, so logic may initially respond with rejection or maybe a "Huh?" As Einstein himself said, "Imagination is more important than knowledge." Knowledge is fixed. The concepts below involve the boundless imagination. Here they are:

Listing: The Muses have you listing throughout the book because it is one of the most effective ways to forge new literal pathways in the brain through which more ideas can flow. Listing helps us go beyond the first five obvious answers that anyone can easily summon. Searching hard for forty-five more ideas flexes muscles of idea fluidity. Listing also alerts the subconscious to keep going with the subject even after you've stopped putting your list on paper. After a listing session, your subconscious continues to work on the subject, and more ideas will spontaneously present themselves in the weeks ahead. Then the resourcefulness you are developing will begin to happen naturally in every aspect of both art and life. You will surprise yourself at the number of ideas that begin to accompany your every day.

To **Quick List**, number your paper to the specified number in each exercise, or to at least twenty. (If you want to really EXPAND your mind's capacity to easily generate ideas, expand THAT number to one hundred.) Then, according to the focus indicated in the exercise, begin listing without stopping to think. If you cannot think of the next item to write on the list, repeat yourself, write gibberish, write complaints about the exercise itself, but keep writing. This method prevents you from prejudging thoughts and getting stuck. More ideas emerge than if we stopped to think at each new number. Surprising, novel, and insightful answers may come up. Garbage may come up, too, but garbage is preferable to nothing in this practice, as well as in the creative process. It means the mind is working. Besides, what we sometimes think is garbage often turns into art or can lead to insight or the next right step. The point is to open the brain's ability to run free without worries or distractions.

Associations: Associations are used as a way to generate new ideas. This process starts by ascribing new meanings to existing concepts. Existing words, images, sensations, thoughts, or concepts can elicit new ideas that are triggered by loosely associating new meanings to parts of old concepts. Imagine how things you see and hear can be construed as something else and that muscle in your mind will entertain you more than any TV show is capable of doing.

Since my childhood I have been creative in weird ways. When I see a gadget, say a blender, I imagine how I can use it for something else.
—Isabel Allende, author

Connections: This is the connection of two previously unconnected words, images, senses, thoughts, or concepts. Try relating cooking to dancing, birds to designing a garden, random verbs to art ideas. You will find more on this in the Brainstorm.

Repetition: This is the creative potential elicited by repeating a word, image, sound, or concept over and over (and over). Rhythm, punch, and artistic tension are created with the throb, throb, throb of bold repetition. The mind will volunteer words and ideas in the midst of repetition because it responds to the spontaneous fill-in the blank structure.

Personification: Bring a concept to life by giving it a personality. The Muses are proud to be an example of this concept.

Relocation: Getting up from your desk and relocating your body someplace else will also relocate your mind out of a limited groove. Moving, working from a café, in an auditorium, or even talking while standing will create many more ideas, techniques, and solutions. I generate richer ideas while talking in class or talking in front of my sink than while sitting at my desk.

Exaggeration: We operate in a narrow range of expression to be socially appropriate. This limits our awareness of ranges past daily acceptability that are filled with new ideas and more artistic methods of expression. Many times, exaggerating an idea, a concept, a dance move, an art approach, a story, or a problem in need of solution can take it to a new level of energy or create new insights by removing it from its designated space. Make it really big, small, dramatic, angry, nice, etc. This breaks you out of a formerly limited range of thought and expression.

Take a problem in your life at present. In your journal exaggerate it way out of proportion. Dramatize your reactions to it. Create new characters if you feel the need. Bring in your own special spirit guides to help out. Invite background singers, firemen, the clergy, police, superheroes, characters from different movies, to join you.

What in your life can you minimize? Talk about an important event nonchalantly.

VISUALIZE CREATIVITY, IMAGINE YOUR DREAMS COMING TRUE

One reason Albert was able to develop the theory of relativity was that he worked on visualizing it. He recognized that the ability to picture things in the mind is vitally important to the creative process.
—Larry and Marge Belliston, authors of How to Raise a More Creative Child

During the thirty years I have been facilitating creativity, the power of visualization has been made clear to me. You have probably seen it, too. When you are taking steps to honor creative dreams, a force outside of logic seems to enter in to assist you, the dream seeker. Although I was once skeptical, the number of times it has happened to students and colleagues has made me a true believer. One thing stands out: When people take steps to be true to their higher self, their power is fortified.

What is a visualization? Visualizations consist of creating the vision, or picture, of what we want in our life in our mind—as if it were already happening. It is like running a movie of your life with the dream already woven. The subconscious creates the conditions for it to manifest. Belief and experiencing the dream in the body as if it is already happening are the fuel.

In the space just below, draw yourself doing something creatively either abstractly or representatively. Stop the inner critic from criticizing or stopping you. Let it be imperfect. Just have fun....A visual of any form helps bring this thought into being, because now you have a conscious image materializing. Images are a powerful force in the weaving of dreams. If you must, give yourself permission to draw like a five-year-old.

Dr. Robert Maurer adds to the discussion of visualization with what he calls, "mind-sculpting," visualizing virtual- change with all the senses, including the way the muscles will be moving during the scene so that real change comes more naturally. Mind sculpting has an added strong emotional component. So, you would be imagining and visualizing yourself engaged in an effortless creative process. Instead of just watching your "mental movie," you are also experiencing each of your senses along with a strong, positive emotional component. You are answering what am I seeing? What do I taste, smell and hear? What do I touch or feel on my skin? And how am I feeling emotionally?

Muse Albert says, "Ze energy ve create by za thoughts ve think makes our visions possible. And za more you are true to yourschelf, da more de energy is coming from a place vhere vhat is visualized can really, really happen because it is coming from da truth."

THINKING ABOUT OURSELVES DIFFERENTLY

Look through new eyes and picture yourself in the best possible light...as creatively expressing your creative passions with effortless joy.

Whether you believe you can, or whether you believe you can't,
you're absolutely right.
—E. M. Forster, English novelist

In his book, *A Whack on the Side of the Head*, Roger von Oech cites a study that concludes that the main difference between people who are creative and people who are not creative is this: Creative people think they are creative while the other group does not. Once again, the power of thought poignantly grabs our attention.

Think this: "I am creative." If that's hard to accept 100%, try allowing yourself to accept if 5%. All of these changes will not happen overnight. Thinking differently takes time. If you can practice it just a little at a time, regularly, you will surprise yourself with how it begins to come automatically over time.

i get to be creative.

MORTALS WHO WERE INSPIRED BY ALBERT

Walking in Albert's part of the garden, you hear the echo of mortals and learn exactly what inspiration there is in learning to think differently.

The real voyage of discovery consists not in seeking new landscapes
but in having new eyes.
—Marcel Proust, French author

A rock pile ceases to be a rock pile the moment a single man contemplates it, bearing within
him the image of a cathedral.
—Antoine de Saint-Exupery, French novelist, aviator

Instead of seeing the rug being pulled from under us,
we can learn to dance on the shifting carpet.
—Thomas Crum, author of "The Magic of Conflict."

A sense of curiosity is nature's original school of education.
—Smiley Blanton, in "My Favorite Quotations" by Norman Vincent Peale

Joy in the universe, and keen curiosity about it all—that has been my religion.
—John Burroughs, author, naturalist

Each one sees what he carries in his heart.
—Johann Wolfgang von Goethe, German poet, dramatist

To look at a thing is very different from seeing it.
—Oscar Wilde, Irish playwright, novelist

There's a wonder in the way we're always free
To change the world by changing how we see.
—Cyndi Craven, singer-songwriter

We are not here to do what has already been done.
—Robert Henri, painter

MUSE PROFILE OF ALBERT

SYMBOL

Albert's symbol is a box falling open releasing the wonder of new possibilities. This happens when we choose to shift our mind's focus to the possibilities outside of the usual predictably packaged thinking.

HOBBIES

Enthusiasm, rule-breaking, daydreaming, laughing, writing on blackboards, walking with a jag, inventing, and practical jokes.

CAR

Albert drives a 1955 Saab.

Take the obvious, add a cupful of brains, a generous pinch of imagination, a bucketful
of courage and daring, stir well, and bring to a boil.
—Bernard Baruch, businessman, statesman

RITUAL TO CALL ON ALBERT

Materials to summon Albert: three yellow candles, a window, music that evokes images, nightfall, your journal.

Start the music and sit by the window. Place the candles in a convenient place nearby and light them. Watch their reflection in the window, then ready yourself for seeing differently. Blow the candles out and shift from seeing the candles' reflection in the window to seeing out the window, and beyond the obvious. With full awareness of the present moment, see as much as you can see that is really outside the window. Then allow your imagination to carry you away for the next five minutes. Make connections to everything you see. Associate with what you see outside to what ideas it can bring up for you. If you can't see anything, just let images arise to the music. Light the candles again.

Write down your experience, allowing the writing to take you further into your imagination. Make it up as you go along. In your journal say to the Muse Albert within you, "I am inspired with a renewed imagination and an endless resource of ideas." Then say one of the affirmations listed below and blow out the candles. Write the affirmation in your journal every day this week or write it on a card and post it where you can see it all week. Start watching for an abundance of different ideas effortlessly coming to you. In the coming week notice yourself thinking in new ways about your world and about creativity and watch for a shift in your point of view.

AFFIRMATIONS AND SMALL QUESTIONS FROM ALBERT

◎ I get to think new ways about my existence.

◎ What's one small way I can think more creatively today?

◎ How can I look at something everyone else sees, and think something different?

◎ I generate many ideas and solutions - there are more than one right answer.

◎ I am open to breaking rules for creative adventure.

The Muse Albert shines his energy on you.

JOURNAL CHECK-IN

☼ Take out your journal and write about the use of Albert's energy in your life now and where you could use more. Make it an Albert Inventory.

☼ Write, draw, paint, or act out some of the things your inner critic has to say about thinking differently, imagination, and breaking the rules. Letting the critic speak on the page without placating its words weakens its effects.

☼ Look over the quotes by mortals who were inspired by Albert (pp. 85-86) and pick one. Use it as a starting place and continue by quick-writing with it or write, paint, or draw your feelings and point of view related to your selected quote(s).

☼ Write, draw, paint, or sculpt as if you were the concept of imagination (see example on p. 84) and continue with one or more of the following:

     as if you were imagination on caffeine

     as if you were an angry imagination

     as if you were a benevolent imagination

     as if you were an imagination stuck in a closet

as if you were an imagination that worked as a waitress in the local bar and grill

☙ Take a few deep breaths to let go of your body's tension and your mind's chatter. Then write a letter to yourself from your Albert energy. Use your nondominant hand if you choose. Let Albert give you some pointers and encouragement on thinking differently, making up your own rules, and being resourseful. Let him counter the inner critic with anything that is needed and praise you for whatever efforts you have made so far.

MUSE WALK 🕺 ALBERT STYLE

Take a walk and be in your Albert energy. Think differently about this walk. Invite connections to come up for you without forcing them. Watch that your mind does not go to default thinking, and if you notice it does, gently shift to possibility thinking: thinking about what's next in your creative project, how you can break the rules, go for the less obvious. Let the walk be an opportunity to exercise different thought patterns. Look for all the patterns, shapes, colors, and symbols on your walk. How does what you see on the walk connect with your creative passion? What other random thoughts do you have while walking that can connect to your creative passion? How can you think differently about this walk? What do you see that you can think differently about?

No amount of skillful invention can replace the essential element of imagination.
—Edward Hopper, painter

BRAINSTORM

MILKING THE ABSURD AND TUNING UP YOUR IMAGINATION

◎ Write, say, paint, dance, or act nonsensical things to move beyond the walls of your previous limitations.

◎ Write a completely absurd essay about what happened yesterday. Go past the boundaries of what's expected of you. Or draw, paint, or dance in an absurd way illustrating the essence of yesterday. Let this stimulate your brain expansion centers.

🌀 Revisit your childhood imagination. What stimulated your imagination when you were little? What books did you read? What did you pretend to be?

🌀 Imagine you are a character from one of your favorite books or movies. How do you approach your creative passion now?

🌀 Imagine you are the most respected artist in the field of your creative passion and write your thoughts about having this position and what you will do with it.

🌀 Listen to all different kinds of music; make yourself comfortable and let images arise from the music. Let the music be a sound track for your own personal music.

🌀 Talk spontaneously about your creative passion and what you plan on doing with it next to an imagined audience in your living room. Do the same for an imagined group of fans, an imagined group of children, an imagined group of aliens, and an imagined group of reporters.

Imagination is the art of thinking inventively and originally. Daydreams flow—the collar of our thinking is loosened so new images form, new sounds are heard, new movements materialize. For me, it is like a movie screen—I project dances or performances or new pictures that I want to paint. My imagination is enhanced with music, heightened awareness, and a dash of the absurd humor. When I practice using my imagination, new ideas seem to be waiting for me.

In our imagination, we can direct the creation of new worlds. We can imagine and create anything, from new characters and their predicaments to worlds on canvas and melodies on sheets of music. We can hear, see, feel, and smell ideas waiting to hatch through our imagination. Much of the magic of imagination is simply making the time to play in the arena of the possible. To defy what exists for something further. To bend open the mind and toy with notions, visuals, music, and movement that, up to this point, did not exist.

Cultivating Resourcefulness

Associations

Humor often comes from the quick association of new meanings to old thoughts, ideas, and images. In other words, breaking the rules of a word's meaning and ascribing another meaning by some idea that comes loosely to mind from a trigger provided by the thought, idea, word, or image that goes along with the word. Whoa. Here's some humor from the Internet. Examining an existing word, ignoring its real meaning, and associating a new definition based on its spelling creates these new words:

Abdicate—(v.) to give up all hope of ever having a flat stomach.
Esplanade—(v.) to attempt an explanation while drunk.
Flubbergasted—(adj.) appalled over how much weight you have gained.
Lymph—(v.) to walk with a lisp.

DON'T SETTLE FOR THE FIRST SOLUTION

Here is one of Albert's most powerful tools. When you start playing with your ideas, make a habit of going past the first solution. Each time you start brainstorming, ask, "How can I take this a step further, and then another step further after that?" Quick Listing comes in handy here by catching your additional steps. Explore mind-mapping - Google Image it.. and see how you can teach your mind to think differently.

ASSOCIATIVE WORD TRIGGERS

I use the following words in my private coaching sessions to create new ideas and fun approaches to practice with artists from all disciplines. Storytellers, comediennes, painters, and writers use them to come up with new ways to think about their craft. To use this technique, associate the word new ways to experiment with your creative passion. You can use the literal meaning of the word or anything the word reminds you of to come up with new ideas. Begin this practice by looking at each word and associating what ideas that word can give you for doodling or moving your body.

exaggerate	hopscotch	electrify
minimize	blow	get scared
relax	vibrate	repeat
make believe	acknowledge	make unnecessary
broadcast	circle	rearrange
reverse	belittle	start in the middle
compound	exalt	shift
invent	improve	subtract
mesmerize	plot	cut in half
improvise	over tell	exclamation point
elevate	under tell	gibber
splurge	confuse	simplify
rest	make weird	

CONNECTiONS

To me books on butterflies or baseball are more legitimate
in terms of thinking about business strategy issues.
—Tom Peters, motivational speaker, author

Here are some examples to help illustrate the exercise of connections:

⟳   Find a kitchen appliance and write a list of how it can inspire you to do your creative work differently.

⟳   Open Scientific American and see what science articles can inspire art for you.

⟳   Open a book, find a line, and copy it down. Add your own writing for the next several lines or until you feel you've gone far enough.

McNeil Sargent teaches how to use the paintings of the masters to develop a new painting style. Her students study the masters, pick one of their paintings, and use the master's colors and shapes with the student's own subject matter. This approach involves connecting an old method with a new style leading to the discovery of another way to paint.

STRiNGiNG JEWELS TOGETHER

Take some of your jewels of existence from Aha-phrodite's brainstorm section and newly associate them by stringing them together in a poem or verse. What you will find is poetry or prose made from the small parts of life that bring you delight. The writing will transport you into a place where pleasure resides: the well-fed mind.

QUiCK LiSTiNG FOR iNCREASED FLUENCY OF THOUGHT

Listing keeps your mind expanding into more flexibility as it participates in mental-nastics. Number your paper from one to between 20 and 100 (the higher the number the more fluency you will develop). Make lists of topics needing several solutions or ideas according to what is going on for you now. Find places in your life where you thought just one solution was enough and see how creative you can get by listing nineteen more. This is where innovation and distinction surface. Use some of the following ideas to warm up your listing skills:

- Small questions that you can constantly ask to keep your creative thinking alive
- How many uses you can think of for an empty egg carton
- Ways you can redecorate your space to reflect who you are
- Ways to reorganize the food in your refrigerator
- Ways you can generate new business (be absurd, silly, break the rules)
- Ways you can enjoy the work you do more

- Things to do on Sundays
- New names for yourself
- Your favorite words
- Pet peeves
- Constructive ways to show anger
- Different ways to show love
- Places you'd like to go
- Subjects you'd like to write about, paint, sculpt, collage, act out, write a song for
- Secret lives you'd like to live
- Different ways you can improve your approach to your creative passion
- Different answers to the question "How are you?"

CURIOSITY AND WONDER

I have no special gift. I am only passionately curious.
—Albert Einstein, Swiss-German-American physicist

Quick List a bunch of things that you are curious about. Number your paper first. Begin sentences with a combination of "I wonder if . . . ," "I'm curious about . . . ," and "What if . . ." Don't stop to think; repeat or write nonsense if you need to; have fun with it. Notice how you feel when you are doing it.

TIPS ON VISUALIZING

Imagine having what you want as though it were taking place in the present. Do not fantasize as if it were a future event. Feel the sensations you would feel in your body and emotionally right now. The universe is a big Xerox machine. It simply copies and distributes back to you what you think. Your future is the extension of your now. Life can unfold as you imagine it if you are a match and are ready for what you call forth.

BREAKING THE RULES

A. Pick a creative outlet that you enjoy and make up the rules and the procedures according to your own intuitive sense of direction. Use a different kind of paper, lose the rules of grammar, and let whatever designs and creations result be experiments with doing things according to your own different way.

B. Take a group of rules or policies or principles and, if they are not based on unchangeable safety or ethical principles, change them for your own definitions. Or take each one of the following New Theories of Relativity and write how they apply to you.

1. You will enjoy life relative to how much you are inclined to think about life in a way that will make it worth enjoying. How can you think of your life differently?
2. You are creative relative to whether you think you are creative or not.
3. We use a small percentage of our brains relative to how much we can use. Journal writing invites a higher percentage.

BACKUP PERSONAS

WARDROBE OF PERSONAS

Come up with a group of personas that serve you. A persona is a different set of personality characteristics summoned to address your present situation. Using a persona is creatively adapting to your world by reinventing who you are. It is surpassing your tendency to be fearful by inventing a confident persona and then wearing it. It is moving beyond your inclination not to believe in yourself as a creative person by wearing a creative persona and then feeling more certain about your creativity. It's like putting on an outfit that better equips you for the world.

I have a friend who is relatively introverted. When she is in social situations, she rolls up her selves to indicate she is putting herself in a socially competent persona. The shift in thinking, accompanied by a symbolic change in her clothing, seems to make her more socially comfortable. Although she is the same person, believing she can be something different, and then becoming it with a developed idea, gives her a greater range of responses for the complex world—a characteristic of a creative person.

What if you had different personas to upgrade your thinking? What would they be and what could you do to indicate that they are in operation? What if you had an imaginary friend who took over when you engaged in your creative pursuits? How would he or she be different from you?

SAGE ADVICE

What if you could get a famous and/or respected historical or present day person to comment on your project? What would the following people or characters say about the creative solutions you are looking for? Don't be too literal. Use your imagination. Take on their persona for yourself and write or sketch from their point of view:

Abraham Lincoln
Audrey Hepburn
Bugs Bunny
Albert Einstein
Marilyn Vos Savant
Mark Twain
e. e. cummings
Dr. Seuss
Character from a current movie
Garrison Keillor
Tom Robbins
Jon Stewart
Stephen Colbert
Your fairy godmother
Rumi
Martha Stewart
Xena: The Warrior Princess
House
Your best friend
The smartest person you know
The most respected person in your life
The funniest person you know
A favorite author
Iron Man
Your neighbor
Owner of the minimart down the street
Lewis Carroll

"Who would you include in a think-tank meeting about your creative project?"

THE DREAM BOARD

Every moment of your life is infinitely creative and the universe is endlessly bountiful. Just put forth a clear enough request, and everything your heart desires must come to you.
—Shakti Gawain, author of "Creative Visualization"

A dream board is a visual blueprint of your dreams. You choose pictures from magazines, photographs, brochures, books, and glue them to foam board or poster board. Then you frame it and hang in a place you see it both consciously and subconsciously frequently.

These pictures become imprinted on the brain as memory, as existing—they are not distinguished from what is already there. Of the twenty pictures I glued on my most recent dream board, fifteen of them have come true in the six months after I made it, including trips to Hawaii and France. I was flabbergasted. If you have made a dream board, you may have experienced the magic of its materializing if you have placed it in a good location and had a sense of belief. There seem to be some other definite conditions consistent in the construction of successful dream boards:

Release the notion of feeling selfish or superficial when asking for material gain. As we feel we deserve fine things in our life, we send out energy of deserving to others. Deserving comes from a deep place of truth as we release the shame that will insidiously sabotage our ability to progress. Releasing shame empowers our higher intentions with focused actions. Receiving material items helps us do more of the work that benefits other people, and somehow the powers that be know this and reward us accordingly. Place your spiritual intention in the center of your dream board.

LIST SOME OF THE IMAGES YOU WOULD LIKE TO HAVE ON YOUR DREAM BOARD:

_____
_____
_____
_____
_____
_____
_____
_____
_____
_____
_____
_____
_____

Looking at a Grocery Story Differently

Embark upon a search for the masked treasures within the mild-mannered grocery store. This is a collector's trip. You will be collecting awe, whim, beginner's-mind delight, triggers for divergent, original thinking, and fun, serious, and yummy viewpoints. Within every ordinary experience is an extraordinary encounter waiting to happen, but it requires the attention of Aha-phrodite, the imaginative thinking of Albert, the playfulness of Bea Silly, and the freedom of Audacity. In the meantime Muse Song may encourage to buy yourself a treat, and Spills the Imp will encourage you to enjoy the process and not worry so much about the result.

Here's what you will do. Give yourself an allowance of $10 - $25. Roam around the grocery store with new eyes. Notice the textures, the colors, the packaging. Look at the people, the stock boys/men/women and the customers. Sneak a peek in people's grocery carts. Converse with the rump roast. Go to sections you wouldn't normally visit. Get a load of the variety in the "Feminine Hygiene" section. Create your own design of traveling through. Fixate on a particular section, the packaging, the ingredients, the competition. Follow one customer in particular.

I used this for a writing class, and these are some of the things we experienced: One student only wrote about pink products. Another student wrote about the bathroom and the conversation she had with the stock boy, and someone wrote entirely about figs. I found myself enthralled by the names of all the hot sauces and the ingredients and decided to contrast my love relationship with them. Someone started a whole novel about a women's preservation society in the South as she glanced at the selection of preserves. Still another student took Polaroid pictures of a lobster. This is truly using the world as your artistic inspiration.

Aha-phrodite would say, "Take notes." Don't be surprised if a grocer approaches you—last time we did this a manager thought we were health inspectors. Just explain you are being creatively inspired by the wonders of the store.

Then write, sing, or paint an illustrative account of your findings. Or be Isadora Duncan and create a dance. Somehow express your particular slant on the grocery store and make a routine activity into art. Don't overthink it. Don't go for perfection—go for novelty and fun. Be a travel reporter, be a news reporter, or be Erma Bombeck—but remember great artists go through many drafts, so just expect your first one to be what it is...I have faith in you. Go out there and be clever, crazy, and fashionable. Open your mind to a different view of a mundane task and you will never, ever, be bored or stuck in a rut again. Life will actually become a daily spectacle of amusement.

Have you been doing your five to fifteen minutes a day of creative passion?

THE NEXT STOP IN THE GARDEN

As you walk farther into the garden, the earth does a "Wordsworth"—it begins to laugh in flowers. The breeze dances in trees and you have an urge to be a little silly. Along the path, a childlike apparition beckons you to leave behind rigid, serious adult responsibilities. With her you climb through a tunnel, down a slide, over a jungle gym, (with a brief stop at an ice-cream truck), to a playground where having fun, being playful, even foolish, is encouraged. She gives you a funny cap to wear backward, a squirt gun to destroy the eminent imaginary monsters along the way, and sneakers to leap over villains. She takes your hand and says, "Let's make believe we are on another planet," "Let's invent a new language," "Let's hide behind that tree and surprise your friends when they walk by."

Pretty soon, fresh new ideas emerge like presents on Christmas morning. She takes you back to where the present moment is open with childlike wonder and uninhibited silliness. Fun is the main goal, because it creates relaxation, new visions, and the freedom to think originally and spontaneously. This Muse is here to set you free from the ties that bind you creatively...namely yourself as an adult. The good news here is having fun and allowing yourself to play have tremendous benefits on enhancing your creativity.

BEA SiLLY: MUSE OF PLAY, LAUGHTER, AND DANCE

It's so much fun being human.
—Rhonda Britten, author

SUMMON BEA SiLLY WHEN

◎ You need to re-learn how to play, lighten up, release rigid thinking, and remember how to make your creative expression fun.

◎ You need to remember and reawaken to the wonder of being a child and know the positive implications this has for your creativity.

◎ You are feeling resistant toward working creatively for one of these reasons:

❀ You just don't seem to want to do it.

❀ You feel a childlike power struggle inside you. You want to do something creative, but you never actually do it.

BOTTOM LINE

Joy, play, laughter, and dance make life lighter and more creative. The cultivation of joy is rewarded with new ideas and fun. Let go of the rigidity of being an adult, find yourself again in play and laughter. Realize play results in productivity and is actually vital to the creative process.

THE BEA SILLY SELECTION

Bea Silly got her name from one of the earlier Modern Day Muse assignment meetings. The Muses were sitting around intensely brainstorming about various possibilities. They wore deep-furrowed brows. Thalia, the Greek Muse of comedy, noticed, "Dudes! Aren't we getting just a little bit too serious?" Knowing that this is unwise in the creative process because seriousness often chokes the play of ideas that generate handfuls of ingenuity, the Muse Albert replied, "Hey, for za next hour, let's just be silly." The experience was rewarding...and Bea Silly was born.

YOUR BEA SILLY ENERGY

All creative people are kids at heart.
—Steve Carmichael, producer, director

Bea Silly knows that the childlike qualities mortals possess are highly responsible for their creative flow. She encourages mortals to loosen up and take creativity less seriously. She is the energy inside mortals that catalyzes play. All mortals have this energy. Yet for some, a strict, uncompromising adult side put the playful side away with the roller skates.

Fun is an elixir of spontaneous ideas. Solutions that seemed so elusive earlier appear effortlessly in the midst of play. To engage in the kind of play that stimulates ideas, mortals need to take themselves less seriously and make room for making things up, kidding, and goofing off. Bea Silly advocates the mortal prerogative to be silly, foolish, and frivolous, and thus have fun. She wants mortals to step out of the adult mode that, because of its tight adherence to unbendable rules, leaves little room for creative discoveries.

A light mind creates an inner playground for ideas. Insecurities that mortals have about letting down their adult guard, and thus looking foolish, need to be reexamined for the benefit of creative exhilaration. Who is the fool? The childlike mortal with a lightness of heart dancing with the spontaneity of mischievous ideas, or the strictly adult mortal who takes himself too seriously?

In her "Creativity at Work" newsletter, Linda Naiman explains, "When people are growing through learning and creativity, they are much more fulfilled and give 127 percent more to their work. Delight yourself and you delight the world. Edison, Einstein, Picasso, and da Vinci all loved to play and they loved to explore. Through play we open our receptivity to imagination, intuition, and daydreams. Play is the root of genius."

THE FREEDOM OF CHILDLIKE ACTIVITIES

Are we having fun yet?
—Carol Burnett, actress, comedienne

Sometimes I ask my classes to draw themselves doing playful things. Most students freeze up at the prospect of having to draw anything. Given permission to draw like five-year-olds, they go at it. When they are asked to scribble, miraculously they dive in with great enthusiasm—the pressure is removed. The end product is fascinating because every person's scribbles are different, although you might think they would all look like tangled-up telephone wire. Even the voices of our scribbles manifest themselves with our unique design. In this simple, unencumbered exercise we demonstrate our diverse voices. There is an audience for everyone's expression if that expression has within it the talent it was meant to embrace—the one that comes from the heart. If we simply express our voice through words and visuals as easily as we scribble, we will share a natural and uniquely wondrous, authentic voice.

Taking the scribbling exercise a step further, we title the scribbles and, on private slips of paper, write down titles for everyone else's scribbles. There are as many different interpretations as there are scribbles. It is another reflection of the diversity of creative voices coming from the artist child within. The creative process works through each of us uniquely.

For you to stay fresh as a writer or an artist, Bea Silly encourages you to experiment with other forms of art, or to wander into stores you would not normally go into but about which you are curious. Be in wonder wherever you go and let yourself be a beginner, over and over again.

PLAYING BLOCKS AND BREAKING THEM

Tom is a stand-up comedian who was experiencing a dry spell. He creates a character onstage that has comical, childlike confusion. His work was getting stale, the lines fell flat, and laughs were decreasing with each show. We experimented with media other than standing up and delivering a dialogue. He found that doodling in a sketchbook right before he goes onstage freed him up to be more in character. The motion of scribbling went beyond the limited warm-up of just thinking about lines. It awakened the child that plays onstage when he is doing his delivery.

Sara was a storyteller who wanted to take her craft to a deeper, more professional level. When she practiced, she stayed stiffly in one place with limited hand gestures. I asked her to play with her story by exaggerating it and making it one of her worst deliveries ever. She varied her voice, moved around colorfully with unpredictable rhythms, made great sweeping hand motions, and basically had a lot of fun. Instead of being one of her worst deliveries, it elicited a whole new style of entertainment and fun. She used much of the exercise's results to enliven her performances.

Susan, a creative writing student, felt she had lost all the enjoyment of writing. She was having a hard time letting go of the rules of writing and what she thought she was supposed to do. She spent too much time listening to others. She did not know where to go next in the development of her characters. I asked her to interview them or have them write her a letter. At first this suggestion perplexed her since her adult side could not comprehend how an undeveloped character could write a letter. Once the idea sank in, she lit up like a child. Each week she brought in a new letter that a character had written her. The characters had taken on such a life of their own and she could not wait to hear what they had to say next. She shared her findings with such excitement. The characters embodied a hidden side of her that had been dormant. Now that they had their own voice, her characters had a broad range of characteristics, and they even surprised Susan. She had returned to the source of her imagination and to the well of ideas that fills when we play. The technique brought fun back into her writing and allowed her to be more productive.

You can do the same with any area of life or art. Figure out how imagination can give you a different viewpoint. As a visual artist, write a letter to yourself from an image ready to come into reality. If you were writing a nonfiction book about trees, Bea Silly might say, "Hey, go interview a spruce and see how you can branch out from the usual dry bark." If you were writing an article about single mothers, she might conjure up play by asking different fanciful questions like "Name a vehicle or a circus character that might describe your experience as a single mother." Bea Silly would also give you ideas for your writing from the curious, innocent, and open-minded child's point of view, a view untainted by narrow and rigid adult views.

Many of the Muse journal-writing exercises ask you to write from the point of view of a quality, emotion, or personality characteristic. If you can have fun thinking from this new point of view, new ideas will tumble free. What in your life can write you a letter to give you more insight? A symbol? A problem you are trying to solve? A creative idea trying to make itself clear? Have your next job write you a letter. Write a letter from characters in your dreams.

In many ways, creativity requires loosening up, otherwise you will become restricted to a tight area of operation. Allow yourself to go out and buy inexpensive materials like tempera and newsprint and found objects from garage sales. For any creative-idea session, you can experiment using these materials without feeling restricted to the careful use of expensive materials. Use the same materials to come up with inspirations for staff meetings, marketing your business, or planning a celebration. Watch the nonlinear, nonverbal nature of the art media give you more ideas than just the verbal realm. If you are excluding play from your life, take a serious look at why. Integrate play everywhere you possibly can. Lighten up, wouldja?

FROM SILLY TO INGENUITY

The creation of something new is not accomplished by the
intellect, but by the play instinct acting from inner necessity.
The creative mind plays with the objects it loves.
—C. G. Jung, psychologist, author

Many times, while in a playful mood, I have thrown comical, absurd, or silly ideas out to colleagues while working with them on a creative team project. Trying to amuse others and myself is a trait that has been with me since childhood. Colleagues sometimes respond, "Oh, come on now, let's get serious." And sometimes I do need to be more serious, but sometimes it is those silly ideas that lead to new, inventive ideas. Often I develop the idea on my own anyway and do discover innovative merit. (So there.)

Ideas often seem silly just because they are new and not something the mind has yet registered as acceptable. They tarry outside the boundaries of what currently exists. This is no reason to reject them. Defying boundaries is a Muse-approved activity. The mind may be stuck in a predetermined set of boundaries so that something offbeat may seem inappropriate when, in fact, it may be the next great idea.

What if in the mid-1990s you were sitting in a Mountain View, California, board meeting when someone mentioned that the name of a major Internet search-engine database might be "Yahoo!"? Would you say, "That's silly"? Now a highly successful endeavor and a household name, Yahoo! obviously came from a fun and playful place. What about Google? Also a seriously profitable enterprise. What about the names: "blogs" "zazzle" "wii". And some of the most expensive TV commercials (such as the ones you see during the Super Bowl) started out with what seemed like a silly idea. How silly is a voice transmitted over a wire to another country or a machine that makes hundreds of supplies in the time it takes an individual to make one? Telephones, TV, movies, and inventions of all kinds were considered silly when they first arrived. Silly is a beacon for consideration.

What silly things in your life camouflage solutions and innovations? What if you had a silly brainstorm? Come up with a problem to be solved on the way to your dream and be a silly kid spurting out goofy ideas. Write them on big paper with crayons. See if something new and wonderful might come from it.

More important than talent, strength, or knowledge is the ability to laugh at yourself and
enjoy the pursuit of your dreams.
—Amy Grant, singer, songwriter

MIRACLES OF LAUGHTER

During my time as a manager for hospital units, I noticed that the tension in meetings was heavy. I had to do something because my brow was getting stuck in a permanent furrow. At the beginning of the meetings I gave out squirt guns or Styrofoam balls to be thrown at judgmental comments to dissipate the tension. The laughter that ensued freed up people's minds to focus clearly on productivity. A Dr. Seuss story illustrated a problem we were having with getting people to cooperate. Hot Tamale candies were given to the staff member who showed the best motivation each week. Everyone was given, and told to peel, a banana while we got to the meat of the matter. A windup bird flapping its wings wildly without flight symbolized being all wound up and not getting anywhere. And so on. Meetings where people are awake, having fun, and releasing tension through humor strengthen team building, commitment, and motivation. Similarly, relationships are strengthened with play (remember the saying "Those who play together, stay together"?). Laughter and being silly are harbingers of collective creativity.

✿ But i Don't Want To ✿

Bea Silly gives us the keys to unlock some of the resistance we may feel toward being creative. Some of the secrets lie in our childhood. If criticism, ridicule, discouragement, or creative neglect came at an early age, they came at a time when we were inexperienced in overcoming conflict. We may have felt threatened and in need of self-protection.

We were delicate, unsuspecting critters not yet mature enough to know how to overcome creative land mines with protective strategies that would not later block our creative flow. Additionally, acts of creativity are fragile and need lots of support to take hold and flourish. Ridicule of any kind can wipe creative interests out for a long time, if not for a lifetime, if we do not explore ways to undo the damage. Creativity can be resurrected again in a supportive environment, and with a sense of adventure, freedom, and experimentation rather than dread. Awareness and deep inner-compassionate work can bring back dormant creative joy.

Often our response to discouragement was simply to stop doing whatever creative activity met with a thoughtless reaction. We were extremely sensitive to harsh opinions from overly critical parents, siblings, peers, or other adults. Or we were influenced by parents who thought they were helping us by steering us away from anything that was perceived as an impractical creative field. We were also at the mercy of the often rigid expectations of the school system, brainwashed away from unique thinking, inventive approaches, or novel behavior. We wanted good grades, so we sacrificed originality. We wanted to be accepted, so we curbed silly behavior. We chose defenses that eliminated feelings of embarrassment, possibilities of inadequacy, and exposure of what we did not want people to know about us. And those defenses were so effective they may also have eliminated our creative joy. If we no longer spontaneously engage in creative fun, we miss out on a whole dimension of life that gifts us with the confidence, ability, and ingenuity that comes from diving into the process unencumbered. And, gee, that's a lot of yucky stuff that has messed up our fun stuff.

> I didn't belong as a kid, and that always bothered me.
> If only I'd known that one day my differentness would be an asset,
> then my early life would have been much easier.
> —Bette Midler, actress, singer

PLAY

Making your approach to creativity fun can rejuvenate powers of the uninhibited freedom you had as a child. By choosing new play techniques that are not charged with painful memories or subconscious baggage that can create resistance, you can begin to express a new childlike side of you. If you are willing to let down your adult facade, you can coast into new playful action as easily as if you were sliding down a slide (unless it is a metal slide on a hot day and you are wearing shorts). Just begin to look for a new child inside you that is ready to create the ease of happiness on the outside. In the descriptions below, and in Bea Silly's Brainstorm section, find what play might be original for you to use for your dream weaving or creative passion.

Play works so well in the realm of creativity because ideas do not just appear when we are sitting down and thinking real hard. Ideas cannot resist playful movement. Play's active spontaneity is the optimal condition for creativity. That's why dance and movement are part of Bea Silly's domain. Exercise and any other kind of physical activity can also elicit ideas. The energy of exercise releases stress so the mind is free to connect to the ideas behind the tension.

> He who hesitates is frost.
> —Eskimo proverb

THE SAFETY OF THE CHILD

The "inner child" has been overly explored as it relates to the wounded part of us. We also have an inner child filled with joy. We can choose to use either one for our creative benefit: the child side that stubbornly refuses to let us be creative or the side that refutes the voices of the inner critic, thereby freeing us to be more creative. The child stubbornly keeps us resistant because we were hurt or are still angry. The child for us is used more effectively, keeping us stubbornly committed to our creative joy. Use of Bea Silly's techniques alchemizes the strength of our child into the conviction to participate in our creative passions no matter what.

FREE YOUR INNER BRAT

> It's never too late to have a happy childhood.
> —Anonymous

Scott was a brilliantly accomplished artist who was trying to reawaken his love of creating large mystical acrylic paintings. He was resistant to returning to his easel and did not quite know why. I prescribed various creative exercises to invite back his motivation, and each were met with a childlike frown and crossed arms. Clearly his artist child inside was not happy. He had been so caught up in the difficult responsibilities of his graphic design business that he had excluded anything fun. There was little time to enjoy the pleasures of his everyday life. Although painting is a pleasure, it takes hard work initiated by the motivation of the inner artist child. If that child has been neglected, he will not be cooperative about allowing the adult side to paint. Scott's child refused to let him paint, retaliating as if to say, "If I can't have fun, there's no way I'm letting you paint. You can't have fun either."

The next week I gave Scott the assignment of stomping around the house like an upset child, playing hooky from his work, talking back to his demanding adult voice by saying, "So what, you can't make me." I told him to rebel against and refuse a list of daily tasks I had prescribed for him. I gave him a lot of tasks so he would have a lot to rebel against. I told him to listen to what the childlike side of him wanted to do and then to indulge that child. As I made these suggestions, his face shifted to a mischievous expression. The next week he came back with a canvas filled with the beginnings of a fabulous painting. His stubborn-child side had been given an outlet and some nurturing attention. The result was a release of resistance and a reciprocation of desired artwork.

Scott also responded to the mystery of the instruction to "start your painting and see where it leads you." He was used to careful planning before starting his paintings, so a childlike sense of wonder was awakened with this instruction and he once again broke through his resistance.

If you are feeling resistant toward starting your creative projects, consider whether you have been doing enough "fun stuff" in your life. Allowing your child side to play and goof off doing anything for just fifteen minutes before you start will make it easier to get to the things the adult side wants to do.

If you were a child right now, what would you choose to do? Ask yourself this question often, and do some of those things—but without the scolding adult throwing guilt and "shoulds" in your direction. Let the adult consciously know that the "shoulds" will only backfire...that it is fine to use a little free time to loaf, water the plants, pet the cat, tamper with some toys, play a video game, or read something frivolous.

You may find yourself in an adult/child struggle. The child watches excessive hours of TV; the adult scolds and says, "Look how you wasted your time!" Bea Silly's distinction is this: You watch infrequent favorite shows or whatever sounds like fun with complete approval from the adult, and the child will then more easily comply with your adult-side wishes. You become more whole and contented. (TV is only an example because it seems pretty dern popular as a time-filler.)

Remember the Bea Silly principle. Give your artist-child side fifteen minutes of play at different intervals during a busy workday. You will be rewarded with more energy and ideas for your work. So THERE!

Play is the exultation of the possible.
—Martin Buber, German-Jewish religious philosopher

It is the shy, little, vulnerable artist-child side of us that is willing, or unwilling, to move forward in creativity, and the strong part of you needs to protect that child in these ways:

What if you surrounded yourself with people with whom the artist child feels comfortable? Reparent your child by providing large gestures of nurturing. Set time for yourself once a week to treat yourself to something your artist child would like. Ask your artist child, would you rather go to the art museum gift shop than the art museum? Would you rather see a frivolous movie than a serious one? Would you rather have a grilled cheese than a tofu stir-fry? As you listen to your artist child and abide by the childlike requests, you will be gifted with the power of creative energy. All of a sudden a stubborn, dormant side of you will open to the festivities of life and your imagination will become spontaneous again. When this happens, the process feels like magic.

Since my artist is a child, the natural child within, I must make some concessions to its sense of timing. Some concessions does not mean total irresponsibility. What it means is letting the artist have quality time, knowing if I let it do what it wants to, it will cooperate with me in doing what I need to do.
—Julia Cameron, author, screenwriter

Time to Play

Allowing yourself to play may take practice if you have been cooped up in a rigid adult stance for a long time, but look at the payoff. You get to enjoy life in a childlike way again, which is worth the price of admission, and you get to reap the joy of a return to creative expression. All areas of your life will be affected positively...you will lighten up, you will feel more giving, less resentful. Others will want to be around you. But if that adult voice throws guilt at you, the child will rebel instead of respond and a power struggle will ensue. Awareness will make the difference.

CATCHING ART FROM CHILDHOOD

Memories of the essences of childhood, and our sensitive response to these memories, are also filled with stories, styles, and art. Reader's Digest sometimes has art and photographs on its back cover. One month's issue had a photograph of a telephone wire running diagonally across the print with clouds and blue sky in the background. The photographer had captured a memory she had of lying in the car while her mom was driving, looking up at the telephone wires as they repetitively flowed by. It was a childhood memory to which many of us can relate. Viewing it can transport us back to a time when this dance of telephone wires gave us a sense of wonder. As adults, most of us do not even see the thousands of wires we pass under every day. Although the spell of newness is over and we have cataloged it away from possibility, we can continue to endow our environment with the wonder we had as a child if we capture it in art. Being mindful of the visual, auditory, and kinesthetic sensations in our environment keeps the magic of the present moment open. You have dozens of similar experiences, and the expression of them in any media you choose, from storytelling to painting, is a validation of your experience as a gift to be savored and shared.

BE FREE

Do what the spontaneous child would do. If you feel an impulse to do something different just because it would be fun and would make you laugh, try it simply because you are alive and you can. Do not worry if it does not make sense. Just have fun.

THE WONDER AND CURIOSITY OF THE CHILD

Ask ten times with wild abandonment, "What if?" For example:
>   What if people who tailgated vanished when they got too close?
>   What if I could sing in a blues club? How about a yellows club?

>   What if bananas flew?
>   What if Jell-O molds talked?
>   What if life were a bowl of eyeballs?
>   What if I could get out of my own way?
>   What if a picture could paint a thousand words?
>   What if a face could launch a thousand ships?
>   What if love were a pile of leaves?

To take the exercise to another level...take one of your "What if" statements and begin writing as if it were true: Life is a bowl of eyeballs and now they all need reading glasses...My Jell-O mold talked to me this morning about how I feel suspended with the fruit cocktail I work with...As soon as I got out of my way I will give myself permission to dance...Love is a pile of leaves and mine has little bugs in it...You will discover new images to paint, poetry, starts to stories, or maybe just amusement.

MORTALS WHO WERE INSPIRED BY BEA SILLY

Listening to these mortals talk, you begin to feel the inspiration of play, dance, and laughter open you to more creativity.

A spirit of fun should pervade every meeting because
it helps people participate and learn.
—Gene Perret, from "Quotations to Cheer You Up When the World is Getting You Down,"
edited by Allen Klein

Serious people have few ideas. People with ideas are never serious.
—Paul Valery, French poet, essayist

People do not quit playing because they grow old.
They grow old because they quit playing.
—Oliver Wendell Holmes, U.S. jurist

Genius is nothing more or less than childhood recovered by will, a childhood now equipped for
self-expression with an adult's capacities.
—Charles Pierre Baudelaire

To stimulate creativity, one must develop the childlike inclination for play and the
childlike desire for recognition.
—.Albert Einstein, Swiss-German-American physicist

He deserves Paradise who makes his companions laugh.
—The Koran

A child's attitude toward everything is an artist's attitude.
—Willa Cather, novelist, short-story writer

Play produces feelings of pleasure which help you escape from two major creativity killers—
stress and self-consciousness.
—Jordan Ayan, creativity consultant, speaker

MUSE PROFILE OF BEA SILLY

Bea Silly's symbol is a playground where ideas are somersaulted into existence without effort. Bubbles passing through symbolize playful lightness and the spontaneous joy of fun movement.

HOBBIES

Laughing, twirling, leaping, blowing bubbles, short-sheeting beds, singing loudly, collecting toys.

CAR

Rides a Schwinn Aerostar.

All creative people are kids at heart. You've got to play—do stuff that's definitely not work to get off the linear approach to creative work. I keep yo-yos in my office and I play solitaire on my computer.
—Steve Carmichael, producer and director

RITUAL TO CALL ON BEA SILLY

Ritual materials: a balloon; pick one: crayons or finger paint or Play-Doh; cinnamon-apple Pop-Tarts; your sketchbook and/or journal; and a glass of milk.

Blow up the balloon but do not tie it. Say this sentence out loud: "Just as I release the messages that come from some strange tendency to be a rigid adult I release the hot air in this balloon. I see the gift there is in thinking and acting playfully." And then let the balloon fly through the air. (This is especially effective in a group of five or more people because as the balloons release, they sound like a bunch of kids sending defiant raspberries to the all-too-serious adult side of us.) Then, for five to fifteen minutes, play with your selected art material. When you finish, eat your toasted Pop-Tarts (or if you prefer a juicy piece of fruit perfectly in season), drink some milk, (milk mustaches are encouraged), and write a statement to Bea Silly in your journal or sketchbook (preferably with a crayon). Say, "I will allow my artist-child side to have more freedom." Then say one of the affirmations listed below, clean up your mess, and take a nap (optional). Write the affirmation in your journal every day this week or write it on a card and post it where you can see it regularly before napping. Watch for bursts of playful energy and an increased willingness to do creative things in the coming week.

AFFiRMATiONS AND SMALL QUESTiONS FROM BEA SiLLY

◉ I release the need to be an overly responsible adult. I will open to my playful side and create a more balanced existence.

◉ I aspire to the freedom of being silly without worrying what people think—because being silly leads to new discoveries, lightens up my day, and is fun.

◉ Like a child, I trust that my world can be filled with wonder.

◉ Where will I find laughter today?

◉ How can I make whatever I'm doing fun today?

◉ What is one small way I can be silly in the interest of creative bliss today?

JOURNAL CHECK-iN

∗ Quickly write or draw your Bea Silly status: What were you thinking about yourself or others when you read the chapter? Can you allow yourself to be childlike? Playful? Funny? Silly?

∗ What does your critic have to say about play, dance, and laughter in your life? Take a moment to give your critic a chance to fully express himself or herself without being held back.

∗ Review the quotes by mortals who were inspired by Bea Silly (p. 109). Pick one and continue in your own words where it left off or write about how it applies to you.

∗ Write, draw, paint, or dance as if you were the quality of play. What would you say from the point of view of being the essence of play? Let the boundaries of your mind extend past logic and into the realm of playful imagination. The piece does not have to make sense.

∗ Take a moment, relax with three let-go breaths, close your eyes, and allow your essence of Bea Silly that is inside you to come to come to your consciousness. Write a letter to yourself from your energy of Bea Silly. What would she (or he) suggest that you do? Write quickly and let her tell you what your own inner-artist child needs to be more cooperative and playful, and less stubborn. Let Bea Silly talk back to your critic. For each discouragement the critic says about your creative process, let Bea Silly respond with "So what, I'm doing it anyway" or "Who cares what you say." Use your inner brat to defent you rather than have a power struggle with you.

MUSE WALK - BEA SiLLY STYLE

Go outside for a Muse walk. Walk with heavy feet the way you might imagine a child would walk. Feel the essence of being a child again. Skip if you would like. See the world around you through the eyes of a child. Enjoy the way your moving body feels. Feel everything that feels good about your body. Embody the feeling of having an inside joke. Let ideas playfully follow you on your walk. Feel optimism, open-mindedness, wonder, mirth. Catch ladybugs. Set them free. Ask yourself: What if I think like a child in this moment?

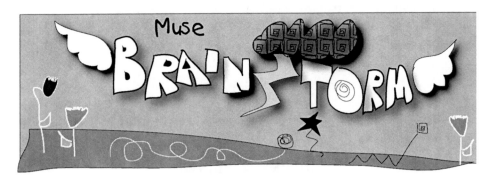

BRAiNSTORM

GETTiNG SiLLY

The best way to break through the rigid bounds of being an adult that repel creativity is to begin to *talk out loud in gibberish using vocal inflections as if you were saying real words.* Do this alone, and notice if you are completely self-conscious even though you are doing it by yourself. If so, your inner critic is policing your freedom to be silly and telling you to stop because it is uncomfortable. That same discomfort will stop you from exploring creative realms. Keep doing the gibberish until you start to feel comfortable with the silliness of it, at least by yourself. Nobody is watching! Silly talk primes your child side for opening up and connecting to great new ideas.

A similar exercise is to just begin *laughing for no reason at all.* At first it may feel contrived, then it just seems to take over. Laughter is cleansing and makes way for new ideas. Do it in the car. Make faces at the other drivers, blow bubbles in traffic jams.

Reconnect with what made you silly when you were little. Did you make spitballs? Did you do imitations? Did you do funny movements, make funny sounds, do double-jointed things? Entertain your parents? Just the memories can help bring back the essence of fun.

Quick List twenty memories you have of being silly. What was your own special brand of silliness? Do not be concerned if you cannot think of all twenty. Your subconscious will work on it even when the list has been put away, and memories of your past silliness will then revisit you at unexpected times. If you weren't silly at all, list how you could have been silly.

SHiFTiNG iNTo THE ENERGY oF EAGERNESS

Kids are often filled with eagerness for what's next. Adults can be filled with dread. Take your "I have to...list," and change it into "I get to…" In other words, notice the shift in energy in your body when you put "I get to" in front of everything on your To-do list. The child-like spirit awakens and somehow the task is made easier. Feel the difference between these two sentences: "I have to write today," and " I GET to write today." The second one is MUCH more likely to have an "oh boy!" at the end of it and we need all the "oh boys" we can get.

STiCKERS

Keep fun stickers handy to reward yourself for engaging in your creative passions. Make a weekly chart and fill it with stickers. Use them on letters to friends. To exceed your play requirements, even seal the envelopes of your bill payments with them. Somewhere inside of you is an artist child who opens up creatively anytime you do something you may have appreciated when you were a child. Stick one on your forehead.

Be aware of wonder. Live a balanced life—learn some and think some and draw and paint and sing and dance and play and work every day some.
—Robert Fulghum, author

MOVEMENT

Inspiration and ideas often come during movement, not just sitting and thinking. In fact, for kinesthetic learners and creators, most creativity happens when they are dancing, gesturing, or moving in some fashion. The walk is included in every Muse exercise section because it is one of the most effective ways for anyone to generate ideas. Instead of taking your dog for a walk, take an idea for a walk. (But don't forget about the dog.)

Experiment with ideas by playing with them in movement. Exaggerate them as you talk about them. Playact every side, everyone involved, anyone who might see the end product. Playact as if you were the problem. Make an announcement about the product. Play with props of any kind for any kind of problem solving.

Stomp around the living room.

Dance in your den to boogie-woogie or some other lively music that gets your feet moving. Get wild, throw your arms and feet around.

Then swing your body back and forth and let your arms swing as if they were just pinned to the shoulders. Have an "I don't care" attitude. (Do not underestimate the power of this one either.)

Go out dancing.

RAMBLINGS

Write in your journal or sketchbook ten times in crayon, pencil, or pen: "I get to do creative things and you can't stop me."

In your daily journal write things a kid might, or write sideways in your journal.

Scribble; comment about the world around you in kid language.

Alternatively: Explain a creative project, idea, or problem you have as if you were explaining it to a child. Explain it from a child's point of view. It is amazing what new ideas come from this childlike frame of reference.

FIELD TRIPS

(Get a permission slip signed by the adult in you.)

Spend a half to a full hour a week with the artist child; get into a childlike mentality and let he or she pick what to do.

Go to the grocery store and let your artist child pick some things to buy. Break down your rigid rules about eating in the interest of creative nourishment just once a week.

Engage in some of the creative projects that you liked to do as a child.

THE UNSENT LETTER AND OTHER GNARLY STUFF

Know that any kind of adversity met during the early years of your creativity may have stifled your creativity. Try to remember voices of the people and what they said to discourage you. If your talents were neglected, acknowledge any related anger you may feel. Let your inner brat write an unsent letter using force, belligerence, and uncensored emotion. Remember, unless you bring unhappy feelings into your awareness, they have control over you. Writing them down helps to banish the resentments from your inner kingdom. Write a letter about any issue in your life that is troubling you. This is a letter venting stopped-up feelings, it is not a letter to send. After writing it, write a transition clause at the bottom that says"Okay, now...that I'm over that, I can go play." Not that the anger will be completely gone, but I bet several layers of it will have evaporated.
"So What, I'm Doing It Anyway!"

Instead of allowing it to prevent you from being creative, use your stubborn inner brat to disobey any deterrent to creativity. When the inner critic tries to stop you, say, "So what, I'm doing it anyway!"

Consider the inner voices and how you can respond:

Inner critic:	"You can't do that! You're not good enough!"
Inner brat:	"So what, I'm doing it anyway!"
Inner critic:	"That's not practical, quit wasting your time."
Inner brat:	"So what, I'm doing it anyway!"
Inner critic:	"You're too old."
Inner brat:	"So what, I'm doing it anyway!"

And so on and so forth.

Have a dialogue with your inner critic right now. Think of the most critical thing your inner critic says to you and then refute what he or she said with the inner brat:

ART THAT'S FUN

Paint as you like and die happy.
—Henry Miller, novelist

"Free drawing," or doodling, is an exercise to shut your brain off and let your hand move across the paper. There is a temptation to feel that a creative session is a failure if we do not create a piece of art—banish those thoughts. When you free draw there is always the possibility of a creative breakthrough. Art is a tactile exercise, and by returning to the basics, our minds will subconsciously create.

Try this exercise in the morning—before the influences of the outside world have diluted your brain and creativity. Paint: Play with paint without judging yourself. Give yourself unconditional acceptance. Title your pictures and hang them on the refrigerator. Say, "Look what I did." Have the Bodyguard sneer at anyone who doesn't absolutely love them.

HUMOR

You can't stay mad at somebody who makes you laugh.
—Jay Leno, comedian, TV host

Do housework or chores to TV, or movie theme songs, or any song that makes them fun.

HANG AROUND FUNNY FRIENDS

Find them. Play with them. Laugh with them. Keep the merry theme of life alive.

Creative individuals place a high value on fun because
it enables then to soar in their other pursuits.
—Jordan Ayan, creativity consultant

Enjoy yourself—it's later than you think.
—Chinese proverb

GUiDED iMAGERY FoR HuMoR RELiEF

This is a guided imagery that illustrates how creative fun can ease in a playfully effective way the tension you have around a difficult person in your life.

Relax. Breathe three deep, let-go breaths. Release all tension from your body. Give yourself a moment to quiet your thoughts and allow stress to melt away with each exhale. Feel yourself open to the innocence of being a child. Imagine an opening in your head. Let everything you don't need drop out of that opening, down to the floor, and see it scamper away. Let your creative centers come alive and welcome imaginative fun.

Notice a group of good-looking people of your opposite sex completely at your beck and call—serving your every need. Pick one of your favorite comedians—Paula Poundstone, Ellen DeGeneres, Jon Steward, Robin Williams, Billy Crystal, Lucille Ball,—and feel the spirit of their humor open you to your own.

Now picture a difficult person in your life. See them standing in front of you. If there is no specific person, make the subject your inner critic; translate it to a human form so that you can see it in front of you. You choose. Now dress whoever it is in a beautiful Ann Taylor suit or deck them out in a Ralph Lauren suit. See the person one of those moments that they have caused you the most difficulty, anguish, and irritation. Feel the emotion they evoke.

Now replace their suit with a pink tutu. Put an unlaced sneaker on one foot and a high-heeled shoe on the other. Add a messy hairdo. Now place them on a cow...riding topless. Whole bunches of people are watching them. If you've chosen a difficult woman, George Clooney and Johnny Depp are in the front row. And if it's a man, some sexy woman actress is watching and snickering. See them ride around you for a while. Now take them off the cow, but only if they are humble and apologetic to you. Now they must clean your bathroom. See them scrubbing the floor, the mirrors, the trash can. See them waiting on you, bringing you tea and crumpets. Check to see if they are performing their duties to your standards. Make them do it over again if they are not. If they have passed inspection, reward them by replacing the tutu with regular clothes from say . . . the Salvation Army.

They seem much more humble now. You decide it is okay to forgive them, but you let them know the spell will automatically come back should they be rude, mean, or unfair to you again. Surround them with white light and send them lovingly on their way. Surround yourself with the power of mirth, love, and the imagination to find something funny in every situation. Then go about your day as if you have an inside joke between you and yourself. Think about the imagery when you see them again.

Blessed are we who can laugh at ourselves for we shall never cease to be amused.
—Anonymous

WRITING

Play with words. Forget rules of grammar. Make up words.
Play with the space on the page. Remember e. e. cummings.
Be silly and see what happens.

DON'T FORGET TO PICK UP YOUR TOYS

Keep toys on your desk: yo-yos, puppets, a Slinky, squirt guns, Nerf balls. I have a ball of clay, glitter, markers, stickers, and doodling paper in my desk drawer. Delight the child in all aspects of your work and play. Release judgment around your artist child's need to be silly.

THE ZEAL OF APPROVAL

Before sharing a fragile, neophyte idea with someone who might shoot it down, fortify it, validate it, and officially proclaim it. Write it down and then add, "I love this idea." Seal it in an imaginary protective coating. Make it pooh-pooh-proof.

Also be willing to let go of ideas or save them for later if they don't work for your current project. Let it be your intuition and heart that you follow, not someone else's feedback.

NEXT STOP IN THE GARDEN

As you walk farther into the garden, voices inside your head mock and annoy you with criticisms and belittling run-on sentences aimed at any attempt that you make toward your creativity. What they are sharing is born out of fear, not reality. You feel rattled and overworked, underappreciated and discarded. You retreat under your blanket with Ben…& Jerry.

All of a sudden, a savory soup scent leads you to the heart of the garden where there is a canopy-covered kitchen with an herb garden nearby. Conjure up the vision of the most nurturing and motherly feminine spirit that you can imagine. This is Muse Song. In her guiding presence, you feel encouraged, taken care of, watched over, and totally appreciated for the gift of who you are. You may know or have known someone like her, or you may want to make a composite of several people from your past who nurtured and/or encouraged you. You may also want to mobilize these same powers inside of yourself and spend some valuable nurturing energy on yourself…your creativity will flourish. Muse Song is the heart of the garden, and walking through the sheltering aroma of her kitchen endows you with her presence from here forward.

Muse Song says, "You are a magnificent creative spirit and trust that what you create from your heart will bless the world. Your true self is beautiful, and we want you to share it."

Here's What I will Do For Myself Today:

_____

(fill in the blank)

MUSE SONG:
MUSE OF NURTURING, ENCOURAGEMENT, AND GOOD COMPANY

A friend is someone who knows the song in your heart and can sing it back to you when you have forgotten the words.
—Unknown

SUMMON MUSE SONG TO...

🌀 Discover how self-love is a conduit for flowing creative expression.

🌀 Shift your self-talk in order to empower your creativity, not squash it.

🌀 Prompt you to choose people who believe in your creative potential and support your efforts.

🌀 Explore the positive effects sharing and service has on your creativity.

BOTTOM LINE

Self-love is vital for creativity. If we do not like ourselves, why would we think we have something worth sharing with others? When we treat ourselves like precious instruments of the Creative Spirit, the result is prolific creative output. Undoing our negative inner talk is vital to move past thinking that does not serve us and to our creative and spiritual growth. Surround yourself with people who inspire and support you. Support others. Stand for a cause, or, make a cause for celebration.

THE SELECTION OF MUSE SONG

The next Modern Day Muse manifestation embodies one of the most powerful influences of creative rebirth: self-love. Mortals seemed to be sadly lacking in this area, a perplexing condition to the Muses, who have another book out entitled Self-Pamper Profusely Without Apology. They thought, "How can a precious instrument of creative expression operate with smooth excellence if it is not properly maintained with praise, pampering, and pleasurably positive experiences?" So they vowed to change the mortal tune of self-badgering to a song of self-praise. They materialized a Muse named Muse Song, whose melodic compassion can soothe the savage beast that sometimes resides in the mortal's own mind. She inspires harmony within us, and in our relationships with others.

YOUR MUSE SONG ENERGY

The energy that Muse Song emits is about care and nurturing. This energy has been considered important enough to be "Muse-worthy" because the art of self-nourishment has a profound effect on mortals' creative productivity. Pampering has not gotten the attention and publicity it deserves since the days of Cleopatra. Both underrated and underused, the nurturing of ourselves for the intention of self-expression is one of the secrets to an enchanting surge of creative brilliance. The explanation is mysterious—it reflects that, if we generously love ourselves, we will be more effortlessly inclined to want to express and share ourselves with others. If you are always verbally haranguing yourself, why would you want to share that beat-up side of you with anyone? It seems that the harangued side is in control of our creativity and can shut down when it is not receiving compassionate care.

You may have a general idea of how nurturing looks to you: Perhaps it is getting to sleep on time, eating thirty percent more vegetables than candy bars, traversing the treadmill with enthusiastic regularity. But listen. This is only minimal baseline stuff. Muse Song requests that you creatively move past the four food groups to self-kindness.

THE SELF-KINDNESS ACCORDS

The self-kindness accords begin with talking to ourselves as if we believe in ourselves. Self-advocacy is an endangered deal in the mortal world. We like to beat up on ourselves. "You can't do this," "You're not good enough," "You are a total dweeb," some of us say regularly, if we have not been enlightened by self-kindness. And some of us like to ridicule the movements of positive thought. We like to remain ignorant of our potential to fly with the penguins.

The mind's default condition is to constantly find fault with ourselves, a provision we needed to stay alert for saber-toothed tigers centuries ago. Today's mind needs serious upgrading if we are to evolve into the best mortals we can be in a modern world where "crouching tigers" is a metaphor rather than an immediate danger. Constant self-criticism smothers the fire of creativity before it has a chance to be anything more than a flicker gasping for air. Self-criticism comes from fear, and fear's imagination is one that rarely serves us. We may have unintentionally internalized and cultivated critical voices in an effort to protect ourselves from taking risks. We imagine consequences usually more terrible than what can really happen. So the result is, we change the way we live our life because a voice in our head tells us a lot of things that are fairly certain not to happen. Or, if they do happen, they aren't as bad as our fear imagined anyway. If I had a flow chart, I could explain this a little better.

Muse Song solicits unconditional self-kindness as a way to excellence. If you follow her prescriptions, you will find some colossal results—as if magic were seeping out of your desk drawers or were wafting through your air-conditioning vents in gratitude for a self well treated.

In classes I teach on creativity that prescribe pampering as a way to enhance creative output, I see students return with stars in their eyes. They cannot believe how far a little pampering can go. It truly seems like magic, and trying to explain it scientifically would be like explaining why water makes a begonia bloom. It happens on a level beyond the confines of our minds. When we begin to treat ourselves with respect, something deep inside feels respected and comes alive with our personal authenticity. This is creativity. Take care of yourself with grand gestures of festivity, and creativity will take care of you by flowing more effortlessly. But the self-kindness accords are not easy when you have a well-developed habit of self-abuse, as many mortals have. It takes patience and practice. If you are game...read on. If not, please just hit yourself over your head with this book and proceed in constriction.

STEPS OF THE SELF-KINDNESS ACCORDS

1. Become Aware of Your Self-Talk

It's eleven o'clock, do you know where your mind is? Do you know what you regularly say to yourself? Or are you just listening to your mind ramble about primitive, worry-based distortions of fears? Or is your ego in control, placing you on a pedestal of grand illusions to keep your insecurities from spilling over into your daily high?

Many minds are abusing the control they have been given. We need to stay aware of this so that we can take charge of our own thinking from a spiritual level, especially since thinking creates our reality. Faulty thinking creates living in a way unbecoming of our grace and potential. Thinking with kindness, patience, and willingness creates a life of open-minded richness. You see the ramifications? It's an engaging equation. The mind is a terrible thing to leave untended...but with a little training it can empower you to tailgate your bliss until you are riding right there in the driver's seat of authentic creative four-wheel overdrive.

One reason journal writing is so powerful is that we can begin to see our thoughts on the page. Our spiritual energies enter in, and we see what we need to do for ourselves. When we are under the control of our fear-originated defenses, we are sometimes not aware that we are not using our power. Having this self-examination on the page effects tremendous growth.

Self-talk is either based on trust or on fear. The difference is clear. Fear will convince us not to take steps that result in our self-realization. Trust will encourage us to follow our dreams, feel fear as an affirmation of growth, and stay true to the paths that are making themselves known according to our unique beauty.

2. Implement Awareness

Start listening to what you are telling yourself as if you were an observer of your own thoughts. By using the consciousness of a witness to watch myself for a few minutes a couple times a day, I am empowered to make changes. If I think, "Oops, there's that thought I have again about being too weird to be a successful professional," I can then think, "Wow, I say that a lot to myself." Just my simple awareness of the frequency of this self-statement weakens the effect my inner critic has by calling me "weird." It removes the inner critic from being the voice of knowledge and demotes it to a voice that is out of control and needs some compassionate quieting.

I relish my zaniness, but the weirdness my inner critic talks about is intended to convince me that people will give each other those worried looks of "We've got a lunatic here, don't we? At the count of three, run!" My inner critic has a more insidious effect on me if I am not consciously aware of its judgments. When I am not aware, I respond by automatically withering in low self-confidence, not quite knowing why. When I am aware, I can retaliate with things like "Oh, give me a break, I'm not as weird as all that." Or "I'm weird, so what? I accept that in myself." Or alternatively, in a compassionate way, responding with "I know you are worried about me, but I am enjoying being fully myself, thank you, now go drink your beer." Listening to the judgmental thought, being aware of it without judging myself for having it, and going on despite its negative tone is what makes awareness of the inner critic so powerful.

Maintain the practice with patience and you will gradually eliminate the inner critic's effect on you altogether. But patience is key. Muse Song stresses the following fine point: If you do not have patience with the process, it can backfire on you and scar your intention. Here's what that looks like. The inner critic says, "You're silly, people aren't going to take you seriously." You respond, "Oh, dang, I keep beating myself up for being weird again! I can't stop beating myself up. I am such a loser for thinking I'm silly and for not being able to stop beating myself up for it!"

Double whammy. Now I am beating myself up—for beating myself up. The spiral continues until I am beaten down so low that the ants are stepping over me on their way to the cookie that crumbled. The appropriate awareness response is "Oops, there's the voice of the inner critic again. I'm being judgmental toward myself, but that's okay.. I'm human and we are hard on ourselves sometimes. My inner critic's power will weaken with my awareness of it." And then I continue moving in a better direction by adding encouraging messages to my awareness and bypassing the criticism.

The key is not to judge yourself for judging yourself. In other words, stay compassionate even when those voices come up, breathe a sigh of acknowledgment, and accept that your self-judgment is part of being human. The struggle then is over, and the inner critic is more likely to stop its attacks because it's not fun anymore.

3. Self-Encouragement and Good Witches

In her book *The Captive Muse*, Susan Kolodny explains that almost every individual who ventures into the creative realm is afflicted with voices that try to torment and discourage him or her. Successful artists, poets, writers, and expressers of creative passions replace the critical, chiding, or discouraging voices with voices that applaud, praise, and encourage. We have that choice. The benevolent new voices come from mentors, teachers, or other guides from the creative individual's past or present. And if encouraging voices cannot be recalled, successful artists invent them. Creating a new reassuring voice to replace the inner critic will make the difference between quitting and triumphing.

Muse Song's voice replaces the voices of discouraging fear, criticism, and mockery. Learning to use the same nurturing voice for ourselves that we often use for others is a skill that takes practice and results in progress unequal to its effort. Find voices that work for you. Hear the benevolent voice in a form that comforts you—a creative advocate, a friend, a mentor, from your past or your present. If you choose to exercise your imagination, your mechanism could be a protective and nurturing image like an angel, a spirit guide, or a big Italian mama showing pride in her offspring with grand gestures and gushing. Find what works for you, and make it a voice from the Spirit inside you.

4. Affirmations and the Right Small Question

Let's visit an old concept in a new way: affirmations. Why? Because the Muses know that affirmations work. Muse Song believes affirmations are a way to undo damage and exercise kindness. When this happens, all parts of the self involved in the creative process will be kind back to you.

Affirmations work if approached in a conscious manner. We cannot change the effect that damaging or traumatic experiences have had on us with a few repeated positive statements. We need to start with statements that our whole being can buy into. We need to start with letting ourselves know we deserve good things in our lives. With the appropriate awareness, intentions, and conditions...affirmations do change lives and are critical to the courage it takes to creatively express.

The Muses laugh at nonbelievers because that very disbelief keeps these mortals from expanding into what is truly possible in their lives. Muse Song remarks, "Goodness, even if affirmations didn't work, what could it hurt you to think positively? And if affirmations do work, the gains that are in store for you are invaluable." My mortal feeling is that we cannot argue with the hundreds of individuals whose lives have been changed by the simple repeating of declarations that undid the thinking that did not serve them.

Small questions also create in huge shifts... but we have to ask the right questions. We don't need to be perfect about this but instead of asking, "Why can't I write as good as she does?" Ask "What's one small talent I can celebrate in myself," or "What's one small step I can take to get better at writing." Your subconscious doesn't know which are the best questions to ask in terms of your self-esteem so it will answer either one - and the answers fuel our action.

"There is nothing that I cannot be or do or have."
-- from the teachings of Abraham-Hicks*
From Rebbie Straubing

"If your affirmations are not working, consider this:
- ◎ Saying words that you do not believe, even though you want them to be true, creates a misalignment.
  Example: You Affirm a higher income than you believe is possible and then feel inner conflict or inadequacy during your affirmation practice.

- ◎ Saying words you do believe, but you don't want them to be true, offers a different flavor of misalignment.
  Example: You reach for some manifestation and fail. Then, feeling defeated, you claim that you don't want it anymore when really you do.

You can speed up this process and make your manifestations even more satisfying by using a well-chosen affirmation.

The simplest and most powerful affirmation begins with the two sacred words, "I am." To find out the most powerful word(s) to place after "I am," follow these four super-simple steps:
- ◎ Look at what is bothering you the most.
- ◎ Find its polar opposite.
- ◎ Now find the word or phase that sums up its opposite quality in a general way.
- ◎ Test the word in the phrase, "I am..."Make sure it feels good to you when you con template it. If it doesn't, if you feel any discomfort whatsoever with the phrase, keep searching until you find a word or phrase that completes the affirmation in a way that makes you smile.

Here's an example. If you are struggling financially, you may be feeling "poor." When you look to it's opposite, you find "rich."

You may say, "I am rich." If that works for you, great. You're done. That's your affirmation. But if the word "rich" bothers you on any level, it is not a good word for you in your personal affirmation. You may want to try, "I am well paid for what I do," or " I am comfortable and secure regarding money." Find words that soothe you when you hold them as your truth.

You can apply this to any aspect of your life from the most material to the most spiritual.

Once you have your affirmation, you can use it in two simple ways:

◎ Repeat it like a mantra. Let this statement set your tone rather than the default thinking that is usually running through your mind

◎ Set aside times for deep contemplation on your statement. Elaborate on it. Look for what it means to you. Meditate on the words.

This simple, "I am...," affirmation practice can change your life. I wish you everything your heart desires.

Find out more about the power of affirmations at the Affirmative Contemplation website at http://www.AffirmativeContemplation.com, and http://www.YOFA.net.

ABSOLUTELY POSITIVELY

Muse Song wants us to know why affirmations are compelling in the creative process: "You must replace the voices that discourage your creativity with the voices that create a belief so strong that there is little that can thwart your intentions to experience creative joy. The creative process is fragile and needs hard-core encouragement from steadfast self-beliefs. Affirmations can build such beliefs."

AFFIRMATIONS MAKE THE NEWS

Although affirmations have sometimes been pigeon-holed into the New Age movement, they are beginning to meet the mainstream. Newsweek magazine ran an issue with the cartoon Dilbert and its creator, Scott Adams, as a cover story. Under the photo of the cartoonist the caption read: "Affirmed: Dilbert creator Adams gets what he asks for."

The August 12, 1996, article explained, "Affirmed? Let Scott Adams explain this, with a straight face. 'The basic idea is that fifteen times a day you just write down whatever it is your goal is,' Adams says. 'Then you'll observe things happening that will make that objective more likely to happen. It's actually a process of forcing your environment to change.' Soon he was writing I WILL BECOME A SYNDICATED CARTOONIST fifteen times a day. He fashioned the Dilbert-esque doodles he had been working on into a slick package and sent it to syndicators. Amid the rejections came one acceptance: United Media, home of his idol, Charles Schulz. Chalk one up to affirmation." The rest is history. He soared to the top as cartoonists Gary Larson (The Far Side), and Bill Watterson (Calvin and Hobbes), were retiring while their cartoons were still popular. Makes you think.

Here are some affirmations that work regarding the creative process and an example of changing your thinking to what will work for you. Although these seem obvious, when working in a classroom, I have found that many students' first formulation of an affirmation is not as powerful as it could be.

When someone's fear is "I'm not good enough," many times their affirmation will be "I will become better at creativity." The power statement is "I am good enough to be creative." Place yourself in an affirming presence.

THE SELF-NURTURING DEAL

Muse Song is delighted to share this stunning secret of creative combustion with you. It is a win-win thing. Here it is: You start doing really nice things for yourself, and the self that is responsible for creative expression begins to unleash itself with ease and delight.

The only problem is that many well-meaning parents, and the movement of Martyrs-R-Us, make self-kindness a hard place for many people to wholeheartedly visit. Treating ourselves like precious instruments of creative expression accelerates our creative output. The results are actually mind-boggling. We are finally coming to an age where we can release the guilt, martyrdom, and feelings of selfishness that used to be associated with paying more attention to ourselves than to others. We can finally see that when we are good to ourselves first, we become better for everyone in our life.

Some of you may need more convincing. Stockpiles of guilt, and the fear of being selfish, may prevent you from operating at your full potential because you underestimate the effect that being good to yourself has on others. Taking quality care of yourself can awaken your higher self. This process has an almost magical quality to it because one of its foundations is the nurturing of our artist's child. When nurtured, we return the favor with grand displays of creativity. When we use the oxygen mask of kindness on ourselves first, we are then able to be kind and present for others. Get it?

THE PEOPLE AROUND YOU: WHO ARE THEY AND WHAT ARE THEY DOING THERE?

Surround yourself with only people who are going to lift you higher.
—Oprah Winfrey, talk show host, actress

When we come up with a good idea, we often have an immediate impulse to want to share it with anyone around. Muse Song advises caution in these circumstances. Share your delicate creative ideas only with people you consider safe. Not everyone is. If a mate or a parent discourages your creativity...keep your ideas to yourself or to your chosen circle of sincere supporters. Or, keep it to only yourself until you have gained some conviction about it. Charles Brower noted, "A new idea is delicate. It can be killed by a sneer or a yawn; it can be stabbed to death by a joke or worried to death by a frown on the right person's brow."

Develop an inner circle of your own creative angels: people who support, believe in, and encourage you. If you don't have these people, find them by taking classes or joining creative support groups and notice which people you gravitate toward. Wake up when you spot people who are encouraging to you and make an effort to bring them into your inner circle. Have a mutual admiration club. Find people who are easy for you to encourage and praise, as well. Watch over your ideas until you feel strong enough about them to be undaunted in the face of anything from a questioning look to downright harsh criticism. Spend more time, thought, and energy on the people who can see your brilliance and can encourage it.

Creating boundaries reinforces your self-identity, your individuality, and your authenticity.

* Who are your immediate muses?
* Who positively influences you?
* Are you open to meeting new people to expand your creative resource bank?
* Whom do you envy and what is it they are doing that is awakening envy in you? (Consider envy a nudge to take your own steps in a direction that you feel passionate about.)
* Where do you need to set boundaries?

Other people can also be a wonderful resource for ideas. You may notice that you feel more creative around certain people in your life. You find that they easily stimulate the juices of fun and clever thought in you. Do you make a point of spending more time around them?

¡INSERT HERE:
A MOMENT OF PONDERING ABOUT PEOPLE WHO STIMULATE YOUR CREATIVITY

When you have a trusted group of creative angels, bounce your ideas off them. I sometimes think I am the only one who can do my creative work, and I am pleasantly surprised when I hear people's wonderful new slants on my projects. Some of their feedback can take what I am doing to a richer, more accessible level. We are creative conduits, each and every one of us, and the source that provides inspiration is greater than us all. The more we contribute to each other, the greater we become ourselves.

In every person who comes near you, look for what is good and strong, honor that; try to imitate it, and your faults will drop off like dead leaves when their time comes.
—John Ruskin, Victorian thinker, author

RANDOM ACTS OF CREATIVE KINDNESS

Often, doing good-hearted things for others is a stimulus for breaking through creative blocks. We may find that we withdraw inside while engaged in creative thought. Shifting our attention toward an outward purpose can bring new juice to old approaches.

Choose those people who are your creative supporters and make a list of what creative things you would like to do for them. Just making the list can create good energy. Picking one of the ideas and taking it further can create synapses of creative congealing.

Try to pick people who will benefit from your inspiration. Sometimes a simple creative gesture toward someone in need will stimulate their creative juices and shift them into a good direction.

Volunteer work ignites to the outward use of our energies. The inspiration of our work can be a propellant for ideas and innovation in all areas of our life. In our selfless work with others, we may discover a new area of creative skill that we didn't know we had.

As we grow in creativity, we positively affect the world around us. We need to remember to put our own creativity oxygen mask on so that we have the vitality to positively energize the people around us.

What three things did you learn from Muse Song?

1 _____

2. _____

3. _____

What actions can you take related to these things?

1. _____

2. _____

3. _____

MORTALS WHO WERE INSPIRED BY MUSE SONG

As you walk through this part of the garden, once again you hear echoes of mortals who validate the inspirations of Muses. This time you begin to understand the importance of nurturing yourself for the creative process.

Keep away from people who belittle your ambitions. Small people always do that, but the really great make you feel that you, too, can become great.
—Mark Twain, U.S. novelist, journalist, riverboat pilot

Flatter me, and I may not believe you. Criticize me, and I may not like you. Ignore me, and I may not forgive you. Encourage me, and I may not forget you.
—William Arthur, author

To give pleasure to a single heart by a single act is better than a thousand heads bowing in prayer.
—Gandhi, spiritual leader

The future belongs to those who believe in the beauty of their dreams.
—Eleanor Roosevelt, U.S. first lady, social reformer

Sometimes our light goes out but is blown into flame by another human being. Each of us owes deepest thanks to those who have rekindled this light.
—Albert Schweitzer, French theologian, musician, medical missionary

Positive self-opinion is worth an infinite number of accolades.
—Emily Herman and Jennifer Richard Jacobson in Stones from the Muse

It is not the critic who counts, not the man who points out how the strong man stumbled, or where the doer of deeds could have done better. The credit belongs to the man who is actually in the arena; whose face is marred by the dust and sweat and blood; who strives valiantly; who errs and comes short again and again; who knows the great enthusiasms, the great devotions and spends himself in a worthy course; who, at the best, knows in the end the triumph of high achievement, and who, at worst, if he fails, at least fails while daring greatly; so that his place shall never be with those cold and timid souls who know neither victory or defeat.
—Theodore Roosevelt, U.S. President

MUSE PROFILE OF MUSE SONG

SYMBOL

Muse Song's symbol is two teacups, inviting the feeling of being nurtured in the company of encouraging friends. Both are in harmony with creative expansion.

HOBBIES

Always having a cup of soothing tea ready, hanging art on refrigerators, writing notes of praise, consulting on the art of luxuriating baths, channeling of exercise and nutrition information, knitting, and karaoke singing.

CAR

A pink-and-white '56 Chevy Bel Air.

When I'm inspired, I get excited because I can't wait to see what I'll come up with next.
—Dolly Parton, singer, actress

RITUAL TO CALL MUSE SONG

Materials to summon Muse Song: A new pot, a plant, some fresh garden soil, four green candles, a floral or earthy incense. Optional: nature-sounds tape or CD.

To summon Muse Song, play the music, light the incense and candles, and take your new plant and re-pot it in a new pot with fresh soil. Make the process symbolic of nurturing your creative process by embodying kindhearted awareness. Blow out the candles and say one of the affirmations listed below. Copy it in your journal or on a card to hang in a place where you will see it often. Then, let go of the process (if the plant dies quickly, this has no additional meaning other than perhaps you may be horticulturally challenged). Your Muse Song energy has awakened.

MUSE SONG AFFIRMATIONS AND SMALL QUESTIONS

- I am gentle with myself and others.
- What does being kind and gentle to myself LOOK like?
- I choose to associate with people who genuinely support and encourage my creativity.
- I am a precious instrument of creativity so I am conscientious about taking care of all my needs.
- I am filled with love for myself and can't wait to see what I have to express creatively.
- What's one small way I can be kind in this moment?
- What's one nurturing thing I can say to myself today?
- Design your own affirmation for creative growth. Write down something your inner critic says to you regularly and then design an affirmation that is the opposite sentiment.

And there ya go. Muse Song is present with you. When you need her just whistle.

JOURNAL CHECK-IN

1. Quickly write or draw where you are with Muse Song. Begin with: In the Self-Kindness realm, I..
   What do you do well in the Muse Song realm?
2. What negative things does your inner critic have to say about taking care of your self, pampering yourself, spending time alone, choosing whom you spend your time with, doing special altruistic gestures for others.

Since Muse Song's specialty is the awareness of the inner critic and other inner voices, she would like to offer this exercise: The voice in our head that prevents us from freely diving into creative pursuits is not coming from a place of higher truth; it is coming from fear. As stated earlier in this book, recording its negativity on paper through writing or art helps you take its power away. Write down some of the thoughts your critic tells you about your creative intention.

⚘ As you operate in the world open your awareness to all the voices inside your head: The ones that encourage you—the ones that dazzle, entertain, and inspire you. The ones that discourage, mock, and berate you—the running commentary. The ones that challenge you to take risks—the ones that know problem solving, strength, and confidence—the wise ones—the silly ones—the intuitive ones.

⚘ Give the voices a vehicle of expression by writing in your journal. Let each of them talk about your creative passion from their different point of view.

3. Look at the quotes by mortals who were inspired by Muse Song (pp. 128-129) and pick one. Either continue the essence of the quote in your own words or speed-write how the quote applies to you.

4. Relax, get comfortable, add some extra pillows, and notice the nurturing nature of your breath. Move into a receptive mode and allow yourself to fully receive the next inhale as if it were a gift of life. Let it go as if you were floating down a river of nurturing golden light - no effort, floating on all that supports who you are.

Embody Muse Song's compassion and nurturing as your own. When you are ready, write a letter from Muse Song to yourself. Let her give you suggestions about taking care of yourself, your selection of friends, support with your journey, and pampering yourself. Let her counter comments from the inner critic's comments written in the exercise above.

MUSE WALK ☕ MUSE SONG STYLE

Take a walk and let yourself fully receive the pleasure and solitude of a nurturing journey. Walk as if you are in the company of someone you enjoy very much, and let that someone be yourself. Let your body take on the feeling of being loved and appreciated. Feel a sense of inner encouragement and notice what changes occur in your posture or in your stride. Take in the beauty around you as if it were a gift created especially for you. Ask yourself, "What in this moment feels nurturing to my spirit?"

BRAINSTORM

To nurture your art, you must nurture yourself.
—Muse Song, Really Kind Modern Day Muse

MUSE SONG PRESCRIPTIONS

Send yourself a cyber card scheduled for a future date so that you're surprised: include a nurturing message.

Buy yourself a magazine subscription to encourage your art or your writing

Send yourself a regular greeting card

Leave little notes for yourself in drawers, pockets, cabinets, on dog collars

Collect compliments and keep them where you can see them or have a book of compliments.. seriously, do it dude.

Breathe in the power of compliments, feel their goodness in your body's energy and if it's hard for you to accept them, accept them just 5% more than you usually do. Compliments fuel the confidence that creative people need.

Leave yourself an encouraging phone message.

Engage in altruism to encourage your creative unveiling and self-discovery.

Write a note to or make something for people in your life who inspire you.

Take moments every now and then to just breathe with nurturing your mind, body in spirit as the only purpose.

ENCOURAGEMENT

Who in your life would you like to encourage? Take time to make or buy that person a special card. Greeting-card counters now have an actual Encouragement Card section.

Or, give a little of your precious time for a cherished friend and make a card. Take magazine cutouts, stamps, or stickers and decorate a blank sheet of paper. Paint a card with watercolors. Manipulate a picture of your friend on the computer and send it. Find a magazine article or a special quote your friend would like and mail it.

Nurturing a friend releases good energy into your life and stimulates creative thoughts.

CREDIT REPORTS AND POWER TOOLS

Many of my clients seek creativity coaching because they feel they are not moving fast enough toward their creative goals. When they do the following exercise, the energy and insight they receive from it propels them forward. Try it yourself. It seems so obvious but it is so overlooked.

Make a list of what you have already accomplished regarding your creative goal. List everything and do not minimize anything. Often what you see is the evidence that you are doing more than you thought you were doing. Seeing some groundwork motivates more and just plain feels good. Ask yourself these questions:

- Where did I get it right?
- What's working?
- What else might work?
- What am I glad I did?

When we stretch wide open the moment that we give ourselves credit, we benefit spiritually, physically, energetically, and creatively. Shifting into

REVERSE LOGIC

Sometimes, nurturing means stopping the work for a while, giving yourself a break, contacting Lull. Other times, a true sense of safety and nurturing comes from getting some of the grunt work out of the way with Marge. This is how Marge works with Muse Song: First thing in the morning you make phone calls, make a list of what needs to be done, and then do some of those items, or you make any kind of concerted effort in the direction of your dream. You then feel a sense of being taken care of that relaxes you the rest of the day and indicates that you know how to take care of yourself. The nurturing is then defined as getting some jobs done in the interest of nurturing your dream. Experiment with this without equating production with worth; just equate it with a little freedom and with the knowing that you are taking care of yourself in a Muse Song manner.

THE PEOPLE AROUND YOU:
WHO ARE THEY AND WHY ARE THEY THERE?

Who are your inner circle of friends? Whom do you need to keep on the outside of the circle?

Draw a circle in your sketchbook so you have a visual for yourself to see mentally as you proceed in your creative process. Include on the inside people who are there,

        For self-esteem;

        For support;

        For ideas.

Who in your life has encouraged you in the past and currently does in the present? Who is taking up a lot of your time at your expense?

Place on the outside, people,

        You love but need to be careful of because they don't yet understand your creativity;

        People you simply need to steer clear of.

Do you need to draw boundaries with anyone or anything, and if so, who, what, and how? Whom do you choose to share your creative work and secrets with?

YOUR PERSONAL MUSES

What real, fictional, historical, or contemporary figures positively influence you? Often, keeping their names where you can see them frequently will instill in you the traits you so admire in them. Take a moment now and scribe a list on a piece of paper separate from your journal. Write it neatly, calligraphically, or type it and place it on the front of your journal or in a picture frame where you can see it.

Here's a partial list of my Muses:

- My friends, Janet Whitehead, Rae Warde, Paula Verdu, and Chris Dunmire.
- Inspirational people, Tina Fey, Eleanor Roosevelt, Audrey Hepburn, Lily Tomlin, Byron Katie.
- Authors, Margie Lapanja, Anne Lamott, Anaïs Nin, Dorothy Parker, Julia Cameron.
- Artists, Saul Steinberg and Fred Babb.
- Performance artist, Laurie Anderson. Speaker, Rhonda Britten.
- Poet musicians, Joni Mitchell, Michael Franks, Tom Waits, Paul Simon, Jack John son and Natalie McMasters.
- Comedians, Ellen DeGeneres, Robin Williams, TJon Stewart, and Paula Poundstone.

Just seeing these names inspires the positive forces of creativity, intelligence, or grace that these people or characters convey. It is like taking a dose of creative medicine just to be reminded of what I like about them, and what I would like to develop more of in myself. Who inspires you? How can you use more of their influence in your life?

MUSE SUPPORT

Write a letter to yourself from each of the Muses, from their point of view of your wonderfulness. Let Audacity get you through any modesty hang-ups.

MAKE YOURSELF COMFORTABLE

Comfort (v.)—"1: to give strength and hope; to cheer 2: to ease the grief or trouble of."

How do you comfort yourself?

We find our own comfort all the time, probably without noticing what we are doing.

Take a moment and think of what you do, where you go, and whom you like to be with when you're in need of comfort. Write a list under each of these categories in your journal: Comforting Places, Comforting Activities, Comforting People, Comforting Quotes or Sayings.

FRUGAL EXTRAVAGANCE

Here is a list of inexpensive things you could buy yourself. Endow each with a little imagination and let the special powers make your day more fun. A little spell of magic in the creative realm goes a long way to give you a feeling of being special and staying in the moment:

◎ A special washcloth: Endow it with the power to wash away your negativity. One big, new special towel: a color different from all the others that you would buy if it didn't clash with your bathroom. Endow it with the power to wrap you in a loving embrace that attracts good people into your life.

◎ Buy a tube sock and fill it with rice. Tie it and place it in the microwave oven for one minute. Put it around your neck for a feeling of the warm arm of a pal.

◎ Although a pint of raspberries may seem expensive, comparatively speaking, for one's pampering pleasure, it's cheap. Indulge your senses with the taste of each one. Let each be a wild explosive pill of creative exuberance.

◎ Buy a nice vase that takes just a few flowers, and make it a ritual to fill it every week. Say an affirmation when you place the flowers in it.

◎ Buy a soft, fuzzy rug to place under your desk so you can take your shoes off and have a pampered feeling. In the winter, place a heating pad under your feet.

◎ Play music that inspires you. Find your theme song. Have your own personal back-up singers.

◎ During your creative times, wear special clothes filled with creativity. Why wear old clothes just in case you get messy? Even for painters: Get fun new clothes meant just to make your creative time more special. Let them take on more character with each mess you make. Or, get a great new apron you can mess up. Even if you are in a non-messy craft, do the same.

A Token of My Inspiration

Creative people sometimes have a totem that brings them more inspiration. Find a picture, statue, button, memorabilia, quote, novel art project, or whatever that will trigger a positive belief and post, it wear it, or string it from your ceiling. Find a little icon of creativity to place on your desk and endow it with creative power.

Writers and other creative people buy a creative think cap, a hat just for your creative session.

Other Pampering Pleasures Without Apology

- Take the day off and relax! If that won't work...take an HOUR off and relax.
- A massage
- A manicure, pedicure, facial
- An hour of reading your favorite magazine
- Find yourself one flower and put it in a wine glass
- Glue-gun beads and silk flowers on favorite wineglasses or mugs
- Buy yourself a special favorite dish on which to eat
- Indulge at the gourmet deli once a week
- Get in pajamas early; set your bed up with books, journal, magazines; light a candle, incense; play soothing music
- Set up the bath with candles and play music...it transforms your bathroom

Other Things

- Write a list of the people in your life who support you.
- Set aside one hour and make one of those people a card.
- Get together for a meal if you haven't recently.
- Get creative by doing something nice for them and leave it without telling them.

Dedications

When engaging in your creative work, dedicate it to someone important to you. This will infuse the process with a power that goes beyond you. You do not even need to tell whoever it is about the dedication. Just knowing you have made the dedication will bring out a sacred quality in your approach to your creativity. Do it for each session and for the finished product.

Altruism

Doing something for another person or an organization often enlivens the heart with a sense of creativity. Brainstorm a list of altruistic gestures. You do not have to do all of them; even the act of coming up with the idea will awaken creative juices from your seat of passion.

NEXT STOP IN THE GARDEN

Across the garden path are strewn waded-up pieces of paper, paint spills, rejected photos, and an occasional banana peel. You hear laughter close by and come to a clearing with a big table filled with media for art, music, and all other kinds of creative expression. An impish character invites you over and asks you to experiment with the media on the table.

"Allow the stumble of serendipity, allow the discoveries that come with imperfections, to happen. In mistakes," she says, "you discover the beauty of unplanned genius and surrender the affliction of control."

You decide to comply, and you gravitate toward your favorite section of art, music, dance, writing, or simply feeling creative. You hesitate because you are a little afraid of doing something that doesn't look good or sound good, or you are afraid of looking like a fool. Spills the Imp convinces you to begin anyway, because it is the process, not the product, that is filled with wondrous joy. It is the fool, not the image-obsessed mortal, who triumphs by risking his or her appearance to live a deeper, more meaningful life.

The Muses were just talking about you,
and they think you are fabulous!

SPiLLS:
MUSE OF PRACTiCE, PROCESS AND
iMPERFECTioN

Process, and Imperfection "He who hesitates because he feels inferior
is being surpassed by he who is busy making mistakes and becoming superior."
–Henry Link

SUMMON SPiLLS WHEN:

🌀 You are avoiding the creative process due to:
Fear of not being good enough
Fear of failure
Fear of change
Overwhelm
Not knowing where to begin
Immobilization
Unrealistic expectations (there is an EPIDEMIC of unrealistic expectations).

🌀 You seem to focus on details far too long; your progress is confined because you
spend too much time reworking things to make them perfect, which they never seem
to be.

BOTTOM LiNE

Both life and creativity are processes to experience, not to judge. Spills the Imp manifests
her energy as the inner part of us that relishes the discoveries that take place in our imperfect approach to the world. We evolve only when we participate, not when we sit on the

sidelines fearing inadequacy. And the more we act, the more wisdom, confidence, and excellence we receive. Trusting the process leads to peace and contentment. Release impatience. Dive in; you will rise to the top. Instead of focusing on the final product, ask yourself how you are becoming a better person by immersing in this divine process.

Decide to align your process with your choice of glorious qualities versus qualities that sneak in when we default to old patterns. Choose a sense of lightness, joy, mirth, mischievousness, irreverence, openness, or wonder. Lose the popular defaults of rigidity, pressure, judgment, torment, and hurry.

THE SELECTION OF SPILLS

Spills came into being purely by mistake. The Muses were playing with the attributes they thought that the next Muse should embody. They kept saying things they really didn't mean to say, but which actually seemed clever anyway. They drew blueprints with a lot of fumbles, yet each blunder led to an insight that led to a consideration of something new, which made them laugh about the serendipity of ideas, which made the process uncommon, which gave them the next Muse. "Mistakes! That's it. Oops, no, that's not it," one of them said, then corrected herself. She had said that by mistake. Here's what was important: They were engaged in the process and not just thinking, avoiding, and fearing it. The result: discovery.

The serendipity of mistakes is part of the magic of the creative process. Within the process, spills, mistakes, and imperfections are a method of discovery. So Spills the Imp was created. Since she's on the uncoordinated side of things, they thought making her an imp would be endearing.

YOUR SPILLS ENERGY

A man of genius makes no mistakes. His errors are
volitional and are the portals of discovery.
—James Joyce, Irish novelist, poet, playwright

The word spills implies "Oops, didn't mean to do that." But when seen through the lens of discovery, spills or mistakes become agents of possibility. Imp is appropriate because it can be an acronym, IMP, for "in mid-process" and "in mid- practice," and "imperfection's merely preliminary." The Muses like the imperfection of having three acronym meanings instead of just one. Spills imparts to mortals the wisdom of loving the process. She emphasizes the importance of releasing preconceptions about, and attachments to, the end result. Practice and patience allow awkwardness to spill into grace.

Spills also advocates the release of perfectionism. She knows that expecting mistakes and inadequacies makes creative genius possible. Expecting instant adequacy or perfection is antithetical to the creative process. Discovery cannot happen without trial and error. Excellence cannot happen without practice. You CAN begin even if at the beginning of a process you don't have all the information, skills, knowledge, tools and materials. The beauty is in discovering, through the creative process, what direction to take next.

Unfortunately, an entire continent of mortals is frozen in perfection's paralysis. Spills's work is not easy and she does not expect it to be. Spills is always in the present moment and believes that the process is a constant state of unfolding discoveries. The results of our efforts may not be great at the beginning, but with practice they will bring a beautiful blossoming of our evolving abilities. All efforts have merit in the unfolding of our beauty. None are meaningless, none are wasted.

The only way to traverse your creative path incorrectly is not to traverse it at all. Spills says, "Hey, mortal, don't have any judgment about what you do. There is no good or bad... are just curiosity and excitement for all the surprises the process brings. All of your attempts and actions are the practice you need in order to be the best mortal possible. Being engaged in the process makes the deepening of your existence possible. The refusal to participate because of your fear of imperfection and inadequacy is the stunting of your spiritual excellence. Peace of mind and creative freedom come with the release of perfection."

Sometimes we strive so hard for perfection that we forget that imperfection
is happiness.
–Karen Nave

The creative process is nonlinear. We do not traverse a straight line to our dreams but, instead, encounter many surprises and new directions. Spills says, "Hey, mortal [she says that a lot], be open to where the process takes you and stay the course that's true to your heart. Striving for a perfect series of results according to calculated actions, and expecting a rigid set of images with no room for variation, is the way of damaging control. Control is not cool. It is used when you don't trust the process. If you fiddle with the process because you are rigid about what your dream must look like, you miss the signs that lead to a more penetrating dream, the one most suited to you. And you miss out on the joy of a process that is filled with the remarkable gifts of your unfolding self." Spills is fairly articulate despite being an imp and all.

Allen Ginsberg talks about his submission to letting go of control. "I really don't know what I'm doing when I sit down to write. I figure it out as I go along. I see the writing is interesting if there are a lot of awkward poetic ideas made up by accident in the course of rapid notation of thoughts. It's usually a subject I've wondered about before, so it's a matter of transcription in visual shorthand of whatever is on my mind, plus spontaneous improvisation and excitement when I realize I'm suddenly talking about something I never did before."

Countless successful artists from every area of expression will tell you it was the process that brought them the most happiness, not the final product. Being awarded an end product still leaves you the week after it is through—requiring that you evolve with new challenges.

Mass media and the school system have contributed to the epidemic of people wanting to look and perform only perfectly. In school we are often judged and graded according to a system of rigid acceptability. Deviations and novel expressions are discouraged, conforming is encouraged. Imperfection is shamed and the unrealistic goal of perfection is promoted and equated with worth and desirability. Imperfect acts, statements, and especially creative expressions are discouraged.

The media bombards us with airbrushed perfection and individuals who convey perfection only through their looks.

PERFECTION PARALYSIS

This needs to be done just perfectly or not at all." Good luck. Perfectionists can be people who strain compulsively and unremittingly toward impossible goals and who measure their worth entirely in terms of productivity and accomplishment. Many people stop themselves from living deeply because they fear looking inadequate or they are impatient with how long it takes to be "good" at something. They live with careful restraint and constipated happiness. It is a sad struggle...but there IS help. You probably know if you are one of them, because you are chronically frustrated with, or fearful of, the creative process. See if any of these sound familiar to you:

- You keep redoing your work over and over and over and over and over, and you are still not satisfied with it.
- You do not begin your creative passion at all for fear of failure or looking inadequate.
- Your mind goes blank at the request or intention to begin anything requiring creativity. You put yourself under so much pressure to perform perfectly that you block doing anything at all.
- You do not enjoy any part of the creative process because it is a constant reminder of how inadequate you are.
- Your expectations are unrealistic. Starting seems overwhelming, so you avoid it completely.
- You think excellent results should happen immediately, and if they don't, you give up. You underestimate the amount of practice it takes to begin to master a creative passion, and you label yourself inadequate way before you've given yourself a chance to flower.
- You insist on doing all the work yourself even when it would make sense to request help from others to ensure your success. You fear that others cannot perform up to your standards.

If you have perfection paralysis, you are not alone. Currently an epidemic, it is responsible for much of life's disillusionment. When you are striving for perfection, your happiness is dependent upon unrealistic goals. Pointless to galactic proportions! Spills directs you through a passage that leads to creative enjoyment. Follow the steps she discovered in her enlightenment of mortals.

- Breathe, and enjoy the process of breathing. Know that releasing the torment of perfectionist thoughts will take practice. Don't expect to be perfect at accepting imperfection. (This may sound funny, but a perfectionist trying to kick the habit will place just as high expectations on herself to do that as anything else.)
- One of the most successful approaches we have in Kaizen-Muse Creativity Coaching is lowering expectations at the beginning. Give yourself permission not only to put less pressure on yourself, but give yourself permission to do things badly at first. Make it fun. Kaizen-Muse Creativity Coach and teacher, Rae Warde, calls this "small and crappy." Try approaching the beginning or process of your next project with small and crappy in mind and notice the liberation and willingness to begin that you feel.
- Step into the process of life and of your creative passion. Exercise acceptance with the knowledge that with practice you will get better at anything. It's a universal law.
- Practice compassion with yourself and others. When thoughts of impatience arise because something seems imperfect, breathe again. Label the thought an "irrational judgment." Embody an air of acceptance even if initially it feels awkward and unreal. You are breaking patterns that are difficult to break because they are old, not because they are right.
- Practice your creative passion without judgment. If judgment arises, breathe and release the judgment with your exhale. Breathe in the present moment and allow yourself the luxury of being a student.
- Have patience: Accept your initial awkwardness with the same compassion that you would accept a small child's learning something new. If you are impatient even with small children, take a step back and pay attention to your unrealistic expectations.
- Have patience with practice.
- And practice patience patiently.
- Relax and let the magic of surrendering to the creative process with grace and acceptance create YOU as a better person. Just be you and know it's all perfect if you don't judge it.

I know you've heard it a thousand times before. But it's true—hard work pays off. If you want to be good, you have to practice, practice, practice.
If you don't love something, then don't do it.
—Ray Bradbury, science-fiction writer

"PATTiNCE" (WORD BY SPiLLS)

Practice and patience are not reinforced in our "have-to-have-it-yesterday" society, and yet, they are required in order to live our truth. We often quit too easily because we have forgotten that practice is essential to get better and that practice takes time. This truth about patience and practice has not changed just because we have invented microwave ovens, cellular phones, and the Internet. New habits, new skills, and quality work take longer to develop than prints at the one-hour photomat. Creative excellence does take time, but wait! It is the process that is important, and in the process joy is instant. Right now you are in a process. You are reading a book, and you are executing a gesture honoring your creative self. Observe what feels good about it because you are here, in the process. Welcome.

> I have not failed. I've just found ten thousand ways that won't work.
> —Thomas Alva Edison, inventor

Thomas Edison tried ten thousand different materials before finding one that was suitable to serve as a lightbulb filament. So if at first you don't succeed, try, try again. We need to set up a system where risk is rewarded. One where we recognize that failure helps us to increase our creativity.

> Nothing risked is nothing gained.
> —Beth Flynn, creativity educator, author of Knock Your Socks off Creativity

THE COMPETENCE ADDiCTiON

Another crinkle in creative growth is the competence addiction—our ego's addiction to competence. We may become attached to skill in one area of our work in order to avoid the discomfort of returning to beginner status in some area waiting to delight us. We may have over-identified with our current limited job description and felt insecure and stubborn about starting something new. We must be willing to be a beginner over and over again in order to live a full life. Otherwise, we will be stuck in a restricted realm of existence. Sometimes we are stuck in the competence predicament without realizing what has happened. If you notice a sense of disillusionment that you cannot seem to put your finger on, consider whether you are willing to venture into something that can widen the range of your existence.

> The power of mistakes enables us to reframe creative blocks and turn them around.... The troublesome parts of our work, the parts that are most baffling and frustrating, are in fact the growing edges. We see these as opportunities the instant we drop our preconceptions and our self-importance.
> —Stephen Nachmanovitch, Ph.D., author, musician, computer artist, educator

Creativity requires foraging into newness. Creativity craves an openness to experiencing initial clumsiness as a method for discovering new ways of being, doing, and expressing art and life. Willingness to be a beginner is rewarded with the expansion and amazement of how much more life continues to give. Profound opportunities dawn regularly.

When you surrender to the acceptance of any result that your participation delivers, you move from judgment to wonder, from fear to ingenuity, and from stunted expert to bedazzled student. The most enlightened beings approach life always as students, open to learning something new about themselves or about their craft. They work not toward one end, but into the bliss of the moment.

ANOTHER VIEW OF PERFECTIONISM

Normal perfectionists are described as individuals who "derive a very real sense of pleasure from the labors of a painstaking effort," while neurotic perfectionists are those "unable to feel satisfaction because in their own eyes they never seem to do things good enough to warrant that feeling."
—Wayne D. Parker and Karen K. Adkins, educators, authors of the article "Perfectionism and the Gifted" (Roeper Review)

Conversely, the quest for perfection has also hurtled many people into new levels of success when they know when to stop. Healthy perfectionism is actually defined as going for excellence, not perfection. It means staying with a project or an idea for a reasonable amount of time in order to get the most excellent result and then saying "close enough!" We can spend an infinity trying to improve works of creativity because, for the most part, all works are works-in-progress.

QUOTES OFTEN CONVEY WISDOM MOST CONCISELY

"Remember the two benefits of failure. First, if you do fail, you learn what doesn't work; and second, the failure gives you the opportunity to try a new approach." Roger Von Oech

"Imperfection clings to a person, and if they wait till they are brushed off entirely, they would spin for ever on their axis, advancing nowhere."
Thomas Carlyle

It's so much easier being coached by someone who is imperfect and comfortable with their imperfections, than someone who tries to appear perfect and is judgmental toward their own imperfections as well as those as those of others. In general, people who are okay with being human are easier to be around than people who strive to hide their flaws. Oh, I don't know. That might have been me!

MORTALS WHO WERE INSPIRED BY SPILLS THE IMP

You hear the echoes of more mortals. This time you feel more brilliantly in tune with what it means to surrender perfection, subscribe to practice, and relish the process. Each step along the way you enjoy compassionately and without judgment, knowing that because you are on the path, you are becoming a better person whether your product shows it or not.

I will take the ring, though I do not know the way.
—Frodo Baggins, from Lord of the Rings

All of life is an experiment. The more experiments you make the better.
—Ralph Waldo Emerson, philosopher, poet, essayist

Now and then it's good to pause in our pursuit of happiness and just be happy.
—Guillaume Apollinaire, French poet, critic

Aim for success, not perfection. Never give up your right to be wrong, because then you will lose the ability to learn new things and move forward with your life. Remember that fear always lurks behind perfectionism. Confronting your fears and allowing yourself the right to be human can, paradoxically, make you a far happier and more productive person.
—David M. Burns, M.D., author of The Feeling Good Handbook

Patience is also a form of action.
—Auguste Rodin, sculptor, artist

"You can't cross the sea merely by standing and staring at the water."
– Rabindranath Tagore

Some mistakes are too much fun to only make once.
—Anonymous

If you can't make a mistake, you can't make anything.
—Marva Collins, from Working Women for the 21st Century

The greatest mistake you can make in life is to be continually fearing you will make one.
Elbert Hubbard

The higher up you go, the more mistakes you are allowed.
Right at the top, if you make enough of them, it's considered to be your style.
—Fred Astaire, actor, singer, dancer

A life spent making mistakes is not only more honorable but more useful than a life spent doing nothing.
George Bernard Shaw

MUSE PROFILE OF SPILLS THE IMP

SYMBOL

Spills's symbol is a spill of discovery.

HOBBIES

Pushing things over, deliberate accidents, exercising awe, espousing patience, lobbying for experimentation in the face of fear, biting bullets, and being tickled at the ingenuity that comes from releasing the fear of being i^mper_fecT. Good humor during failed attempts.

CAR

Spills the Imp drives a beat-up, yellow '65 Ford pickup.

The greatest mistake a man can make is to be afraid of making one.
—Elbert Hubbard, publisher, author

RITUAL TO SUMMON SPILLS THE IMP

Ritual materials: your favorite music, an imperfect candle, a lemon, hand lotion, chalk pastels, water soluble crayons and paper or malleable clay like Sculpey or Fimo, your journal or sketchbook.

To summon Spills the Imp, play the music, light the candle, and cut open the lemon. Smell the scents with focused attention. Notice every nuance. Look at the inside of the lemon as if it were the first time you've ever seen one. Can you view it with a state of wonder? Do you feel impatient or silly? Allow yourself these, and any other feelings, as you watch yourself as a compassionate observer. Slather your hands with the hand lotion and notice how it feels. Take ten minutes just to enjoy playing with chalk pastels, water soluble crayons or clay with no finished product in mind. Write a statement in your journal with your Spills energy: "I will turn over to God my fears of imperfection. I will practice acceptance and embrace the process of life and creativity in the interest of becoming a better person." Say one of the affirmations listed below, then blow the candle out and watch for inspiration. Write the affirmation in your journal every day this week, or write it on a card and post it where you can see it regularly. Be ready to feel less pressure and more joy in living and creating during the next week.

AFFIRMATIONS AND SMALL QUESTIONS FROM SPILLS THE IMP

What would it feel like if I were free from the need to be perfect?

I get to be imperfect in the creative process!!!

I am evolving into someone I love for who I am, not for what I do.

What mistake will I make that results in a new discovery, direction or the perfect process?

I am the joy in my journey.

What would it feel like to truly enjoy the process?

I am willing to be a beginner at my craft, starting with beginner's results on my way to getting better. I am getting better and better with regular practice.

When I find myself working too hard to reach my unrealistic expectations, I will just stop and say "Close enough!"

And there you go. Spills the Imp is with you.

JOURNAL CHECK-IN

1. Take out your journal. Write or draw about your Spills the Imp status. What thoughts did the chapter bring up for you? Start with one of these unfinished sentences: Giving myself permission to do things imperfectly… or I am jumping right into the process by…I shall season my process with…

2. Write down what your inner critic has to say about starting projects, about inadequacies. Is the criticism "You're not good enough" one of the regular messages you get from your critic? Give your inner critic a chance to fully speak its mind on the page. This practice will help to diminish its power over you. At the end say "Thanks for sharing, but I'm pretty okay with small and crappy as a place to start."

3. Review quotes from mortals who were inspired by Spills (p. 146). Pick one and keep writing where it left off, continuing with your own thoughts. Or quick-write about how the quote applies to you.

4. For the next five minutes imagine you are a "mistake." Write, draw, dance, or paint as a mistake would. See if there are any discoveries. What are your feelings in the process? Is it easy to create from this point of view?

5. Relax. Take some deep let-go breaths and embody your own Spills energy. When you are ready write yourself a letter from her, let her comment and encourage you in areas of perfectionism, practice, and being in the process. Let her counter what your inner critic said and be an advocate for your progress.

PERMISSION TO BE IMPERFECT

Purposely perform below your standards in any creative activity just to experience the "permission to be imperfect." Title it when you are finished. Notice how it felt. If it was difficult, write an affirmation to help advance you to a more process-oriented place.

MUSE WALK   SPILLS STYLE

Take a walk simply to walk. Have no destination in mind and notice what that feels like. Allow yourself to wander off your usual path. What thoughts does it bring up? Feel the breeze created by your walking wash across your face. Feel your feet caress the earth. Match the rhythm of your breathing to the rhythm of your walking. Look for different colors. Focus only on reds, then greens, then blues. Listen for every sound you can hear. Then listen for only one. Feel yourself perfectly imperfect and let that relax you. Ask: What does feeling no pressure at all in the creative process feel like? What does trusting the process feel like? How can I reframe how imperfect I am so that I feel it's gift?

BRAINSTORM

If I had to live my life over again,
I'd dare to make more mistakes next time.
—Natine Sanger, writer

What a wonderful life I've had!
I only wish I'd realized it sooner.
Colette

If you look closely at a tree you'll notice it's knots and dead branches, just like our bodies.
What we learn is that beauty and imperfection go together wonderfully.
Matthew Fox

BREATHING

Breathing is under both automatic and voluntary control. The act, feel, and art of breathing are overlooked by many of us as some of life's most powerful and pleasurable processes. The creative importance of breathing, as far as Spills goes, is in using the pleasure of breathing to open our awareness to other enjoyable processes. As we learn to find pleasure in something as natural and available as the breath, our pleasure awareness will begin to apply to other areas of our lives. As we practice focusing on the pleasure of an automatic process such as breathing on a conscious level over and over, the pleasure itself can become automatic. Then, the state of contentment and relaxation will be as effortless as breathing. At this point, we are more able to engage in creative passions.

When you breathe as a conduit for the creative process, it serves as a release for fear that comes up around performing perfectly. Focusing on the breath joins us with the present moment. In the pure mindfulness of this very moment, there is no fear. The breath is a remedy for many of the reasons the mind is not present. In the creative process it can energize the magnetism of our inspirations.

Take a moment and return to the breath. Follow its process and notice how the simple shift of focus from thought to the process of breathing relaxes mind and body. Inspiration and joy are now more accessible.

A grounding Breath

The following breath exercise brings alive appreciation of breathing. It relieves anxiety and returns our focus to the eternal flow of the here and now.

1. Inhale halfway and hold for four seconds.
2. Inhale again and hold for four seconds.
3. Exhale halfway and hold for four seconds.
4. Exhale to a natural stopping point and hold for four seconds.
5. One more time, exhale, squeezing the air out as the abdomen pushes in and hold for eight seconds.
6. Inhale halfway and hold for four seconds.
7. Let go of the control of the breath and stay with the feeling of the breath's unrestricted flow for the next two cycles of inhale and exhale.
8. Repeat twice.

This breathing exercise is a metaphor for the flow of the creative process: taking an inspiration, holding it, bringing more to the inspiration and holding it, exhaling as it is expressed, and stopping and exhaling again, and again letting go of the idea. Then letting go of control and surrendering to the sweet, unobstructed flow of both breathing and creativity.

The Alternate Nostril Breath

This is an ancient yogic breath exercise, or pranayama. Medical science has recently discovered the "nasal cycle." Yogis have known about it for thousands of years. We know that we don't breathe equally with both nostrils. One nostril is much easier to breathe through than the other at any particular time, and this alternates about every three hours.

Studies have shown that the nasal cycle affects brain function. The electrical activity of the brain was found to be greater on the side opposite the less congested nostril. The right side of the brain controls creative activity, while the left side controls logical verbal activity. When the left nostril was less obstructed, the right side of the brain was predominant. Test subjects were found to do markedly better on creative tests. Similarly when the right nostril was less obstructed, the left side of the brain was predominant, and test subjects did better on verbal skills.

Benefits of the Alternate Nostril Breath are as follows:

! The exercise produces optimum function in both sides of the brain: this is optimum creativity and optimum logical verbal activity.

! This is the best technique to calm the mind and the nervous system, thus making focus and concentration for creative pursuits more accessible.

Method:

1. Close the right nostril with your right thumb and inhale through the left nostril. Do this to the count of four seconds.

2. Immediately close the left nostril with your right ring finger and little finger, and at the same time remove your thumb from the right nostril and exhale through this nostril. Do this to the count of eight seconds. This completes a half round.

3. Inhale through the right nostril to the count of four seconds. Close the right nostril with your right thumb and exhale through the left nostril to the count of eight seconds. This completes one full round.

    Start by doing two rounds. For optimal results add one per week until you are doing seven rounds.

PRACTICE MAKES PRETTY DERN GOOD

Nature without exercise is a seed shut up in a pod,
and art without practice is nothing.
—Pietro Aretino, Italian poet, writer, dramatist

Choose an aspect of one of your creative passions. Find steps that you can begin, and then for twenty-one days (not necessarily in a row but fairly regularly) have no product in mind; just practice. Fit it into fifteen-minute spans of time, more if you like, but fifteen minutes is all that is required. Do not judge yourself, and if you find you do, write down what you hear yourself say and then throw it away. After twenty-one days decide whether you want to continue.

Here are some suggestions for things to do: Write personal essays or short stories (making sure you allow yourself to start out with first drafts that may be pretty bad). Engage in any art modality, such as drawing, painting, collage, mosaic, paper making, human-figure drawing, photography, writing letters, making cards or journal writing, learning dance steps (modern dance or freestyle), playing a musical instrument, making a film, practicing a walking meditation, gardening, decorating, or throwing parties. Pick something your intuition feels like doing.

Get resourceful about how you will spend your fifteen minutes. Just reading about what you would like to do counts, as does shopping for supplies, calling about a class, or getting equipment ready. Just consistently stay with any part of this creative endeavor's process, and you will be pleasantly surprised. (Reading about it more than a year may mean it is time for the next step.)

MAKING PRACTICE FUN

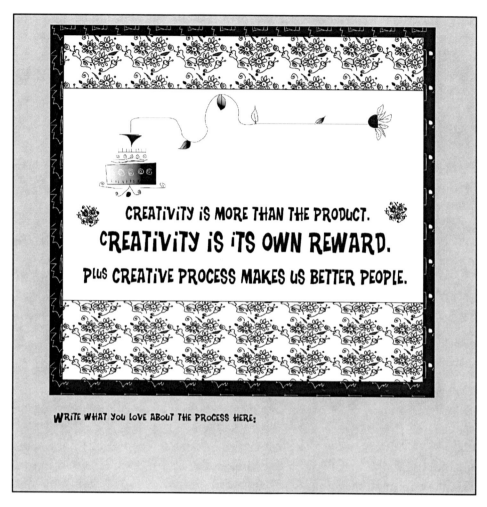

CREATIVITY IS MORE THAN THE PRODUCT.
CREATIVITY IS ITS OWN REWARD.
PLUS CREATIVE PROCESS MAKES US BETTER PEOPLE.

WRITE WHAT YOU LOVE ABOUT THE PROCESS HERE:

If you dread practicing, use some Muse techniques to make it enticing. See some of Albert's ideas. Use his associative word triggers during your practice for new ideas. Imagine you are practicing in front of different audiences. Dress up the environment. Warm up to practicing by playing. Talk to yourself as if you were talking to a TV audience about what you need to practice, and how. Practice with friends. Play music, burn incense, wear a special fun outfit that is just for practicing. Reward yourself for practicing. Just practice. Experiment with attaching feelings of play, mischievousness, zaniness, and wild abandon to your process.

SIMPLY FOR THE PROCESS

Be aware of how you feel when thoughts of perfection flare up. Shift to being completely engaged in the process of breathing. Allow yourself to be a beginner again. Be unattached to the results of these activities.

Finger paint: Feel the textures, use different instruments. 🖐 🖐 🖐
Use color pencils: See how many different looks you can create. ✏ ✏ ✏
Make a collage: Tear the paper instead of cutting it. ✩ ✩ ✩

Experiment with using art media completely different from what you normally use.
Do not plan; just engage in the process.
Start writing as if you were in the middle of an essay or short story.
Dance in your living room in a sloppy way with no concern for perfection.

When you decide to season your process with intentions that delight you, joy is more prevalent and with joy the results are better. Decide on your intentions: joy, lightness, curiosity, eagerness, openness to the unexpected, mischievousness. And if you stray from these feelings, think the thoughts or find the reminders to take you back to your intention.

QUICK TIPS AND MUSINGS

🕯 Change your standards to eighty percent. Notice relaxation set in as you do.
Let go of unrealistic expectations and decide to allow the process to be pressure-free and enjoyable.

🕯 Write a list of five things you would do if you could do them perfectly. Take note whether you could do any part of anything on the list just to experience the process. Take note if you are avoiding something because you want to be instantly good at it. If you gave yourself one year to be "good" at it just for the fun of it, would you change your mind about trying it?

🕯 Spend time with someone engaged in his/her craft who is not a perfectionist. It is SO freeing!

🕯 When you finish something and you are critical of it, check to see if your criticism is realistic. Figure out what you learned from it and what part you do like; be reasonable and compassionate about what you don't like. You can like some of it and not all of it... and still accept it.

🕯 Develop compassion for yourself and others. Compassion happens quicker through trial and error. Find people who are compassionate toward you.

🕯 Be willing to look like a beginner in order to become an expert. Understand that this is common sense.

🕯 Examine how perfectionism affects your ability to experience all of your feelings, including inadequacy, guilt, shame, anger, inferiority, jealousy, and envy. Experiencing all you feelings can move you more deeply into creativity. Allowing the

imperfection feelings to surface also gives permission to joy.
- ✝ Read *Bird by Bird* by Anne Lamott, for perfection breakthrough strategies.
- ✝ Read *Drawing on the Right Side* of the Brain by Betty Edwards.
- ✝ Make up a book (or story or poem) called *Drawing on the Wrong Side of The Bird.*

SPILLS SPEAKS SOME MORE

1. If you do something over and over, trying to get it perfect, set a time limit and stop. Come back to it later, but at one point know what you have done is enough and then let go of it. Generally, we have a hard time stopping when we are too attached to the end result. Know that there is a time to release and move on.

2. Release your need for you, or your work, to be accepted. It is a wonderfully freeing feeling to give yourself a designated work period, then to set free your completed result. This makes rejection or criticism unimportant since you have done your best during the process and have now decided to be unattached to what happens. If the results meet with success, the process again is the most important part.

3. Be aware if you spend a lot of time on details that are unimportant or that you can return to once the bulk of work is done. Focusing on unimportant aspects of your project is usually an avoidance strategy. You may do it to avoid harder work, responsibility, or the discomfort of forging into the unknown. Explore these possibilities and make sure you are prioritizing and focusing on what is most important to the project's process. If you feel you are losing sight of what is significant, a trusted opinion from someone safe, whom you respect, can be helpful.

Pursuing perfect creative efforts is missssssing the point of the creative experience. Live with wild abandon. You are not being graded.
—Spills the Imp, muse

NEXT STOP IN THE GARDEN

You are starry-eyed from what you have seen so far in the garden. You feel inspired to share more of yourself with the world, whether it is through art or writing, or the splendid unique way you express yourself daily. You know the Bodyguard is there to protect you, but you still feel constricted, vulnerable, and shy. You wonder how people get up the courage to be creative, or more authentic. The inner critic taunts you by saying that your desire to be creative is not worth the risk.

The trees restlessly wave about because a Muse of great authenticity is about to assist you. The garden is alive with her energy, her ability to seize the moment and set it on fire with unbridled enthusiasm. She is alive with the desire to share her energy. She cannot wait to help you share with the world your unique way of being and your creative expression: art, writing, dance performance, letter writing, just being you. She will help you move forward with confidence, courage, and genuine expression.

"Her most ardent messages: "Be yourself!" - and -
"Share yourself with the world without hesitation."

AUDACITY:
MUSE OF COURAGE AND UNINHIBITED UNIQUENESS

"My darling girl, when are you going to realize that being normal is not necessarily a virtue?
It rather denotes a lack of courage!" Practical Magic

SUMMON AUDACITY WHEN:

◎ You need to boldly move beyond the insecurities you have about creatively sharing yourself. You want confidence and courage to proceed with your creative dream.

◎ You want to be yourself, but feel inhibited by, or at the mercy of, what other people think of you. You also feel at the mercy of your own excessive self-criticism.

◎ You need to accept and use your own power as an individual.

BOTTOM LiNE

As mortals who are given creative propensities (ALL OF US), we have the ability to manifest our divine authenticity and unique form of creative brilliance. Through our willingness to share our originality we share with the world the beauty, insight, and ingenuity we were born with. We must share with audacious courage, believing that, as we do, we make a sweeping statement that can change the world around us.

THE SELECTiON OF AUDACiTY

It took little deliberation for the Muses to come up with this modern equivalent. Trying to stay nonjudgmental, the Muses kept correcting themselves when they referred to mortals as "those wimps." "Oops, we mean mortals," they would correct themselves time after time. Muses are compassionate beings, but they often err on the side of being a little too brazen. They just cannot believe how many mortals sell out their creative brilliance because they are afraid of what other mortals might think.

Because look, here is the reality—mortals think judgmental thoughts toward another mortal's creative expression substantially less often than imagined. If another mortal does think something judgmental, that thought process usually takes up mmm, maybe thirty seconds AT THE MOST. Think about it—self-conscious mortals hold back their destined creative exaltation, often for their entire lives, because they fear a thirty-second judgment from other mortals who don't deserve that much power in the first place. Or mortals refuse to engage in their creativity because a misguided mortal from the past WAS judgmental and given too much power for those judgments. These timid mortals just need a little more moxie, a little more...audacity. And when the Muses reached that conclusion, Aha-phrodite said, "Yes...audacity is exactly what they need, so let's make 'audacity' a Muse." The others concurred unanimously with catcalls, a few whoops, and one somersault.

Your Audacity Energy

Power is the ability not to have to please.
—Elizabeth Janeway, writer

The word "audacity" is a synonym for boldness, daring, and courage. Other synonyms include grit, guts, and appropriately—patience. The Muse Audacity is here to inspire these qualities in order to endow mortals with the courage they need to be creatively liberated, and to be themselves without explanation or apology.

Audacity wants mortals to know that being genuine frees others who need a beacon to guide them. Then we will have more authentic mortals running around, and fewer cranky, confused, and painfully shy ones.

Audacity brings to us a knowing that reflects a strong sense of certainty that comes with intuition. When we listen to the wisdom of intuition conveyed to us from our inner resources, we find that listening to ourselves, rather than to others, is the most important way to know and trust the truth of who we are. Likewise, we will know how to share this truth in whatever way we are inspired to do so. Intimately knowing and trusting ourselves is a form of overcoming barriers created by thinking someone else has to approve of us or of our creative work. Our consequent power dwarfs the effect of opinions, criticism, or negativity.

We learn to know ourselves by experience, awareness, and acting according to what we feel is right in the moment and then weighing the consequences of our actions from an objective standpoint. Success in the form we visualize is not guaranteed. Constant success is in fact contraindicated in both creativity and the growth of an individual. So much more insight and depth of living arise, so many more ideas are discovered, from the balance of successes and failures. If the decisions from our own wisdom result in success, we feel more confident. If they meet with failure but we remain tenacious, focused, and committed to a path true to ourselves, our self-respect grows. Self-respect results in personal freedom and confidence. Steadfastly following our own wisdom in the realm of creativity, to the degree that we can without expert opinions, is a win-win confidence builder.

What Does It Mean To Be Audacious?

To thine own self be true.
—William Shakespeare, English dramatist, poet

Have you heard someone exclaim, *"Well...the audacity!"* about someone who had the nerve to do something bold and perhaps rude? Audacity in the case of Muse-creativity is not disrespect toward other mortals or toward oneself. Audacity's influence includes respect—yet this does not necessarily mean positive public opinion is needed. In fact, one of the favorite things Audacity encourages mortals to say is "Listen, if everyone likes what I've done, I haven't gone far enough. It is not possible to be liked by everyone if I am deeply authentic and true to myself." And this is perfectly okay.

Oprah Winfrey, a former people-pleaser addict, says that now, if she is being completely true to herself, there is usually someone mad at her. It is most important for her to follow her intuition about what is right for her, not the words of others.

So long as they don't get violent, I want to let everyone say what they wish,
for I myself have always said exactly what pleased me.
—Albert Einstein, Swiss-German-American physicist

When we are completely ourselves, we grace the world with a uniqueness that colors it with the interest and variety brilliantly possible for us as humans. We live a more fulfilling and energetic life because we are not using all the energy it requires to constantly please others. We also do not have to deal with the disappointment we have in ourselves about a putting a lid on our true expressions. Singer, songwriter, and actress Madonna reinvented herself many times. At first, she met with a lot of criticism because it was new for a celebrity to stray so much from a consistent, mainstreamed image. She commanded respect and attention for her willingness to follow her love of remaking herself.

The audacious have always been pioneers in the world of art. The ability to be one's self in the face of critical public opinion is a freedom that results in new ways to be, new ways to see, and deep admiration by those who are touched. Whole movements are many times created from one individual's risk taking. Freely expressing individuals, who are not afraid to stand by their beliefs, are inspirations. They keep us awake and share the potency of self-commitment.

We love to watch movie characters who demonstrate audacity because then we can vicariously experience their freedom, confidence, and ability to share with the world their earnest convictions in a bold and sometimes outrageous manner. From Fame, Strictly Ballroom, Norma Rae, Harold and Maude, Erin Brockovich, Billy Elliot, Maximus in Gladiator, Juliette Binoche's character in Chocolat, Mel Gibson's characters in Lethal Weapon and in Braveheart, Kevin Spacey's character in American Beauty, Robin Williams's character in Dead Poets Society...the list goes on and on. They are heroes that go against previous limits of acceptability to stay true to themselves or to their cause.

LiViNg oN THE EDgE oF FREEDoM

The joy of living comes from not being afraid to risk living fully. This does not mean risking life and limb by taking foolish chances, but rather risking acceptance in order to be real. It means risking being vulnerable and sometimes uncomfortable, in order to be free to act spontaneously. We can never be truly free unless we are fully ourselves.

Gertrude Stein said, "Let me listen to me and not to them." To be true to one's self means ignoring the advice of people who uphold a certain way to do, and to be, as the only way. These are the people who fear change or feel threatened by the creativity of others. Many people care too much about what people think at the expense of sharing their uncommon gifts, unique views, and distinctive lifestyles. They also sacrifice a lifetime of living their sublime destiny.

THE BLUNDEROUS PHENOMENON OF HESITATION

Only those who risk going too far know how far they can go.
—T. S. Eliot, poet, playwright

We might also feel we are disdainfully presumptuous if we take creative work we have completed and submit it for publication, show, or sharing. We think that it might not be good enough, or we might be judged and rejected. Yet, many times the only thing that differentiates a successful artist, writer, rugged individualist, is audacity, taking the extra step of sharing and submitting work without the restraint that comes from worrying what people will think.

The cheeky prevail and reap the benefits of courage, notoriety, and growth. These first steps of putting our work and talents out there propel us to better ourselves to meet that mark and then rise to the next. The countless artists and creative individuals who have a standard that must be reached before they are willing to share their work miss out on the experience and amazing insights for growth that come from sharing their work. And the standards they are waiting to achieve may never arrive without the necessary tension of showing their creative expression. Audacity terms this the "blunderous phenomenon of hesitation." It is a Muse crime requiring the attention of the Creativity Police Force—a faction you do not want to contend with.

We must be willing to fall flat on our face. Fearlessly putting ourselves out there is simply a required part of the process. At the very least, it results in the gift of humility and, at best, the triumph of our human spirit. Both are pretty good rewards.

SELFISHNESS VS. SELFLESSNESS

You may be stuck in what Audacity calls selfless blind-spot muck if:

- You are feeling selfish about spending time on your creative work.
- Everyone and everything else comes before your creative work.
- You worry you will "show up," intimidate, or lose people with your talent.
- You are self-conscious about appearing presumptuously good.

You need a little more audacity. When this is the case, pull out this emergency passage from Marianne Williamson's book A Return to Love:

"We ask ourselves, who am I to be brilliant, gorgeous, talented and fabulous?
Actually, who are you not to be?
You are a child of God.
Your playing small doesn't serve the world.
There is nothing enlightened about shrinking so that other
people will not feel insecure around you.
We were born to make manifest the glory of God that is within us.
It is not in just some of us; it is in everyone.
And as we let our own light shine, we unconsciously give
people permission to do the same.
As we are liberated from our own fear, our presence
automatically liberates others."

When we are true to our own creative light, others will be true to theirs. If not, they will be left in their shy and shallow places of muck until they are ready to emerge. The Bodyguard tells us we need to be shielded from people who discourage our decision to live a creative life, and the strength to do this needs to come from deep inside.

Modesty has its place in the social graces, no doubt. Being humble expresses approachability and refinement. Yet, in moving toward self-realization, it can limit us if it is overused. For instance, if we say, "Please look at my work of art, I think it is very good," we may worry that someone will label us "conceited." Generally we try to avoid being labeled conceited, obviously, because it has a negative connotation. This avoidance controls our actions. In this case, we are holding back against our inner wisdom, our better judgment, and our authentic voice's desire to share itself.

This is not to say pleasing others is unimportant. But one must start with the self to be truly available for other people. Many people believe that they are being responsible when they martyr themselves, taking care of everyone around them, and continually depriving themselves of their own time, energy, money—even their health and peace of mind. This is the opposite of being responsible—because doing too much for others can deprive them of the privilege of meeting their own challenges in their own way and prevents them from becoming independent and responsible themselves. As with many aspects of life and love, it is all about balance.

CULTIVATING AUDACITY

We all have equal access to the energy of Audacity. This energy animates us to be more "uniquely" ourselves! It starts with a little courage to go beyond what any voices in our head tell us not to do because of fear. After a while, those voices give up when they see we have the courage to act in spite of their taunting. And when we subscribe to the spell of Audacity, at last we begin to listen to the authentic voices that celebrate our flowing expression of existence. We begin to honor what we have to say. We build momentum and liberate ourselves from unreal-fear-driven obstacles. We are free to dance to our own unique music and inspire those who are ready to dance to theirs.

> Those who danced were thought to be quite insane
> by those who could not hear the music.
> —Angela Monet, author

FEARS ARE BALLOONS

Robert Genn, the painter and on-line columnist, notes that the loss of our power in the creative process can many times be attributed to our fears, fears that "float up in the mind and obstruct the free flow." He suggests that people identify their fears, list them out, and then float them in the air like balloons and pop them. Audacity concurs with this idea and even encourages you to buy or designate your own personal-power sharp thing, decorate it or have a place of honor for it, and pull it out anytime a fear floats up in front of your magnificence.

Emerson said, "He has not learned the lesson of life who does not every day surmount a fear."

Robert Genn notes, "The following are multiple choice. There are more. Go for it. Fear of failure. Fear of success. Fear of competition. Fear of play. Fear of joy. Fear of work. Fear of plagiarism. Fear of learning something. Fear of being an impostor. Fear of not being paid. Fear of being paid. Fear of being ridiculed. Fear of being noticed. Fear of not being noticed. Fear of being copied. Fear of making a mess. Fear of being wrong. Fear of the unknown. Fear of commitment. Fear of getting excited. Fear of wasting time. Fear of irrelevance. Fear of fear itself. Pop, pop, pop."

AUDACITY'S EMPOWERING PURPOSE

When we commit with strength and conviction to our desire to share our creative ideas or our creative purpose, our purpose becomes more important than the opinions of others. It is a choice where you place your power. When you are eighty years old, where do you think you would wish you had placed your power?

AUDACITY CONDEMNS COMPARISON

Comparing your work, intentions, talents, to others is a sure way to invite a creative clog. Comparison is one of those temptations on the journey that mortals need to refuse. It has no place in the creative process except to thwart it. When you catch yourself in a comparison situation, work to replace your thought with an affirmation that works for you, such as "I am on my own path of magnificence and what she/he has done is only proof that I can do it, too," or "I'm traversing my path in my own way, little by little," or "I have everything I need and I trust I am moving forward." Ask yourself the question: "What would it feel like to feel as if I am doing just fine just the way I am?" Just this question can tame the comparison animal.

INTUITION

Your vision will become clear only when you look into your heart. He who looks outside, dreams. He who looks inside, awakens.
—Carl Jung, Swiss psychologist and psychiatrist

Intuition originates from our deepest truth. The discovery of our intuition as the voice of authenticity paves a path clear for our desire to express who we are. The discovery of this unique voice of the spirit inside us is, in itself, motivation to share. Sharing ourselves creatively is what we were designed to do. Why else would we all be so different?
Practice your confidence of intuitive knowing:

Number from 1 to 20, then fill in each of these incomplete sentences twenty times:
   I think...
   I sense...
   I know for sure...
   Then write about how it felt to make the distinction between thinking, sensing, and knowing.

Be You to Full (Beautiful)

MORTALS WHO WERE INSPIRED BY AUDACITY

As you walk through Audacity's part of the garden, you see her teachings seem to have freed many bridled souls to speak their truth. Notice how you feel more willing to take risks in line with your divine authenticity (and then take one if big and two if small).

If you pay nervous attention to other people's opinions, maneuver to obtain their indulgence and to stand high in their esteem, you will be whisked about
in their winds and you will lose yourself.
—Jo Coubert, from www.CreativeQuotes.com

The modes of expression of men of genius differ as much
as their souls, and it is difficult to say that in some among them,
drawing and color are better or worse than in others.
—Auguste Rodin, French sculptor

If people can cultivate inner security and develop a commitment to their own talents, in this
path they can earn as much money as they need or want.
Once involved in this path, they go beyond the goal of money to the
goal of authentic self expression.
—Marsha Sinetar, educator, author of Do What You Love and the Money Will Follow: Discovering Your Right Livelihood

Courage is doing what you're afraid to do. There can be no courage unless you're scared.
Eddie Rickenbacker

If an idea does not appear bizarre, there is no hope for it.
—Niels Bohr, physicist

Courage and perseverance have a magical talisman, before which difficulties disappear and
obstacles vanish into air.
John Quincy Adams

The most common form of despair is not being who you are.
—Soren Kierkegaard, existential philosopher
If you are going to walk on thin ice, you might as well dance.
—Anonymous

The successful man is the one who had the chance and took it.
—Roger Babson, entrepreneur, educator, philanthropist

To be nobody-but-yourself—in a world which is doing its best,
night and day, to make you everybody else—means to fight
the hardest battle which any human being can fight;
and never stop fighting.
—e. e. cummings, poet

I don't know the key to success, but the key to
failure is trying to please everybody.
—Bill Cosby, comedian, actor

If you're not having fun, reconsider what you're doing.
—Audacity, muse
Take risks. If you win you will be happy. If you
lose, you will be wise. author unknown
Only when we are no longer afraid do we begin to live. —Dorothy Thompson:
When you can do the common things of life in an uncommon way, you will command the at-
tention of the world.
—George Washington Carver, U.S. chemist, educator

To go against the dominant thinking of your friends,
of most of the people you see every day,
is perhaps the most difficult act of heroism you can perform.
Theodore H. White

MUSE PROFILE OF AUDACITY

SYMBOL

Audacity's symbol is a dazzling marquee sending a message to the world to shamelessly share talents in an authentically personal way.

HOBBIES

Freedom, parades, body painting, tight-rope walking, dancing on tables, baton twirling, performance art, taking fashion risks, inspiring mortals to be themselves with verve, exhibitionism, and talking over a PA system.

CAR

Drives a red 2012 Maserati with a gold vanity license plate that says SOARRRR.

To change one's life:
1. Start immediately.
2. Do it flamboyantly.
3. No exceptions.
—William James, psychologist

Ritual To Summon Audacity

Ritual materials: ten candles (splurge), a mirror, some audacious music. Light the candles. Look in the mirror. Embody your own persona of Audacity by adding elements of someone you know who is audacious and bold. Think of a charismatic public speaker, a certain friend of yours, someone you know who is unafraid of what people think. If you can't think of anyone, conjure up the spirit of a movie character who is outrageous or audacious: Robin Williams's character in Dead Poets Society, Sandra Bullock in Blindside, Juliette Binoche in Chocolat. If you need to rent a movie, do so to feel the audacious attitude but make the energy your own, draw on your own audacity.

When you have embodied your dauntless energy, turn it up ten notches and notice how that feels. Feel what makes you, you. Say to yourself, "I'm good! And I'm going to _____." Then fill in the blank with a convincing statement about your creative dream. Repeat it out loud until you hear the courage and conviction in your voice. Write it on a note card or take up a whole page in your journal and write whatever else you wish to say for at least five minutes based on where the attitude takes you. Then write a pledge to the Muse Audacity: "With patience and compassion each new day will be an opportunity to be more and more true to who I am." Then say one of the following affirmations and blow the candles out.

Affirmations and Small Questions from Audacity

- ☦ I am true to myself.
- ☦ What would it feel like to be true to myself?
- ☦ What's one tiny courageous step I can take today?
- ☦ As my intuition strengthens, I am confident about the decisions I make.
- ☦ I have the courage to express my talents.
- ☦ I love shining my light so that others can find theirs.
- ☦ I release the restraint of believing taking creative time is selfish. Creative time is divinely spent and makes me a better person for all other areas of my life.
- ☦ Being my authentic self invites the spirit of creativity to express through me.

And so it is. Audacity is with you.

JOURNAL CHECK-IN

1. Take out your journal and write about where you are with audacity, courage, and authenticity. List examples of audacity in your life.

2. Quickly fill in this blank at least 5 different ways: If I were true to myself I would. Keep going with this unfinished sentence: With more courage I get to...
   Let your inner critic say his or her piece about being fully yourself, sharing yourself with the world, and taking time for your creative work despite what others say.

3. Take a look at the quotes from mortals who were inspired by Audacity (pp. 165-166). Choose one or more and pick up where the quote stops and continue with your own thoughts or simply speed-write about how the quote applies to you.

4. Get comfortable, and close your eyes. Embody the essence of what you know about the Muse Audacity. Feel her strength fill your body. Contact your own Audacity energy and then write a letter to yourself. What would she say specifically to you about being yourself and authenticity? About courage? Let her counter what your critic said. Let her praise your efforts.

Courage is being afraid but going on anyhow. Dan Rather

MUSE WALK - ✺ AUDACITY STYLE ✺

Go outside for a meditative walk. Walk with a feeling of courage in your body. Feel a sense of audacity arising from inside you. Think of what you might do if you had ten times more courage than you have now. Do you walk differently when filled with outrageous energy? Do you think differently? Do the neighbors feel greater respect for you?

BRAINSTORM

BELIEFS

Identifying our beliefs strengthens our motivation to boldly be ourselves. Quick List fifty of your beliefs. They can be as small as "I believe in the blessing of the first sunlight in the morning" to "I believe in world peace." Write them quickly, feeling your conviction for them grow by increasing the pressure of your pen, pencil, or crayon.

To live creatively free,
do what you know how to do now then
"act as if" you know how to do the rest.
—SARK, author

"ACT AS IF"

Audacity loves this "act as if" exercise. Act as if you are an artist, a writer, or an authentically expressive person, and you will convince yourself that you truly are and begin to fill the form. During the writing of this book I consulted a coach to help me focus. She asked me, "What is it that authors do? Find out and do it." It seemed like such an easy concept, but the truth was, I was doing what people who procrastinate do, not what authors do. As soon as I gave myself the label "author" and "acted as if" I were one, confidence surfaced and the conditions came together to help me to focus on the right activities.

What are five things you can begin "acting as if" in order to weave closer to your dream?

1.

2.

3.

4.

5.

TIPS FROM AUDACITY

- Say what you really mean in a compassionate manner.
- Ask for what you want.
- Don't agree when you don't - just disagree kindly. Say nothing rather than cave to something you don't believe.
- Act based on your best judgment.
- Speak up at the risk of appearing foolish and see if you survive.
- Redefine "foolish" as self-confidence and creative freedom. Drop your preoccupation with what people think
- Talk back to your inner critic: Say, "Thanks for sharing now bye-bye!"
- Share your art, submit your writing, share dance, music, song, and reap the benefits of strengthening your character. Share at an open-mike event.

† Show the world who you are from your truth, feel the freedom, and notice how people begin to relax more around you.

† Do those things that your heart desires without guilt, apology, or self-consciousness.

† Give yourself permission to do these things imperfectly and in a small, non-linear way...5% more each time.

In a world where you felt freer and more confident to be yourself, where would you be more audacious?

1.

2.

3.

4.

5.

What are three of the greatest joys in your life? Are you paying attention to them?

1.

2.

3.

Close your eyes and picture yourself doing those activities while being supported by a strong spirit and the Muse Audacity. Draw yourself engaging in at least one of those situations in your sketchbook. (Permission to draw like a five-year-old granted.)

In your journal, claim what you do really well—bypassing your inner critic and releasing inferiority, insecurity, false modesty. Write boldly. Use a permanent marker.

Put outrageous music on and move with your deepest-seated audacity.

List seven of your audacious-fantasy personalities. Give them a name, a hobby, or an occupation. Here are some of mine:

Disagreement Diva: Is not afraid to disagree with someone at the risk of making him or her mad.

Ballsie Betty: Pulls a chair up to a table of strangers in a restaurant and is so charming they buy her dinner.

Monica: Jumps out of birthday cakes and throws frosting at the onlookers.

Angie: Is a fireman.

Rocky Renee: Ushers mothers who mistreat their kids to the bathroom for a good talking to.

Angela: Paints with pistachio, banana, and cherry pudding on white linen pants and wears them to the grocery store.

Make a list of twenty or more preferences that, at least for today, you want to claim for your own (e.g., I like vanilla shakes better than chocolate, I prefer tulips to carnations, I like reading better than football, I like plays better than opera, I like The Grinch Who Stole Christmas better than A Charlie Brown Christmas). This helps you make a small stand for the moment, empowering the convictions of your authentic identity.

Give yourself the title of your heart's choice—artist, writer, screenwriter, woman extraordinary, Warrior Princess, Brilliant Decorator, Titillating Conversationalist, Chocolate Cake Olympic Gold Medalist, Sensual Goddess, Love God.

SiGN HERE WiTH YoUR NAME AND YoUR TiTLE:

Begin to believe that you are talented in your mind and body. Begin to resolve not to hide it. Have the audacity to call yourself talented and look for ways that the world complies with your wishes.

Believe in a leap of faith. Picture it and do it. (Small leaps at first.) Do not quit your job or your relationship unless intuitively the gut feeling says, "Absolutely, go for it." Set up conditions to do it first. Have a plan. Make connections that will support you. Sometimes taking a leap too quickly is not as successful as the gradual leap. Small steps make your leap possible from a common sense point of view. Excavate who you are by making a list of those things you find endearing about yourself from the past. If you can't remember many of them, remember comments from other people. I forgot I was funny in high school, but with some contemplation I remember the cutest kid in the school told me he voted for me as the funniest girl in my senior year. If you can't remember any of these things, know this is an exercise to prime your subconscious for remembering more. You may find two days or one month from now you do remember. Go through the drill so as to make future discoveries. What accomplishments are you proud of? Use these age ranges to structure your responses:

From age 10 and under, age 11 to 15, 16 to 18, 19 to 24, 25 to 30, 31 to 35, 36 to 40, etc.

When you have the money, go out and buy a piece of clothing you really like but would not normally wear. See how it feels.

Try speaking up where you are usually silent even if it is to thank someone or appreciate someone out loud.

Are you doing your daily routine fifteen minutes a day?

NEXT STOP IN THE GARDEN

As you walk farther down the path, you come to a hammock. Here stretched out in the bliss of reverie is yet another Muse. The trees have lost their leaves and the weather creates dormancy. It is the winter of creativity—the creative cycle decrees rest, diversional activities are encouraged, and catching the breath is in order. During the pause, the grace of gratitude is also addressed.

Come and sit in the lull between the labor. Submit to the influence of letting go. Upon return, you will then be refilled with the fuel of dreams, with a renewed perspective, and often a clear sense of what needs to come next. Ideas will be more immediate if not virtually parading around you for your attention. "Yo! Over here!" New energy and fresh approaches will make your ideas sparkle. Accept rest.

LULL:
MUSE OF PAUSE, DIVERSION, AND GRATITUDE

To do great work a man must be very idle as well as very industrious.
—Samuel Butler, English novelist, satirist

SUMMON LULL WHEN:

- You are having a creative dry spell.
- You are stuck in similar themes, repeating previous ideas, and having difficulty coming up with something new.
- You feel creatively blocked, burnt out or you've come face-to-face with a quagmire.
- You are losing energy toward, or have stopped enjoying, your creative passion.

BOTTOM LINE

Sometimes in the creative process, the next right step is to let go, pause, and give time for our vast resources to connect and spring into new ideas. Surrender to the natural cycle of creativity. Fill with new sensations. Meditate. Turn your attention to mind-stimulating activities. Let go of trying to control things. Trust in the process. Celebrate the creative rejuvenation of rest and pause. Say thanks.

"Here's To Enjoyable Moments of Solitude,
Focused on Creativity!"

THE SELECTION OF LULL

So the Muses were working incredibly hard to reinvent themselves into these modern versions of the Greek inspiration brokers. They had successfully come up with five Muses when, zap! Muse revamping came to an abrupt halt. They still had some slots left to fill, but they could not think of what would work next. They made all sorts of facial contortions, had a few brain strains, and Bea Silly's attention span was completely shot. They tried hard to control the process by auditioning various Muses, hiring a Muse from an escort service, and attempting to rehabilitate a Muse with a bad reputation. They were trying too hard—then it dawned on them: "Duh! We need a break!"

As often as it happened, they were still surprised when the juices dried up without warning. So they took a break. One of them went skiing in the French Alps for a while, and one of them lay in the grass and looked at the pale moon in the daytime sky, but most were fine with just being still. They just stopped doing what they were doing to rest, to let go, to listen, and to receive. That's how they came up with the next new Muse, Lull.

YOUR LULL ENERGY

Stop. Breathe. Allow yourself the luxury of doing nothing for a moment, or an hour, or even a day. It is in emptiness that inspiration will appear. Carole Katchen

The word lull, according to the mortal Word-Weaver, Webster, means "quiet, stillness, pause, short period of calm; to bring repose, rest." The Muse Lull embodies and inspires all these definitions in the interest of the release that mortals need when their brains get stuck. It is a time of no action, of listening, of releasing, and when the time is right, of receiving.

In addition, a creative lull is a time to look in a different direction to activities unrelated to the primary creative passion, process, or problem. It is the phase of a cycle that involves turning away and filling the inner well with more experiences, sensations, and emotions from which to draw upon, enticing back creative vitality, direction, and insight.

A note from Lull to those mortals in "permanent lull": "Taking a break before engaging in the process would be categorized as avoidance...the Muses do not support avoidance activities...it is a foiled rationalization. But nice try."

The lack of directed thought that comes during a creative break creates a chance for ideas to connect on a subconscious level. Breaks result in "eureka" experiences of solutions, plans, or definitive directions. Profound discoveries make regular appearances during a pause. This is the mystery of inspiration, and one of the joys of being a creative mortal.

Lull lets us know that at certain points in our creative process we cannot make more progress unless we honor the part of the cycle where the unconscious processes of spirit and intellect have a chance to connect. This natural element of the creative cycle is often mistaken for a block when sometimes it just indicates that it is time to let go for a while. Sometimes when we go blank, it is simply Lull reaching to replenish the resources of our creative magic. She has removed the process to freshen and load it with abundant wonder and untold inspiration. Mandatory goofing off is in order here. At last, we have actual permission to skip out.

I handle the notes no better than many others, but the pauses—ah! that is where the
art resides.
—Arthur Rubinstein, concert pianist

If there has been no focus, no collection of data, pondering of a problem, working hard, or experimenting with solutions, Lull is not going to appear. (Dull may appear, but there's no Muse magic in dull.) Lull usually springs up either in the middle of an intensely focused phase of a project or between the end of one project and the beginning of the next.

If mortals get to know their patterns of creativity and are honest with themselves, they pretty much know when they are rationalizing their procrastination behavior versus when they've worked intensely hard, are up against a wall or showing signs of depletion and need to take a break to replenish. Sometimes however a needed break does masquerade as procrastination among those who are diligent about being engaged in the process. A true call from Lull usually does not happen with those who succumb frequently to a habit of avoidance. A creative lull, is a part of the creative cycle and if the other parts aren't attended to, the lull won't feel right.

Some usually hard working mortals might THINK they are slacking off, when in fact, they are answering the call of Lull. In that case… be easier on yourself during a lull. When we honor a lull, it passes quicker and we feel refreshed and a new tide of inspiration slides into shore.

Rationalizations are known to come from the brain and are close cousins to fear, laziness, and addictions to distraction such TV and the Internet. The need for a break is born of the spirit. The feeling between these two origins is dramatically different. But because many mortals have unrealistic expectations of themselves, they may call a lull - goofing off instead of the divine break it is.

Individuals in a creative job with deadlines that don't allow for long breaks may need to take short ones: walks, drives, hikes, complete release of a project for an hour or so; exposure to activities, visuals, music, even a breathing meditation that can quickly reboot their idea reserves. Flowing into a magical, energizing and light daydream can help as can a juicy nap.

TAKING A BREAK

I asked poet Lizzie Wann what she did when the inspiration dried up. Calmly, without great concern or panic, she said, "Wait." Honoring the creative process means letting go.

Kerry Vesper, a wood sculptor and furniture maker in Tempe, Arizona, says he struggles with a problem until he starts repeating himself. "At that point I let it go," he says. "I put it away and do something else."

WHAT'S THE DIFFERENCE BETWEEN BEING BLOCKED AND HAVING A LULL?

Being blocked, and needing a break, can be the same thing—in this case the block is telling us that a break is needed. Being severely blocked is a little more complicated. Accompanied by heavy resistance and anxiety, severe blocks manifest as all sorts of chronic avoidance strategies. This severe and irrational fear of failure can benefit from professional relaxation techniques or counseling. Blocks due to long-standing depression, constant fatigue, or unhealthy addictions also need more than a break to be resolved. Find someone to talk to, your creativity is waiting.

In a temporary block, the next step is not apparent, the creative juices are not flowing, or we seem to be repeating old ideas over and over. We may not enjoy our work anymore, or we may become anxious each time we approach it. Before seeking the professionals, explore Lull's inspiration and honor the rhythm of the creative cycle. See what effect a break has on you.

Just as there is a cycle to the seasons, to the moon, and to the tides, there is a cycle to the creative process. Makes sense to me. Many times after an intense creative project has been completed, nothing seems to happen next. Ideas are missing in action; a HELP WANTED sign is hanging on the door of our mind's idea centers. This is where it can get tricky. Some people fight against this void, and the result is often strained efforts devoid of the juices they remember having had before. They think, "That's it. I only had one work in me. I'm just a blunder in the blue of the universe." Similarly, after expending a lot of effort collecting information and striving to bring a project together, other people might reach an impasse. Knowing where to go next seems so out of reach. At this point, when it becomes tempting to abandon the project, consider it time for a lull.

When you recognize that letting go is part of the cycle, and is beneficial, a break can be met with sweet relief. We have a choice. We can choose to surrender to the break, or we can beat ourselves up, thinking we could be doing better or pressuring ourselves to keep going when, in fact, continuing will not get us anywhere, anyway. Surrendering fills us with optimism and ready energy. The latter subjects us to frustration, quitting, and a whole lot of wasted energy. If we willingly let go, understanding that letting go is part of the cure, we can fill the time with other pursuits that will bring richer results when the spring of our creativity returns. So, as Lull would say about the winter of our creativity, "Chill! Relax."

Once we have surrendered to a break, we will know when it has done its wonders—a surge of enthusiasm will send us into a delightful jump-start and we will once again be flabbergasted by our creativity.

"There's a misconception that artists are constantly making things. We all go through cycles," says Carol Grape, a sculptor and instructor at the Art Academy of Cincinnati and Thomas More College, and author of Handmade Jewelry. "Sometimes that creative block scares people. But actually, maybe you're just observing things around you or taking care of other things in your life."

FEED THE BRAIN

The mind's bank of resources is another magical and enigmatic quality of the creative process. One of the wonderful functions of the mind is to store an incredible amount of data. Myriad sensations and feelings can combine with our immediate thought flashes to create the chemistry of ingenuity. In other words, when coming up with an epiphany of ideas and their subsequent cultivation, we use lots of mental art supplies—illustrious experiences, rich facts, absorbing emotions, casual interactions, ardent desires, sudden shifts in routine, and idiosyncratic insights. Our subconscious collection of universal themes is also tapped. The richer the depth of our experience, whether it be in the inner world or the external world, the more we have to pull from in order to invent, create, and self-express.

We can overdraw from that bank of resources. This will cause creative dry spells, stale ideas, and blocks. So during our breaks we need to refill. This is one of the principles of Julia Cameron's powerful experience of creative recovery in The Artist's Way. She prescribes a weekly "Artist's Date," an hour's solitary and festive excursion. During such events the Artist Way followers experience synchronicity, the seeming coincidence of events whose relevance to our needs is uncanny.

When we feel overdrawn, the Muses recommend "diversional" activities to restore creative abundance. This comes in the form of any experience that diverts our attention from our intense work and that is desired by the artist child inside us. Lull calls it the Surreptitious Adventures of Sacred Solitude (SASS). She calls it SASS to conjure up the attitude of secret self-adventure, which makes the experience entice us with fun and appealing adventure. But you can call it whatever you wish… just give yourself this time and watch the magic.

With SASS, mortals can shift into the frame of mind of being brilliantly in the present moment. One student said pleasant experiences she regularly engages in become special, filled with sensation, deeper and more alive when she can just change from an attitude of being half awake to being fully present as if it were a first experience. This feeds the brain with the feeling of wonder—a feeling that vitalizes our creative possibilities. To do this, merely tell yourself, here is a special experience for me - I wonder what it will inspire.

¡NCUBATE

Another service Lull brings us is the incubation, percolation, and gestation of an idea. Ideas need some time to connect with other ideas or to new insights and experiences. So having an idea and then letting it go for a while, returning to it in thought, taking it for a walk, sleeping on it, knocking it around with some friends, dreaming about it, reading unrelated materials and referring to it—can give it juice and make it ready for its next step. This is a valid and important part of the creative process.

gRATiTUDE

Gratitude unlocks the fullness of life. It turns
what we have into enough, and more. It turns denial into
acceptance, chaos to order, confusion to clarity. It can
turn a meal into a feast, a house into a home, a
stranger into a friend. Gratitude makes sense out of the past,
brings peace for today, and creates a vision for tomorrow.
—Melody Beattie, author, from Gratitude: Affirming The Good Things in Life

A magical experience happened for me once during a Lull-prescribed pause when I looked at all the blessings in my life. I started to fill with what was already there, and the feeling of neediness disappeared. The most profound part of the shift in my thinking was that I filled with the wealth of my own creativity and realized that being engaged with my creative passions made me incredibly content already. Material wealth lost some of its driving allure. Nothing else except the basics was really necessary for my happiness. I still wanted to continue manifesting my dreams, but I felt the desire coming from an already filled place. Both spiritual and material abundance began to appear more effortlessly.

Every night I started writing down two reflections of the day: (1) What I'm glad I did that day from the tiny details to great deeds, and (2) the things for which I feel gratitude. This simple exercise, I am convinced, created whatever energy there is out there waiting to be accessed. The energy brings more things to be thankful for, and abundance seems to gravitate toward me, enabling me to work more effectively toward my creative dream.

And 'tis my faith, that every flower
Enjoys the air it breathes.
—William Wordsworth, English poet

In her book *Simple Abundance*, Sarah Ban Breathnach reinforces the power of gratitude. She writes, "Simplicity, order, harmony, beauty, and joy will not flourish without gratitude— after consciously giving thanks each day for the abundance that exists in your life—you will have set in motion an ancient spiritual law: The more you have and are grateful for, the more will be given to you."

Gratitude has a compelling role in creativity. Energetically, we repel matter when we are needy. We repel situations, people, and interestingly enough, creative inspiration. When we shift our thinking and have a sense of appreciation, we fill, and from a filled place we have a desire to share our joy and creative expression.

SiGHTS ALONG THE WAY

My soul can find no staircase to heaven unless it be through earth's loveliness.
—Michelangelo, Italian painter, sculptor, architect, poet

An alternative to taking a break is slowing down. Slowing down allows the senses to drink in the copious gifts of the moment. Multi-tasking might be fun and effective in certain realms, but it also robs us of the possibilities that reside in a moment given undivided attention.

We have gained time and lost out on the sensations, smells, tastes, and sounds that could coalesce for creative output. The sun sets in pinks and golds, tangerines and cadmium blues, and the harried still race by, gobble down their prepackaged processed cheese, and collapse oblivious.

MEDiTATioN

Meditation is not as elusive and out of reach as many people seem to think. I use meditation more than any other method to access ideas for writing, paintings, performance art, classes, and issues needing creative problem solving. Meditation is a time to focus on the present moment and clear the mind so that our divine creative resources from within can find and fill the void. It can also be a time to say thanks.

Once you start meditating regularly, you will discover the incredible effect it has on centering you and opening your mind—but do not expect it to be easy at the beginning. Quieting the mind is a skill, and just like art, music, or acting, it requires patience and practice. Have no expectations, no judgments about your practice. Accept where you are, which at the beginning will be like listening to the running commentary of your mind. When it has not been trained to release the control it has over you, the mind will intrude soon after you have just quieted it. This is normal and is not a product of your particular oddness.

The practice it takes to find peace will be profoundly rewarded. In the mystic calm of your inner world, you will meet your heart. You will more easily open to the voice of intuition and draw upon the vast resources of your inner wisdom. Moving from a state vulnerable to distraction and superficiality, you will begin to recover the still and shining mind that lies beneath the chaos of default thinking. This rediscovered mind is filled with bubbling ideas.

Sometimes I sits and thinks. And sometimes I just sits.
—Anonymous

WHAT ABOUT MARGE?

You'll meet Marge later on, but I need to mention her here. The Muse Marge tells us to work and Lull tells us to take a break. Is there some Muse discord here? Well, no. Marge and Lull are simply in different parts of the amazing garden path of creativity. Experience with our own process gets us acquainted with which Muse is needed at the time, and which makes the most sense for us. In this case, honesty is key because Lull could be used as an excuse not to do the work. This is called Lull exploitation.

We don't need to fill every space of silence with stimuli. Silence and stillness can be quite medicinal. Here is some empty white space for you to clear your mind and surrender to nothingness for a moment. Stare here and breathe:

EMPTY WHITE SPACE

MORTALS WHO WERE INSPIRED BY LULL

Now, a lot of mortals have been influenced by these Muses already. You can truly savor what Lull has inspired mortals to say:

The harder you chase something, the faster you go and the less you're able to let life
meet life. If you're having difficulty coming up with new ideas, then slow down.
—Natalie Goldberg, author

Life is hurrying past us and running away, too strong to stop,
too sweet to lose.
—Willa Cather, novelist, short-story writer

In the depth of winter, I finally learned that
within me there lay an invincible summer.
—Albert Camus, French philosopher, novelist, dramatist

Adopt the pace of nature.
—Ralph Waldo Emerson, philosopher, poet, essayist

If I think, everything is lost.
—Paul Cézanne, painter

It takes a lot of time to be a genius; you have to sit around
so much doing nothing, really doing nothing.
—Gertrude Stein, author

A daydream is a meal at which images are eaten. Some of us are gourmets, some gourmands,
and a good many take their images precooked out of a can and swallow them down whole,
absentmindedly, and with little relish.
—W. H. Auden, poet, dramatist, editor

Vision with action is a daydream; action without vision is a nightmare.
—Japanese proverb

I was trying to daydream, but my mind kept wandering.
—Steven Wright, comedian

Yet it is in our idleness, in our dreams, that
the submerged truth comes to the top.
—Virginia Woolf, author

MUSE PROFILE OF LULL

SYMBOL

Lull's symbol is a hammock filled with flowers, symbolic of a place to rest, daydream, and ponder the fullness of our existence.

HOBBIES

Lull's hobbies are pausing, daydreaming, meditating, loitering, seeking out atypical festive experiences, climbing trees, watching a play, reading obscure magazines, visiting a nursery, lying on the grass looking at the clouds through the trees.

CAR

Lull drives a white convertible Volkswagen Cabrio, but only on the weekends. Sometimes, she just sits in a hammock.

> If you take a flower in your hand and really look at it,
> it's your world for the moment.
> —Georgia O'Keeffe, painter

RITUAL TO CALL ON LULL

Materials to summon Lull: five candles of any color, silence, a flower of any kind.
Light the candles and simply stare at the flames for five minutes, letting your mind wander where it will. Then, using the light of the candle, stare inside the flower. Enjoy the feel of your breath. Feel the temperature of the room. Hear sounds and experience them with your whole being: your heart, your mind, even your body. If any insights flare up, savor them. But feel no pressure to do anything right now. Say one of the affirmations listed below, then blow the candles out, place the flower in some water, and relax. Let go of the process this week.

Affirmations and Small Questions from Lull
- ◎ What does rest or a creative break look like and feel like to me?
- ◎ What idea is calling for me to daydream about it and where might a daydream lead it?
- ◎ I release the creative process and trust that inspirations are on their way to me now.
- ◎ I trust the process of letting go.
- ◎ I enjoy this space between creative activities and fill myself with new experiences, sensations, and feelings that result in a fresh creative flow.
- ◎ I am so thankful for the abundance already in my life.
- ◎ I get to take a few minutes today to tune in to my inner self.

And there ya go. And your Lull energy is awakened.

JOURNAL CHECK-IN

1. Take out your journal and write, draw, or paint about where you are with Lull: How is your Lull energy? Have you allowed yourself to feel the sensations of a colorful diversion? Are you able to let go and let it be?

2. Continue one or all of these unfinished sentences: In the space between the worlds…When I let go…Give your inner critic the day off.

3. Write as if you were a "lull," talk about your qualities and intentions. e.g., I am a lull, a pause pregnant with possibility. I float through space and land on flowers… I dream of meadows with dancing light . . . Something like that.

4. Look at the quotes by mortals who were inspired by Lull (p. 182) and pick one. Continue the essence of the quote in your own words or simply speed-write how the quote applies to you.

5. Write as if you were Lull talking to you. What would she say specifically to you about taking breaks, meditating, giving thanks, and finding ways to refresh yourself with new experiences? What do you need to learn from her purpose and powers? Have her compliment you on how you are including her in your life and counter what the critic said above.

MUSE WALK - LULL STYLE

Stop and go for a walk. Choose someplace different to walk. Find a different part of your neighborhood, or walk your usual walk backward. Wear something different when you walk. Walk through a store you don't usually walk through. Walk through a clothes store and buy something different. Embody the sense of someone who has truly let go of whatever process is the focus of your life right now. Or do not walk this time, just sit instead.

BRAINSTORM

REGULAR WALKING

If you are seeking creative ideas, go out walking.
Angels whisper to a man when he goes for a walk.
—Raymond Imon, short-story writer, novelist

Natalie Goldberg walks her dogs for inspiration. Wolfgang Amadeus Mozart said he could hear his compositions all at once, "in a pleasing, lively dream," while he walked. Poet A. E. Housman said this about a brisk walk: "As I went along, thinking nothing in particular... there would flow into my mind with sudden and unaccountable emotion, sometimes a line or two of verse, sometimes a whole stanza at once." All sorts of revelations happen during walking. Take index cards and a pen with you!

GOOFING OFF

In your journal, write twelve ways to fulfill the Art of Goofing Off. (Include your favorite goof-off activities with a sentence about each.) Make a goof-off theme for each day of the week—e.g., Monday: daydreaming; Tuesday: sitting on your balcony; Wednesday: watching TV...You don't have to do them, just write and contemplate doing them.

DAYDREAMING

While the rational mind is important, we gain a new perspective when we learn how many of the greatest scientific insights, discoveries, and revolutionary inventions appeared first to their creators as fantasies, dreams, trances, lightning-flash insights, and other nonordinary states of consciousness.
—Willis Harman and Howard Rheingold, authors of Higher Creativity

Let your mind have free time to wander. As with Aha-phrodite, empty the mind of worries and chattering. It takes practice, so don't be discouraged if at the beginning your mind does not seem to stop. Make believe the noise of the mind is coming through an imaginary Walkman, and to physically reinforce your intention to quiet the mind, pantomime taking the Walkman off. This often gives a momentary relief from the pressure of thought. You may have to take the chattering headphones off several times.

Also, allow yourself to daydream while performing tasks that do not require a lot of thought, such as regular household chores, driving, bathing, or fixing something. Again, make sure the mind is not falling into the default thinking of worries, judgment, and plans. Have a creative idea that you allow to visit you during your tasks and see what happens when you let your mind wander around it. Your preoccupation with the task will occupy one part of your brain while the creative part has freer access to your consciousness. This works while closing your eyes and writing on your word processor.

MEDITATION

Practice consciously associating empowering messages with your breathing for a while, and soon your breath will be the automatic circulation of effortless, ongoing positive fuel.
Examples:

◎ Imagine exhaling all negativity and inhaling creative energy.
◎ Inhale and allow yourself to fully receive this inhale as if it were a divine inspiration. Fully feel every sensation of the inhale. Your practice of fully receiving your inhale is practice for fully receiving divine goodness.
◎ Exhale with a feeling of letting go, releasing control, surrendering the need to be constantly doing something.

GRATITUDE

If the only prayer you said in your whole life was "thank you," that would suffice.
—Meister Eckehart, German theologian

† Take a moment and Quick List one hundred things for which you are grateful. This exercise magnetizes you to the abundance in your life and attracts more. (If one hundred is overwhelming, start with twenty-five.)
† While you are at it, engage in a powerful sense of gratitude toward yourself. List, in this lull, all of the creative activities, thoughts, and events you have participated in recently.
† Make a daily list of what you are glad you did during the day. The power of this exercise will surprise you.

SURREPTITIOUS ADVENTURES OF SACRED SOLITUDE (SASS)

❧ Steal away into your bathroom with fragrant bath oils, salts, and bubbles. Light candles, play music. Take your time. Do this twice a day if necessary. Let your mind be as light as the bubbles. Feel the warmth of the water and the body's inner recognition of being nurtured.
✳ Take a walk on the beach, in a garden, through a garden nursery. Give yourself $15 to spend however you wish. Practicality is not a requirement.

- Go to the theater by yourself and notice the explosion of new sensations you feel when you are not in the more contained world of being with another person.
- Load the cooler with cold drinks and sandwiches, get in the car, put on some favorite tapes, and just drive, destination unknown.
- Or, drive to a nearby town and explore.
- Put some music on or listen to books on tape while making a collage, watercolor, or finger painting.
- Hike. Go to a lake. Find a field. Commune with a tree.
- Put together a scrapbook.
- Give yourself an uninterrupted hour to roam around a bookstore, art store, or hardware store. Have your senses on high and really pay attention to the details, colors, and possibilities.
- Give yourself a pressure-free hour to sit on your front porch or balcony or in your favorite chair. Feel free to do nothing, or read a book or favorite magazine.
- Write a delicious letter to someone.
- Go to the animal shelter or a pet store and pet the animals. Walk your neighbor's pet.
- Take a walk accompanied with small, curious questions like "What message is out here for me today?" "What creative call is about to look me up?" (let go of the need to have an answer).
- Take the day off and switching up your routine.
- Listen to music.
- Walk in a bookstore, asking a question and opening a book randomly to find the answer.
- Simply ask small questions like: What will fill me with inspiration?
- Find large empty spaces (literal, metaphorical, or imaginative) where your mind, spirit, and body are free to rest in the space between the worlds.
- Go to an art gallery. Go to the art gallery gift shop.

> Benches are my bliss, I sit on every one of them.
> —Nicole Moore, editor and mom

- Find a bench. Sit down and write the first thing that comes to mind about anyone whom you can see.
- Go to a coffee shop and eavesdrop on conversations for dialogue ideas or simple, mischievous amusement.
- Make yourself a wonderful dinner. Try new recipes, buy a new place setting, and get out the candles and wineglass. Experience it, replacing any negative thoughts with gratitude for the experience of celebrating being alive. Sing loudly to a favorite CD while cooking.
- Sleep somewhere else in your house for a change—bring a blanket. Build a pillow fort.

- Make a cheese-and-crackers tray for yourself.
- Have a luscious, guilt-free nap (a favorite of mine).

WRITE DOWN YOUR DREAMS

That seems to be fairly self-explanatory. As you may know, as you write dreams down, you remember more of them. You also open yourself up to more messages during the day that come from the wisdom of the unconscious. The centers that open up when you pay attention to your dreams feed your knowing ingenuity, creating new creative connections. The world of the imagination comes alive as you open to the vast amount of archetypal, symbolic, and metaphorical language of dreams and the dreams' subsequent opening to self-knowledge. Have the intention to remember your dreams and you will. Write or draw a picture of tomorrow's dream in this space.

THE MUSES ARE TAKING A BREAK

Here's a break space. Doodle on it. No really, go ahead. Take a break from reading and just doodle. Let your doodle reveal how you feel in this moment. If you are worried about defacing the book, live on the edge. Do it anyway. Or just doodle really, really small.

NEXT STOP IN THE GARDEN

You are noticing that the creative journey is bringing up some uncomfortable feelings. You feel like eating more, watching more TV, or biting your nails. You are discovering parts of yourself that you do not really want to know, or new parts that are unrecognizable from the former definition you had of yourself. Your avoidance strategies are spinning—but you hold on in order to check out the mystery. Since you met Albert, you realize that there is a new way to look at things. And as you walk on the garden path and think this, your shadow grows long and you turn to see that your shadow is actually a Modern Day Muse, too.

Raw creative energy has been known to come from a mortal's darkness, so the Muses added a Shadow to remind you to alchemize the darkness into art and personal freedom. Underneath our veneer of "nice" is another side that is ready to release some really juicy creativity.

"REAL ACTION IS IN SILENT MOMENTS."

~RALPH WALDO EMERSON

The Shadow Muse dares you to come closer
and examine a side of yourself
that you may not realize is alive with possibilities.

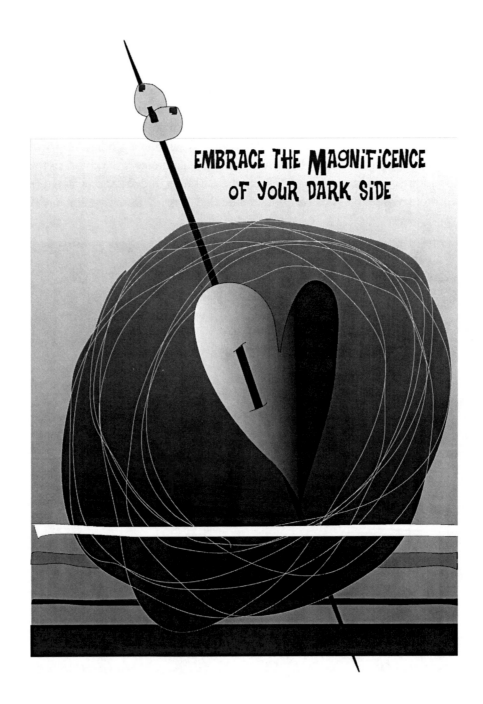

SHADOW:
MUSE OF THE DARK SIDE

One must still have chaos in him to dance with a shooting star.
—Friedrich Nietzsche, German philosopher, poet

SUMMON THE SHADOW MUSE WHEN

- ◎ You want to explore the potential of creativity contained within "the dark side" of your personality.
- ◎ You are prone to dark moods, pain, and sensitivities that you would like to metabolize into poignant self-expression or to see in creative perspective as gifts of strength.
- ◎ You are curious about the fine line between creativity and madness.

BOTTOM LINE

Shedding light on our darkest qualities releases the energy of creativity. Honoring all the aspects of that which we are rewards us with compassion, and insight. Revel in your rarities. Release the restraint of your insecure ego. Find art and freedom in your Shadow.

THE SHADOW SELECTION

The Modern Day Muses were almost finished coming up with the upgraded versions of the original nine Muses. They were on number eight. They wanted the next Muse to have a little depth—some intrigue—be a bit mysterious. And they thought and they thought.

And then the Muses started to get a little crazy and sinister. The side of each of them that is naughty and not-so-much-nice started to appear. They rather became controlling, intolerant, and one of them started spitting. Personality blemishes broke out in complaining, whining, and not making sense; they slipped revenge, vindicative, and punishment. And in the midst of the darkness, they noticed the creative brilliance that's possible when our slips are showing. Hence, I, the Shadow Muse came into being. [maniacal laughter].

Your Shadow Energy

The dark sides of personalities are always present, just as light invariably casts a shadow. When the light is brightest, the shadow is deepest. When mortals explore their hidden shadow side, there is a power, a liberating freedom, and a creative release. Carl Jung opened mortals to this idea, and the Muses want to elaborate in the interest of creative expression.

The Shadow Muse casts her silhouette across a mortal's path for three reasons. For one, mortals keep distasteful parts of their personality buried deeply inside. They fear what they might do, who they really are, and what others might think about the sides that society says are undesirable. Freedom and power are right around the corner when the Shadow Muse sheds her light.

Secondly, the angst of the mortal condition is a canvas for creative expression. Creativity often comes easier in difficult times. The Shadow knows and inspires mortals' artistic expression through unleashed emotion and pain, alchemized to beauty.

And third, creativity has been described as a quality close to madness. Although many artists and writers have led an unstable life, this is not a requirement for creativity. However, to be open to our quirks, idiosyncrasies, and uniquely eccentric interpretation of life can provide us a channel for our originality.

The Potential of Creativity Contained in Your Shadow

A bunch of subliminal selves are congregating inside the waiting rooms of our minds. Some of them serve us better than others. Just as we possess the positive traits of goodness, we also have the whole spectrum of the opposite qualities. Where we surface on the spectrum is a function of our adaptability, our growth, our genes, our preference, and our awareness. We have selected a range on this scale of lower and higher selves, but we fluctuate according to stress, inspiration, or conscious control. Subpersonalities surface according to our inner needs and outer desires. Cultivating different aspects of our higher sides makes life a more adaptive experience.

Most of us do not like to admit that we have the uglier parts of the personality-trait spectrum, so we deny, repress, or keep those parts from showing—sometimes we are not even consciously aware that they are there. Some people will begin to open and accept their shadows more than others when they discover the sense of humanity and expansiveness in self-acceptance.

The very characteristics that annoy us about others are the ones we suppress the most. We validate the existence of these traits within ourselves by being perturbed and annoyed by the people who mirror us. The characteristics we disown may look a little different in ourselves than in someone else's display, or they may lurk in a camouflaged version beneath the veneer of our cover-up. But if we have an emotionally charged response to someone, we can be sure it is a reflection of ourself. Characteristics in others that are undesirable to us, but are not charged with emotion, are usually not reflecting our own traits, just our values.

Keeping the aspects of ourselves that we do not like suppressed encloses us in a restricted space of awareness. Keeping the less desirable sides of ourselves out of sight takes a lot of energy. Exploring this shadow side to the point of acknowledging and accepting our disowned parts can give us a tremendous release of energy, freedom, and power. Acknowledging, accepting, and integrating that energy can result in a new lease on life and can open a reservoir of creative expression—not to mention acceptance, compassion, and forgiveness.

ME AND MY SHADOW

This was a difficult but transformational discovery for me. I was so proud of how flexible I thought I was, especially because my life work is about enhancing creative flexibility in others and myself. I reveled at how I could change my class activities in the flash of a moment if I sensed the class would benefit more from something different. I could invent activities on the spot that coaxed people into wondrous discovery. I could switch from going to the theater to watching the moon rise if I sensed that watching the moon might be more fulfilling. I could adapt to almost any task I was given and could deal with just about anyone unless they were—rigid. I could not put up with how unwilling some people are to altering their plans, even if it meant something better was sure to ensue with the new plan. It frustrated me when people refused to deviate from book instructions or rules when other techniques and rules would clearly benefit their unique situation. Some people could not break the rules in the name of creative experimentation. "Uhhh! So rigid," I thought.

So imagine my dismay when my friend called me—you guessed it—"rigid." At first I was stunned and perplexed at how little this guy knew me after three years of experiencing my impressive flexibility. Then, reluctantly, one self-look at a time, I gave it some thought. I could not believe it. In other areas of my life, I was incredibly rigid. What I realized was that I would not engage in anything except planning an hour before one of my classes. After a yoga class, which I teach twice a week, miles away from my workplace, I would come directly home and go to work. No stopping for a spontaneous walk, sight-seeing, or restaurant exploration. I felt I had to work as much of the day as possible or I would be anxious about money and unmet potential. I was not taking advantage of the perks of adventure and free time that come with inventing one's own schedule. I would not even talk on the phone with friends for more than five minutes. And these were just a few examples. I had to admit I was RIGID. Awwhhhhhhhhhhh! It was like a horror movie. And here, someone else could see what I felt was a horrendous trait even before I realized I had it. I instantly flogged myself with my yoga mat.

There's nothing like a hardship song to set my toes a-tapping.
—Roseanne Barr, actress, comedienne

Having read some wonderful books about the shadow side of our personalities, I realized I either had to look for the gift in being rigid or join the army. I am "so not" army material, so I looked for the gift. I got quiet, went inside, and asked the rigid part of myself, whom I named Rigid Rita Rutbutt, what she was adding to my life. (I found that making up goofy names for the parts of my personality that I am not fond of lessens the anguish of ownership.) Rita replied that my being in charge of my own schedule created the possibility of a completely wasted day. Rigid Rita Rutbutt surfaced from my anxious side and felt she needed to work overtime to keep some order in a free-floating day. She was exerting control to save me from the complete chaos my life had the potential to be. There was no leeway for flexibility because of Rigid Rita Rutbutt's need to alleviate my fears about meeting the daily steps that could lead to my potential—not to mention to being paid, which can sometimes be unpredictable in self-employment.

I asked Rigid Rita Rutbutt what she needed to feel secure enough to integrate into my personality in a way I could tolerate. She knew exactly what I needed, and the message came as if she were a friend with an obvious solution for my dilemma. She wanted a written schedule that designated work time as well as free time; something in writing so at least there was a plan to work the best I can. The schedule would not have to be followed exactly, but just making it created a semblance of control that could free up energy to spend enjoyably during the scheduled free time. She also wanted a little more self-acceptance. I thought that might be a good idea. Then, I felt this instant liberation of tremendous energy and relaxation. Compassion grew for people I previously viewed as rigid.

In my world of art, I discovered that when I exaggerated Rigid Rita Rutbutt, I had a new comically neurotic character for my performance art and for storytelling, as well as a visual for my whimsical paintings. I also noticed similar neurotic characters of others that now served as comic relief for me.

Some contend, in poetry, that the mind is dangerous and should be left out.
Well, the mind is dangerous and should be left in.
—Robert Frost, poet

Viewing our weaknesses with compassion and possibility is profoundly liberating. It gives us another creative mechanism with which to deal with life's complexities and the pursuit of living deeply. We can embrace the world with a lightness of being and witness the beauty of our humanity.

METABOLIZING PAIN INTO POIGNANT SELF-EXPRESSION

The cyclone ends. The sun returns; the lofty coconut trees lift up their plumes again; man does likewise. The great anguish is over; joy has returned; the sea smiles like a child.
—Paul Gauguin, artist

Many people find that creative release comes easier in times of poignant emotion: after a romantic breakup, a loss, during moments of anger or confusion. All of a sudden, words and images flow, or expressing one's pain is simply easier. Sorrow and anger lay dormant much of the time, so when unexpected hard times break through the defenses, the emotions sometimes spill forth in beautiful words, visions, music, feeling, and insights. Paul Simon said, "My words trickle down from a wound I have no intention to heal." Alan DeNiro said, "Fall in love, then have a breakup. Plenty of writing material there." What wounds do you have that can serve your soul through creative expression?

Accessing your emotions at times other than a crisis can also be a doorway to creative expression. Creative people have a reputation for having an increased sensitivity to experiences and a heightened awareness of sensory stimuli. Sensitivity opens us up to deeper feelings from the sights, sounds, and movements around us. The observation of a cloud, the cacophony of automobile engines, or a simple grimace liberates metaphors, emotions, poetry, or song from within. Staying on the surface of emotion may be socially more adaptable, but it keeps us from tapping into and siphoning out the art that can touch and transform others and ourselves. If you are open to the sensitivity of your human nature, it can become a channel through which heartfelt expression flows. Rich voices of deeper feelings weave the common threads of our humanity into the divination of a healing tapestry. Art is exalted. Others are moved.

Besides, if you keep your feelings in control and under wrap, the longer they stay there the more they will fester like mold on an abandoned tuna casserole. They will develop into illness and tension. Stifling feelings keeps you further away from the acceptance that rallies you into easy self-expression. And as we relieve and heal ourselves through self-revealing expression, we touch and heal others who come in contact with our work.

MADNESS AND CREATIVITY

There is a link between madness and creativity. Everyone knows creative people such as Nietzsche, Poe, and Hemingway who later went crazy. And we know of crazy people who produce amazingly creative works as part of their therapy. As a former mental health professional, I have seen many emotionally disturbed patients produce works of profound depth and quality. Creativity that tarries on the edge of sanity is the breath of daring. It is the uninhibited display of the unseen, unsaid, and the not yet experienced. Loose ego boundaries can set free the avant-garde.

Hieronymus Bosch, surrealism, dadaism, Edvard Munch, and other unconventional art and artists have a sense of madness to them. Expressionists and abstract artists such as Pollock and countless others broke tradition by sublimating their madness in revolutionary new forms born of their deep inner turmoil. Musicians from Tchaikovsky to the Doors have elevated derangement to art. Listening gifts us with poignant effects unrealizable through sanity. Creativity is both a strategy and sublimation for inner turmoil.

The fascination of this perspective is part of art's mystique. But do we need to be mad to be creative? It depends on your definition of madness. Creativity can often feel like madness because what we conceive creatively has not yet been processed by our rational minds or met with acceptance by others. Creative energy may come from parts of us that remain unexposed, and we may wonder if it is revealing something about ourselves that we should not be showing. If we expand our definition of acceptable and give ourselves license to create without judgment, we reach a liberated release. We all have a little bit of crazy in us, in terms of idiosyncrasies, quirks, preferences, and neuroses. These hidden parts of us contain a great deal of passion because of the energy it takes to suppress them. When giving voice without censorship or modification, we are capable of original expressions that excite and provoke. This is the voice we have heard countless times in the art and writing of others.

It is under these immense stretches of wheat, under these troubled skies, that I am unhindered in expressing deep sorrow and extreme solitude.
—Vincent Van Gogh, painter

THE TAINTED SHADOW

There are shadow emotions that specifically block our creativity. Anger is one—when we view our past as unfair. Frustration about not having the time, skill, or confidence is another. Resentments that our creativity was not nurtured more at an earlier age. Jealousies toward others who seem less worthy or remind us of our lack of prosperity can stand in the way of the creative flow. These are all natural feelings in the world of the mortal. Compassion, acceptance, and understanding can turn their venom into fuel.

Anger is energy with enormous power. Actual physical strength can be quadrupled when a mortal is angry. You can imagine how much energy is sapped by keeping that anger inside, not to mention the health complications it can cause. But when expressed, it can result in masterpieces of art. Or, it can be used as fuel to get started and keep going. Anger has been the stimulus for incredible music, exciting art, powerful dance, and poignant theater.

Jealousy is simply a nudge to look at our own neglected potential. Comparison is deadly to the creative process. Brush it off when it pierces your confidence with the spikes of its primitive claws.

Any emotion we enter into has great potential for self-expression. The body and the subconscious hold emotions as visual symbols. Unrestrained expression from an emotional, rather than an intellectual, avenue can tap into these visuals. During dark moods, the availability of inspiration can exceed that of sunny moods. Giving voice and image to these palaces of darkness can turn misery into a productive artistic celebration.

Creative expression requires an ability to work with feelings and channel them. Frustration, dissatisfaction, and even a sense of desperation may help you access an eloquence you never knew existed.
—Shaun McNiff, author of
Trust the Process: An Artist's Guide to Letting Go

MORTALS WHO WERE INSPIRED BY THE SHADOW MUSE

This part of the garden is dark. Wandering branches of towering oak trees that reach in all directions have Spanish moss blowing from their limbs in forewarning. It's at once ominous and beautiful. Mortals touched by the Shadow Muse lend their voices to these ponderings.

A great artist...must be shaken by the naked truths that will not be comforted. This divine discontent, this disequilibrium, this state of inner tension, is the source of artistic energy.
—Johann Wolfgang von Goethe, German poet, dramatist

It is, after all, the dab of grit that seeps into an oyster's shell that makes the pearl, not pearl-making seminars with other oysters.
—Stephen King, author

Conflict...that's where we find art.
—Garrison Keillor, author, radio-show host, storyteller

The controversial aspects of our personality may be adding a needed color, tone, or impetus that energizes our movement toward

selfhood and the life/creative statement of our very selves.
—Marsha Sinetar, author of Do What You Love and the Money Will Follow

Your pain is the breaking of the shell that encloses your understanding.
—Kahlil Gibran, poet, artist, philosopher, writer

"Creativity – like human life itself – begins in darkness."
– Julia Cameron

There came a time when the risk to remain tight in the bud was more painful than the risk it took to blossom.
—Anaïs Nin, author

There was never yet an uninteresting life. Such a thing is an impossibility. Inside of the dullest exterior there is a drama, a comedy, and a tragedy.
—Mark Twain, U.S. novelist, journalist, riverboat pilot

THE LIGHT SIDE OF THE DARK SIDE: THE SHADOW ACTUALLY DOES HAVE A SENSE OF HUMOR

Of all the things I've lost, I miss my mind the most.
—Anonymous

Things may be strange, but, hey, listen, they are weird, too.
—Anonymous

Why be sane?
—Anonymous

The only normal people are the ones you don't know very well!
—Joe Ancis, author

I can't always handle reality, but it's really the only place to get a good cup of coffee.
—Jill Badonsky, muse channeler

Reality is the leading cause of stress among those in touch with it.
—Jane Wagner, playwright

The nervous breakdown is highly underrated.
—Anonymous

Every writer is a narcissist. This does not mean that he is vain; it only means that he is hopelessly self-absorbed.
—Leo Rosten, writer, scholar

Never moon a werewolf.
—Mike Binder, writer, director, comedian

It's been fun, but I have to scream now.
—Anonymous

Going Crazy, Back in Five Minutes.
—Anonymous*

MUSE PROFILE OF THE SHADOW MUSE

SYMBOL

The Shadow's symbol is a window looking upon the moonlight amidst a dark night. As Allen Ginsberg says, "Follow your inner moonlight: don't hide the madness."

(*This guy named "Anonymous" is at once brilliant and comically dark. A true Shadow Muse follower.)

HOBBIES

Opening closet doors, playing evocative music, materializing mirrors for a closer look, inviting mortals to walk through the darkness and to find the light.

CAR

The Shadow Muse drives an ebony '67 Jaguar XKE.

Everyone has talent. What is rare is the courage to
follow the talent to the dark place where it leads.
—Erica Jong, author

Ritual To Call On The Shadow Muse

Materials to summon the Shadow Muse: musk incense, two black candles and two white candles, your journal or sketchbook, chalk pastels or any other art materials.

Light the incense. Light a white candle and repeat, "I radiate warmth to myself and others." Light a black candle and repeat, "I am open to meeting, and accepting, my dark side. As I become more aware, I become more whole and centered." Light the second white candle and say, "I radiate compassion and acceptance." Light the second black candle and read this poem paraphrased from Tao Te Ching aloud:

If I want to shrink something, I must first allow it to expand.
If I want to get rid of something, I must first allow it to flourish.

In your sketchbook or your journal, depict what you feel your dark side may look like abstractly or representationally. The less art skill you bring into the expression of emotion, the less you will be hindered in your free expression. When you finish drawing, have a dialogue with your drawing in your journal to find out what your shadow side has to bring you in terms of power and what it needs in order to integrate. Blow the candles out and write any note of gratitude you feel from this exercise. Pick one of the affirmations below and write it in your journal or on a card and place it where you can easily see it this week or however long you need it. Feel the energy and power of your shadow side arise to meet your needs in grace and kindness.

Affirmations From The Shadow Muse

☾ I allow the voice of creativity to express through my emotions.
☾ As I discover and accept my dark side, I build compassion and feel a sense of union with all mankind.
☾ I have the courage to explore my pain and my fears.

And so it is. And the Shadow Muse is here to free you.

Revealing the dark side of human nature has been, then, one of the
primary purposes of art and literature. As Nietzsche put it:
"We have art so that we shall not die of reality."
—Edward C. Whitmont, Jungian psychoanalyst + homeopathic physician

JOURNAL CHECK-IN

Marybeth Webster, a Grass Valley, California, art therapist, who often works with artists, says writing in a journal can often clear a creative block. "In a journal, you set aside time to focus on yourself, and there's a freedom to tell the truth," she says. "It's a real opportunity to face the shadow." To break through an agonizing writing block, she kept a journal to record her dreams.

1. Take out your journal and write about where you are with the Shadow Muse in your life. What is your dark side like?

2. Write some of the things your critic has to say about your dark side's undesirable traits and its role in your creativity. Let the critic tell you exactly what he or she thinks without mincing words. This will decrease its power over you.

3. Look over the quotes by mortals who were inspired by the Shadow Muse, (pp. 198-199). Pick one that has a special charge for you and continue where it stops or write how it applies to you.

4. Write, paint, or draw as if you were the dark side of the world.

5. Take a moment to relax and embody the essence of your own Shadow Muse from what you have learned about it. Then write yourself a letter as if the Shadow Muse were speaking. How would she encourage you in drawing on your dark side? What would she praise you for in your shadow work?

MUSE WALK - SHADOW STYLE

Stop right here. Go outside for a meditative walk. Embody the Shadow side of yourself in your walk and your posture. Let yourself view the world from your dark side. What do you feel? Write about it when you get back.

Take A Deep Breath And On The Exhale, Let Go...

BRAINSTORM

DIPPING INTO YOUR SHADOW

The next two exercises will generate ideas, entertainment, humor, or poignant insight. If they don't, I'll suck eggs.

List what you believe to be the shadow sides of your personality. Now write from one of those sides without censoring or softening. Write about your opinions, preferences, and desired actions. Let pour out that side that you use so much energy to keep safely stored away. After finishing, smile, sigh, and write, "I accept all sides of myself and I choose to operate from my highest self."

1.
2.
3.
4.
5.

DARE TO DO THE ADVANCED VERSION (OPTIONAL).

Write down an attribute of people who get your dander up (especially if your dander's been down).

1.
2.
3.
4.
5.

Now write "I am" and that attribute and write the feelings this exercise brings up, or write as if you possess that attribute, again expressing opinions about one topic in particular or free-associating about many.

Try on feelings of acceptance and curiosity about this exercise. Stay in a place of compassion toward yourself and choose to see this as another welcome to the land of being human. Quiet your mind and relax your body and dialogue with one of your shadow sides:

1. Asking for the benefit that part brings to you.
2. Asking for what that side might need to balance your life for greater expression.

EXPRESSIVE DRAWINGS

☁ Do a drawing of yourself from your shadow's point of view (no talent required, use chalk pastels or paints). Do one from your lightness.
☁ Then do a drawing that integrates your shadow and your light together.
☁ Do a drawing, sculpture, collage, or other artwork of you from your shadow's point of view of anything.
☁ Dialogue with the inner critic. Let the critic have at you with a list of shoulds and shouldn'ts even beyond the journal exercise above. Brush it away when you finish.

HARNESSING THE POWER OF SAVAGE EMOTION - ANGER

First get in touch with any anger you have around a creative block, missed opportunities, bad decisions, obstacles, or creative neglect you incurred as a child.

A good way to do this is to list the reasons you are angry or resentful, feel where the emotion is located in your body, breathe into it, and allow it to be unbridled. (If you have been holding a lot of emotion in for a long time, it is a good idea to do this with a professional.)

Then see if you can funnel that energy straight into your creative passion:

Move with it and talk about it, paint it, draw it, dance it, sing it, even make a list of the next steps you will take to bring your creativity to fruition allowing the spell of anger to give you clarity and heated insight in the direction of your dreams. Follow Julia Cameron's advice and "skewer the bastards. Create right at them." Many successful song artists, playwrights, and actors have used the power of anger to bring their art to new levels. Rod Serling channeled his anger into the plots of The Twilight Zone. Rock stars are known for letting out anger in their songs and acts, and stand-up comedy is one of the most used outlets for social outrage and personal anger. The sarcasm of many comedians is anger clothed in humor.

If the above does not work, for your benefit and the benefit of the people around you, channel your angry energy in one of the following ways:

Vigorous exercise: running, weight lifting, kickboxing, martial arts.

Pounding a pillow.

Taking a rubber bat to your sofa.

Screaming obscenities in your car or in an isolated field close to an airport when a plane takes off (especially effective because the power of the plane parallels that of anger).

Buy some old dishes at a garage sale, get some goggles, gloves, and a tarp. Place the tarp at the edge of a wall with lots of space in front of it and throw the dishes at the wall. Enjoy the freedom of breaking through to an expressive release.

Then write about each activity, or talk with a counselor.

RELEASING EMOTIONS NO LONGER SERVING YOU - ANGER AGAIN

Exercise: As mentioned above, exercise is recommended to dissipate anger. Exercise is important to the creative process. Exercise energizes ideas and clears the head. It releases the reign that emotions can have over your creative expression.

The unsent letter: One of the most powerful tools I use over and over with both classes, clients, and myself is the unsent letter. Do not underestimate the power of having an uncensored dialogue on paper with someone who still fuels anger, sorrow, resentment, or other emotions that eat away at your creative energy. Use the pressure of the pen, the size of words, and third-degree profanity to sock it to the felon of your choice. These letters are not meant to be sent. They release emotions and help dissipate their grip on you. You may still have feelings toward these persons, events, or things you have written to, but a layer of their control over you has been freed.

At the bottom of your letter write: "I now release your power over me and make space for new energy and possibilities."

Here's an exercise that is so incredibly effective it's mind-boggling.
You must try this if it applies to you.

REVERSE PSYCHOLOGY

This is for that self-talk torment we often put ourselves through like constant self-criticism over a particular action or project, guilt, thoughts of inadequacy, obsession about what someone said or did to you.

Take away the pull and resistance so the feeling can get through, and keep on going so that you can be freed and move on to more lofty obsessions. Those agonizing thoughts float up into our consciousness; we hate the feel of them knocking around in our mind—we attempt to avoid the feeling or try to get it off our mind, then start at the beginning again, fueling the misery-go-round. This process actually keeps the thought around longer—remember, what we resist persists.

If you give yourself just fifteen minutes a day to feel fully guilty, to think continuously about what you're trying not to think about, or to be self-critical—no matter how irrational and untrue the thoughts and feelings and without trying to placate yourself with pleasantries—many times this release of resistance creates a thoroughfare for the thoughts to get through, completely disarms the feeling, and lets it pass through without its toxic toll.

Freedom!
—Mel Gibson's character in Braveheart

SHAME

The courage to be is the courage to accept oneself, in spite of being unacceptable. Paul Tillich

Shame is an insidious emotion that has control over us in a way that sabotages our efforts. If we have a hard time starting or finishing projects, we may have a deep-seated sense of shame. Shame installs in our mind a subconscious belief of being undeserving. If you have done things in your past that your inner critic has labeled shameful and has blown out of proportion, you may sabotage your efforts because you feel undeserving of success. This is a hard one to connect to because it is buried under layers of good intentions. A sure indicator that you are sabotaging yourself is finding yourself advancing in the direction of success or creative project completion and completely derailing yourself by stopping, quitting, or taking a job transfer to a place you hate.

Write down five of your deepest regrets. This is not easy but it is powerful.

1.

2.

3.

4.

5.

Estimate how many times you have punished yourself by bringing these regrets into your consciousness and scolding yourself harshly, saying anything from "You are sooo stupid" to "I cannot believe you did that! What were you thinking?" Chances are that the number of times you have said these things to yourself could be labeled cruel and unusual punishment. This keeps shame alive. Resolve that you have punished yourself enough and are now open for good things to happen to you.

After you have written your list write: "I give myself permission to move past these regrets. I was only human to do these things and I accept myself in both good and bad times.

I now receive the good that is waiting for me.

NEXT STOP IN THE GARDEN

So you are walking along your garden path thinking, "Ya know, it's not like I don't want to engage in creative ideas, I have wanted to do it all along. Yes, creativity is definitely on my gonna-maybe-do list. The only problem is I don't seem to be doing it. I am just having problems getting started."

You are not alone. Creative-ignition difficulties are more common than stuffed-up noses. The Muses are here to help clear your passages.

One of the Greek Muses updated herself into a reliable, strong, and focused straight shooter, boycotting the whims of moods, the paralysis of perfection, or the distraction of anything that steals mortals from their creative passion.

Unless we act on our creativity destiny, we will sink into the depths of a mundane existence. Yuk. The strength of this Muse's conviction reawakens our conviction so that nothing can hinder us from starting or following through with our creative endeavor and rising to celebration. Good thing, because as Bob Moawad says, "You can't make footprints in the sands of time if you're sitting on your butt, and who wants to make buttprints in the sands of time?"

MARGE:
MUSE OF
OKAY-NOW-LET'S-GET-STARTED

It's a job that's never started that takes the longest to finish.
—J.R.R. Tolkien, author

SUMMON MARGE WHEN

- ✝ You are having a hard time getting started on your creative passion. Resistance and procrastination seduce you to their place of discontent.
- ✝ You are overwhelmed with the task before you—you feel immobilized, frozen, inert, and not quite sure where to start, so you reconsider starting at all.
- ✝ Chances are good that you will just give up or put your creative passion off indefinitely even if the voice of inspired reason continues to call to you.
- ✝ You always read books on creativity, but do none of what they recommend.

BOTTOM LINE

We are here for a divinely creative plan. There are oodles of things that can steal us from creative expression, and we have the choice to do our work anyway. The discipline to engage in our passions can be made easy with routine, reasonable goals, small steps, and focus. The result is that the magnificence we are meant to create comes to life. We glow.

THE SELECTION OF MARGE

In 1996, the Muses went to see the movie Fargo. In the movie an unflappable sheriff named Marge Gunderson resolves the gnarly crimes that happen in North Dakota despite her challenges of pregnancy, snow, dense deputies, and an uncooperative car salesman. Marge's no-nonsense Midwestern attitude gets the job started and, without moodiness, complaints, or drama, gets the job done. The Muses feel they ended up going to that movie because the Marge character was a good inspiration for a Muse. Especially because the modern mortal is constantly caught in crimes of the creative process: procrastination and avoidance.

YOUR MARGE ENERGY: MUST-SEE CREATIVITY

Planning on starting a creative project and instead finding yourself removing fleas from your dog? Are you making unimportant phone calls when you intended to write? Putting projects off until you have "a block of time" that never seems to arrive because the next episode of The West Wing is crucial?

Instead of listening to the little voice right inside your soul that is asking you to creatively express yourself, you veer left...toward the crisper bin in the refrigerator. The mold in need of cleaning is coaxing you away from your passion. This is not a good sign because, before this moment, cleaning mold was the last thing listed on your to-do list. You have been derailed. You have fallen prey to the avoidance dilemma. When you are in avoidance, you wear earplugs and can't hear what your good intentions are trying to tell you. You get a lot of cleaning done.

Sometimes we avoid creativity because we do not want to do something that is not as easy to manage as the remote control. Other reasons are not as simple to figure out, mainly because we are not even conscious of them. How can we be so resistant to a process that we were so excited about at the beginning? Or why don't we finish the projects we were so agog about when we started? An invisible force grips our good intentions and threatens them until they give in to "must-see TV." Yet, the voice inside lobbying for creative expression persists, and you still squirm with a guilt you cannot even hide under the mold in the crisper bin. When you ignore the desire of your soul to express the gifts you have been given, the ideas that chose you for their vehicle of release, chances are that you will wear unrest like a perpetual itch.

> It does not matter how slowly you go, so long as you do not stop.
> —Confucius, Chinese philosopher

Many mortals struggle with getting a start on their creative passions because of the weight of creative expression. Creativity goes deep into the well of who we are, dipping us into the unknown, which is sometimes scary—and "sometimes scary" is a stimulus for resistance. Are you resistant?

INSERT HERE: A MOMENT OF PONDERING ABOUT YOUR RESISTANCE.

Creativity taps into our deepest insecurities. This is good. Fear is a sure indicator that we are in store for growth if we accept the call to go beyond the mundane and into new possibilities strewn in the unrevealed. When we answer our soul's request to surrender the safety and security of the known, for the precarious unpredictabilities of the unknown, our strength, confidence, compassion, and self-knowledge cannot help but grow. The creative journey brings up fear. Fear of exposure, fear of failure, fear of inadequacy, fear of undeserved good things, fear of responsibility, and fear of hard work. All of these fears may rear their prickly heads at the onset of creative acts. Also, creativity requires a change in patterns that don't serve us. Even a positive change from negative patterns can result in resistance when we are unsure of the new ground on which we stick our big exploratory toe.

The Muses have spent endless nights devising solutions, potions, and resistance removers in Muse laboratories because the problem seems widespread. Frankly, it really infuriates the Muses. They hate to be ignored when they send out sizzling sparks of electrified epiphanies. An infuriated Muse is not a pretty sight...sputtering, cursing, and potential staining has been sighted in these cases.

MARGE SEZ, "WELL, OKEYDOKE THEN"

Marge's approach is definitive but nonjudgmental. Connecting with action is the only thing that will guarantee to get mortals going creatively. Got fear? Are moods, insecurities, distractions, habits, addictions, overresponsibility, or the illusion of not having enough time preventing you from getting started? Here's how Marge would respond, "Hey, thanks a bunch for sharing, but I've got a date with my creativity. So, I appreciate the offer, but I'm gonna have to turn you down." Do the same and then set yourself in action. Do not look back. Do not dust the top of your refrigerator.

Small actions are at the heart of kaizen.
By taking steps so tiny that they seem trivial or even laughable,
you'll sail calmly past obstacles that have defeated you before.
Slowly — but painlessly! — you'll cultivate an appetite for
continued success and lay down a permanent new route to change.
Robert Maurer

How-To-Get-Started Awareness

Awareness of your resistance will begin melting down the formerly unconscious blocks that hinder your creative progress. Although most of your dynamics remain in a mysterious place, exploration can unleash the power of recognition. If you are unaware of resistance, you have no control over it. Recognition results in a gradual process of choosing what works and relinquishing what does not.

Come Back!

If you have been refining the title of either procrastinator or avoidance-aholic, believe that you can now leave that title behind. There is no need to continue to identify with bad habits or to beat yourself up. The urge to do this will come up again and again, until you develop a routine that makes your creative passion easy to access. Start where you are in this moment. Some of the energy of the Muse Marge is already inside you. Concentrating on the times when you just went ahead and got started and then successfully finished projects will serve you more than labeling yourself a terminal procrastinator. At times you actually did start things without a struggle. What did they look like? How did "starting" work for you before? Can you implement in the present what worked for you in the past? Listed below are a few of the things that have helped creativity seekers get to their craft. Sometimes we know what works for us but are simply not doing it. Take the extra effort to dust off and reimplement jump-starters that worked for you in the past.

Habits

If you engage in your creative passion fifteen minutes a day for three weeks, you will have created a daily routine. Habits are helpful in keeping the creative progression going.

Habit is what keeps you going.
—Jim Ryun, congressman

If you are not taking regular classes in your creative passion, creating a habit is the next easiest way to maintain creativity in your daily schedule and keep it there. And if you are not in the habit of getting right into your work, do not expect that it will be easy. "Starting" gets easier the more you do it. But at the beginning it is like a huge aircraft taking off. It requires a lot of momentum...it rolls slowly down the runway until it lifts off the ground and is on its way. When you have made a routine or a habit of your creative passion, you will shift into autopilot, where you will then soar with your passion. Once this happens, it takes little effort to stay aloft.

It takes little thought to maintain a routine. Less energy is spent on thinking about getting started than when browbeating ourselves when we procrastinate. We barely think about brushing our teeth every morning and evening, and we certainly do not employ all sorts of avoidance strategies or power struggles around this healthy daily habit. If you know creativity like the Muses know creativity, you know that it is daily hygiene for the soul, spirit, and heart. Creativity is responsible for our mental, emotional, and spiritual vitality. Thus, a daily habit of creativity is vital to our fulfilled existence. A routine similar to teeth brushing deserves installation into the daily schedule.

If creativity is a habit, then the best creativity is the result of good work habits. They are the nuts and bolts of dreaming. Twyla Tharp

Mornings work for many artists...getting up a little earlier is a sacred act that becomes easier as the momentum of the ritual takes over. Performing your creative passion first thing in the morning is a message that the sacred act of creativity comes first. However, several artists observed by Marge agreed that any time you can make regular is a good time. At first, be prepared to use a little awkward force to start the routine. Know that unless you work even when you do not "feel like it" you will never achieve that dream or drink the delicious wonder of the process. The common rule is that twenty-one times of consistent performance makes a habit...and the payoff is that a positive, life-changing reflex will become automatic, (with regular maintenance and starting over when needed). Your work will have a time and space to slowly and dependably flourish. Over time, you will generate and refine abundant creative output. The heavens will applaud and you will indeed experience the miracles that creativity bestows.

To honor the routine completely, and to diminish the pressure, sometimes the starting place is simply showing up. If you decide your routine is to work from 7:45 to 8:00 A.M., the requirement is to be there, even if you are just sitting and staring. If your resistance is caused by overresponsibility in other areas of your life, see Bea Silly in order to warm up to your serious creative-passion goals with play.

Creativity is an organ that improves with use and
when fully engaged is difficult to wear out.
—Robert Genn, artist

Creativity is a muscle. If it has not been strengthened, it is a little weak. If it has not been exercised, stamina is low. If you do not have space in front of you, you will hit the wall (huh?). Just as a sedentary person cannot immediately get up and run in a marathon, an individual without a creative routine cannot engage in an endeavor for great lengths of time without some conditioning. This truth is more obvious for the runner. Physical limitations make themselves known in inarguable ways—collapse, exhaustion, aches, and pains. In the creative process, the necessary conditioning is not so obvious. So when trying to stay with your passion longer than is reasonable, you may think your lack of stamina, or your difficulty with starting, is a lack of ability or a failure. Annnnnnkkkkkk! (Game show buzzer.) Wrong answer. You just need conditioning and patience. Start small and repeat often. Be gentle and without judgment and believe that you can do this.

For of all sad words of tongue or pen,
The saddest are these: "It might have been!"
—John Greenleaf Whittier, poet, essayist

Be open to solutions that you have not tried, but know that what worked one time may not work every time. The creative process is fickle. Honoring a routine, whether or not you feel like it, is the most consistent key to success.

I produce more consistently when I am taking an inspiring class. When in a class, those around me create an energy that inspires my diligence. I also do better with a deadline. I work amazingly well when I'm working at the same time someone else who agreed to work with me is working too. Knowing these truths about myself gives me options to use when I am struggling to get started.

¡GNiTioN

Just as appetite comes by eating so work brings inspiration,
if inspiration is not discernible at the beginning.
—Igor Stravinsky, Russian composer

If you are waiting to get in the mood for creativity before you begin your work or start your changes, you may be waiting a long time. Sometimes after Aha-phrodite's energy opens your eyes to a new inspiration, you will feel driven to begin. Sometimes there is no inspiration . . . until you begin. Many times, in fact, the act of beginning starts the inspiration flowing and you wonder what took you so long in the first place. Action begets action. Motion creates inspiration. Keep the pen, the brush, and the intention in motion, and it will soon reward you with inspiration that keeps you going.

MARGE'S STARTER KIT

Often the best way to produce a block is to sit down with a blank sheet of paper and expect inspiration. The pressure to produce without the aid of inspirational triggers can be daunting. It's not to say that it can't be done . . . for many that's the way. Marge has some suggestions for warming-yourself-up activities and thoughts that stimulate creative action. Look at the list. Many are from the domains of other Muses. Write down on a card what you think might work for you. When you have empirical proof of which of these tools work best for you, list them artistically or with your favorite font on a four-by-six- or five-by-seven-inch piece of paper, buy a fun little frame, and keep it in your work space.

- ✰ Meditation—with a request for new inspiration, a visualization of the project forming.
- ✰ Write a letter from the project to you having it tell you the next step.
- ✰ Scribbling nonsense words to get the pen going.
- ✰ Reading from one of your favorite authors. Talk about it to a trusted friend or creativity coach.
- ✰ Listening to lyrics of a song that inspires you.
- ✰ Flipping through art magazines, postcards, catalogs, or unrelated sources to see how they can inspire you.
- ✰ Reading Albert's chapter again and listing which tools you get energized by.
- ✰ Pulling words randomly out of a dictionary and playing with them.
- ✰ Looking at work you've already done to reignite your passion.
- ✰ Taking a walk with an idea.
- ✰ Taking an outing and letting everything you see give you potential ideas about your project.
- ✰ Taking a drive, a shower, a shave, with your idea.
- ✰ Visualizing, with as much detail as possible, your project finished and the feeling of accomplishment and satisfaction you will feel.
- ✰ Remembering that your project will be a beacon of inspiration for others.
- ✰ Remembering what energizes you about your creative passion and slipping into that energy.
- ✰ Listing the next steps for your project and then embarking upon them, one bite-size step at a time.

INFINITESIMALLY SMALL BABY STEPS (ISBS)

Even if you are on the right track, you'll get run over if you just sit there.
—Will Rogers, actor, lecturer, humorist

Feeling overwhelmed is another creativity stopper. Our society, as a whole, has adopted the let's-make-things-really-unrealistic practice. We want everything now and we set our goals too high too soon to be reasonable. We have good intentions, but why try if it is too hard to complete?

Small goals are easily met. We like to be the taskmasters from hell and set lofty goals, which then backfire on us. They are too lofty to even attempt to try. If we did a little at a time, we would get there. When we give up because our only goal is unrealistic, we do not even get close. When a small goal is met, a feeling of success ensues. Success releases motivation and increases interest. More action is likely to occur when success is reachable.

Here's the Equation:

Small goals met = a feeling of success = beaming motivation = increased interest in dreams and pursuits = more small goals set = advancement toward dreams = celebration and gratitude and an occasional "Yes!" = results

This is Marge's "Most Treasured Trick": BREAK IT WAAAAAAY DOWN. That's six A's in WAAAAAAY, emphasizing the importance of really, really, really, really, really, really small steps. Change your definition of small to even smaller. And I say this because this is a central blockbuster with the private clients and classroom students with whom I work. Even when I ask, "So, what is your next really, really small step?" they still respond with something too unrealistic for starting up a creative process. Together, we decide on something about sixty percent more reasonable, and they are relieved. Then, they are actually able to take an action that enables them to reach their initially unreasonable goals.

So I ask you to reexamine your own small steps and consider making them smaller, because I don't know who you are, so reaching you on the phone may be a little more difficult. We have been brainwashed into being delusional about what we will accept from ourselves—take your brain back! Small means as small as sharpening your pencils or even walking toward your work space and not expecting anything else from yourself that day. It may seem ridiculously small, but it is just the ignition, it is the key to breaking through the awkwardness of getting started. Once we have started and are in a routine, progress happens naturally.

Unreasonable goal = overwhelmed = less chance of doing it = less chance of reaching the goal = overwhelmed = "Oh, just never mind" = absence of creative joys = crankiness and disillusionment

Once, I asked one client to set a writing goal for the following week. She replied, "The completion of a chapter." This may be a good goal for an experienced writer, but an unrealistic goal for the newcomer or the returning writer. She came back with no progress. My countergoal for her was one page of awful writing. She came back with a solid first draft of five pages.

The freedom not to be good, as well as setting a very small goal, can jump-start any creatively blocked person and create the energy needed to go further. We create a success experience even if we stop at the small goal. Success leads to more action.

PERSEVERE

Learn to self-conquest, persevere thus for a time, and you will perceive very clearly the advantage which you gain from it.
—Saint Teresa of Avila

1 The formula for success in a creative endeavor is this:
2. Have a passion for a creative interest (required).
3. Make sure there is a need for it.
4. Have skill in it or practice and train and get good at it.
5. Engage, persevere and stay the course...voilà—it's yours.

"YEAH, i GOT TiME": MARGE'S FiVE To FiFTEEN-MiNUTES PLAN

Five to fifteen minutes a day can fit into anyone's schedule, and it really is all the time you need to work toward creative excellence. Put it this way: If you are not finding the time for creativity, you are not finding the time for one of the main reasons you are on earth . . . to fully allow the creative force of your divinity to connect and move through you. Can you take five minutes a day to do that?

Instead of envisioning spending an hour a day on your creative passion, start five to fifteen minutes three or four times a week. You can find five to fifteen minutes to sketch or write down ideas, to set up your work space, to read about your craft to invite more enthusiasm, to write affirmations or journal, etc., etc., etc. Your creative passions then fit into a full schedule of other activities. And secondly, it takes the pressure off what we expect ourselves to do. When fifteen minutes is achieved, success is experienced. You may have noticed that fifteen minutes is repeated ad nauseam in this book to drive the point home (like repeat advertising).

Individuals can work longer, which often happens because the momentum has been initiated, or they stop, knowing they have received a sense of mastery and completion because they have met their goal. Your success will increase your chances of returning to your creative passion soon. Conversely, if a goal of an hour is set, the highly impressive accomplishment of forty-five minutes will fall below the goal and you may feel a sense of failure. Failure experiences drain energy, reduce motivation, and over time result in the abandonment of creative satisfaction. I know I keep saying the same thing—Marge told me to keep repeating so you will get it.

- Just set up your easel. Let the paintbrush lead you to where it wants to go for fifteen minutes. Do this four times a week, and the second week look for an image that might want to be painted. Experiment for just fifteen minutes.
- Take one prop and experiment with it fifteen minutes for a performance art piece.
- Work on finishing that quilt for just fifteen minutes.

- ꙮ Begin your interior decorating passion by looking at a magazine for, yes, fifteen minutes. Next goal would be to wander in a store and get ideas and write them down.
- ꙮ To add more humor to your life, your goal might be to read a humorous quote book for fifteen minutes. Look on the Internet for humorous Web sites for another fifteen minutes on another day.
- ꙮ Practice your musical instrument just fifteen minutes a day. It will get you where you want to go over time.

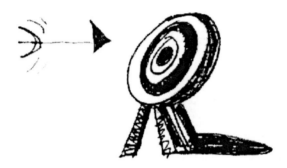

These small goals actually get people excited about starting. Rather than dreading what and how much to do, and wondering if what they have done is enough, small goals motivate people. Then, they are more likely to continue and gradually build the momentum they need to finish. Excitement is what the Muses want you to have. That is what makes the process so precious. Darn tootin'.

Follow the advice of artist Fred Babb:
"Go to your studio and make stuff."

What is the next very small step you can take toward your creativity?

When will you do it?

How will you reward yourself?

JUST 5 minutes, 5 minutes, 5 minutes, 5 minutes, does it.
Sometimes just 2 minutes can get you started.

MORTALS WHO WERE INSPIRED BY MARGE

In Marge's section most of the echoes you hear are of people not so much talking but working. But here's what some of the mortals have to say about what they've learned from Marge.

When you're following your energy and doing what you want all the time, the distinction between work and play dissolves.
—Shakti Gawain, author

All good work is done the way ants do things, little by little.
—Lafcadio Hearn, lecturer, author

Affirmation without discipline is the beginning of delusion.
—Jim Rohn

Burning desire to be or do something gives us staying power –
a reason to get up every morning or to pick ourselves up
and start in again after a disappointment."
—Marsha Sinetar

Ideas won't keep; something must be done about them.
—Alfred North Whitehead, English mathematician

You are desperate to communicate, to edify or entertain, to preserve moments of grace or joy or transcendence, to make real or imagined events come alive. But you cannot will this to happen. It is a matter of persistence and faith and hard work. So you might as well just go ahead and get started.
—Anne Lamott, author of Bird by Bird: Some Instructions on Writing and Life

If you believe in what you are doing, then let nothing hold you up in your work. Much of the best work of the world has been done against seeming impossibilities. The thing is to get the work done.
—Dale Carnegie, teacher, writer

Action may not always bring happiness, but
there is no happiness without action.
—Benjamin Disraeli, English statesman, novelist

MUSE PROFILE OF MARGE

SYMBOL

Marge's symbol is the release of an arrow toward a bull's-eye (action to goal).

HOBBIES

Accomplishment. Being, doing, having. Eating.

CAR

Marge drives a Jeep with big flood lights on the top of it. It just keeps going and going.

If you're dedicated, if it's something that lives and breathes in your heart,
then you've simply got to go ahead and do it.
—Rodney Crowell, singer, songwriter

RITUAL TO CALL ON MARGE

Materials to summon Marge: any color candle, your work space, your journal or sketchbook. Light the candle. Write in your journal or draw in your sketchbook what small step you can take next in this moment toward your creative dream. Then, for five to fifteen minutes, organize or make your work space a little more inviting. The point is to simply start "doing" something related to your next step. It is the ritual of beginning. Take the step without a lot of preparation, deliberation, or opportunity for procrastination. When you are finished, reward yourself with a written or sketched compliment. Then write this: "I give permission to the power of Marge to just get me started and stick with my creative passions." Pick one of the affirmations below and repeat it out loud, then blow the candle out. Watch in the next week how much easier it is to get started.

AFFIRMATIONS AND SMALL QUESTIONS FROM MARGE

- ❀ What's one small step I can take today in just 5 minutes?
- ❀ What's one small thought I can be having about my creative project?
- ❀ I do one thing at a time in very small steps. Breaking things down makes engaging in my creative passion easier and more desirable.
- ❀ Darn tootin' I'm getting started and staying with it until it is done.
- ❀ I am inspired and energized to start working on my creative endeavor.
- ❀ What would make it easier to engage in my creative passions?
- ❀ Okeedokee, I'm getting started now.
- ❀ The hell I'm NOT getting started. Step aside.

Well already then. So it is.

So what do we do? Anything. Something. So long as we
just don't sit there. If we screw it up, start over.
Try something else. If we wait until we've satisfied
all the uncertainties, it may be too late.
—Lee Iacocca, auto business executive

JOURNAL CHECK-IN

1. Take out your journal and write about what you know about your own experience of the Muse Marge. What thoughts did   reading the chapter bring up for you? Continue with this sentence: To get started...
   Complete these sentences quickly five times: I'll make it easier to get started by... In just 5 minutes I can…

2. Write some of the things your inner critic has to say about your ability to get started. Let the critic tell you exactly what he or she thinks on paper without mincing words so that stuff will quit eating at your energy.

3. Look over the quotes by mortals who were inspired by Marge (p. 217). Pick one that has a special charge for you and continue where it stops or speed-write how it applies to you.

4. Write as if you were the quality of procrastination. Start with "I am procrastination..." and continue with quick-writing. Do the same with "effortless action."

5. Take a moment to relax and embody your own essence of the Muse Marge. From what you have learned about her and know about her powers already present within you, write yourself a letter from her. How would she encourage you in the area of getting started? What would she praise you for? How would she counter the voice of the inner critic?

MUSE WALK - MARGE STYLE

Go outside for a meditative walk. Feel your own getting-started power grow. Think about what project you are working on and what next small step you will take. Picture yourself doing it. Make an analogy of your taking steps in your walk with taking the next steps in your creative passion. Taking one step at a time, feel the quality of moving toward your destination. Feel the confidence of action running through you, and when you return, go straight to the project or process you are working on and do one small part of it—or clean the work space for it.

"I long to accomplish a great and noble task, but it is my chief duty to accomplish small tasks as if they were great and noble."
—Helen Keller, author, lecturer

BRAINSTORM

ADRENALINE

If you are like me, you respond to deadlines. I like the adrenaline of having to meet a time frame or else! Adrenaline sometimes provides the creative tension we need to get going. Setting deadlines is a popular way to jump-start creative energies. Here are Marge's suggestions for creating them:

- You and a creative friend set deadlines for each other.
- Enlist a group of friends to meet and set creative deadlines week to week.
- Work with a creativity coach.
- Submit works to publications, places, or people who require deadlines.
- Have a show for your talent or work—set the date and time.
- Attend events to share creative work—open mikes, other people's parties, your parties.
- Set a deadline for yourself and wait until the last minute to meet it.
- Become a member of a club like Toastmasters, a play group, a writing club, or an art society that sets deadlines.
- Get a deadline-oriented, creative job.

TAKING A CLASS

Many people take classes primarily because the structure of having a place to go for creative expression helps them just do it. These people respond to the structure of time, space, and the energy of other people engaged in working that the classroom situation provides. If classes have worked for you before, make it a routine to check out catalogs, newspapers, and other periodicals. Make sure the teacher is one who is validating and inspiring, not dismissive and derailing.

PARALLEL UNIVERSE TIME

Go beyond being social with your friends and be creative together. Find times that work best for all concerned, then meet weekly, bimonthly, monthly.

The parallel-buddy system: Set up a time that a friend and you can work on your separate projects. The energy of working together gives the work staying power. This works even if your workplaces are in your separate homes in distant spaces. Simply decide on a time to begin and end. Call your friend before you start and at the end of the time limit. Start small. Compare notes about how much was done and how you felt. Chances are you will have created momentum so keep the check in call at the end short and keep going. Even reward each other. Knowing that someone else is working at the same time will help you work more effectively. Parallel universe time can have a magical feeling to it.

A CREATIVITY COACH

If you want to advance more quickly toward your creative goals, a creativity coach can help. A creativity coach differs from a life coach in that the deadlines a creativity coach sets honor the nonlinear, unpredictable nature of creativity. Kaizen-Muse Creativity Coaches offers experiences during the phone call itself and gives people permission to be imperfect. Methods also include the activation of intuition, imagination and confidence in guided imageries, tools that make creativity easier to engage in and as well as prescriptions from the Muses geared toward your individual needs.

FIND YOUR PASSION

If you have been courting your true passion, it will not leave you alone until you engage in it. Doing what you love just makes you want to do it more. There is nothing like wanting to spring out of bed in the morning to see the work of art, the writing, the craft—the results of what you started or finished the night before. Court your passion by playing and dabbling in it. Think about it whenever you can: while waiting in line, in traffic, for your computer to warm-up. A little creative foreplay creates the heat that lures more action. If you do not know what your passion is, explore various media. Take classes if you feel awkward initially. Focus on inspiration and play.

HAVE A CAUSE

Make something creative for the purpose of making someone else feel better. Get involved in a higher cause. It will get you started, and the energy will flow to other areas of your work.

WARM-UPS AND EXPOSURE

Warm up: Begin with indirect techniques—like playing with something unrelated to your project. Water your plants, sharpen pencils, or simply sit with nature. Do whatever sounds fun.

Play: One of the most successful ways to get started is to use play as a warm-up activity. Doodle, scribble, and play with ideas, whatever looks like the passion of your choice.

Exposure: Read works by the authors who inspire you. You are drawn to them because they may reflect the same creative chords you have inside you. Reading them will call on your voice. Visual artists can glance through art pictures. Listen to tapes from motivational speakers. Watch videos of your area of creative passion. Look at work you made have started or completed in the past that reminds you of that which you are capable. This kind of exposure can be effective in lighting your starting fuel. Then, cross-fertilize yourself by looking at creative works you wouldn't normally notice.

JUST GET STARTED

Several artists I interviewed admitted that sometimes force is the only way to get started—until momentum makes it possible for the passion to take over. Simply start, despite the resistance. Be aware of its presence, smile at it, and just do the work. Strengthen your tenacity, build your will, and elicit self-respect for your staying power. The motion will register, and the resistance will fade, leaving you in blessed action. The easiest way to keep going is to turn on what Marge calls your "passion-automatic." This involves creating a habit.

- Figure out what time of the day is best for you creatively and install your fifteen-minute ritual in this time zone. If you don't show up one day, do NOT beat yourself up...just start over. Be gentle.
- Make a list of the next steps you need to take on your journey to your creative dream. Then break those steps down. Then break them down three more times until you have a very, very small task to do. This is where you begin.
- Try mind mapping. Google it if you don't know what that is.
- Do one of those tasks now. Praise yourself for your efforts in your journal or sketchpad even if it was a really small step. Soon you will be doing steps without so much thought, because praise on many levels conscious and subconscious creates energetic inspiration to do more. After all, it is the artist child within you that oftentimes is doing the creative work. Fun rewards will also result in repeated and sustained efforts.
- Just start work on your creative endeavor or journey knowing that through the work the inspiration arises for the raw material used for later in revisions. Just starting creates self-esteem, which then becomes fuel for motivation and for creating the momentum, and the routine that makes returning and restarting easier.

Tricks For Breaking Through Resistance

Be aware of the resistance. Begin to listen to what you tell yourself when you are ready to begin a creative endeavor and then end up doing something else. Get in touch with the fear. Write down all the fears you have around this project. (Pop them with your Audacity pin.) Take a breath and decide on the smallest possible step you can take. Let this step be the only one that exists for you. The step following it does not even need to be in your mind. Just the one phone call about a class, the decision about where your work space will be, the fifteen minutes you spend cleaning the work space, or the five minutes you spend engaged in your craft.

If you are avoiding a task, it may be because you are overwhelmed. Being overwhelmed often comes from looking at everything that needs to be done to reach your dream, instead of just the next step. Feeling overwhelmed comes from setting unrealistic standards. Go back then, to infinitesimal baby steps. This technique is consistently a resistance breaker.

Have an affair with your passion. Proclaim that you are going to work on one thing like scrapbooking… and then sneak off and write in your journal. Put on your to-do list: Clean the fridge and then rebel and make some progress on your photography project. Remember to put "I get to.." in front of your creative passions on your to-do list. "I get to write a book" is much more enticing than I have to.

Make Starting Over A Routine, Too

If your goal was to work fifteen minutes a day for three days and you only worked two days, this is not failure—it is process. There is a big difference. Even if you haven't worked for a month, you still can return to the process and start over. Make your life a laboratory, not a class. Our experience in school sometimes leaves us feeling that learning something new is like taking a class: there is a limited time frame in which to complete the assignment, there is a grade (or judgment at the end), and there is the possibility of failure.

In the laboratory of creativity, experimentation is the agenda; trial and error is the rule. There is room for lapses without judging yourself. Simply go on from where you left off. So if you miss an entire week of your allotted time to work on your passion, do not harass yourself and proclaim failure. Just begin again, and keep beginning until you have enough beginnings to call it a habit. And if you lose the habit, keep starting over.

The No-Nonsense Tool

The Midwestern value of committing one's self to get to the work no matter what, will create better efficiency for our creative process. Great self-respect and the reward of moving forward result in the adoption of this value. This deep force will then take you to new places in your life experience. Another payoff for hard work, of course, is that periods of play are richer and more valued.

List moods that usually stop you from your work. Write a letter to each of them. Accept them for the sweet slice of human nature that they are, ask them for their creative input, and let them know you will be getting to work with them, or in spite of them.

_____
_____
_____
_____

Be there in a jiff.
—The character Marge from the movie Fargo

NEXT STOP iN THE gARDEN

Here at this point in the garden you see a bench. You sit and all of a sudden it dawns on you that you, too, have inspirational abilities. It is a time of self-reflection as you strengthen your knowledge of yourself as the creative being you are.

Celebrate yourself as the muse you are!

WHAT MUSE ARE YOU?

Truths cannot be acquired from words out of other people's mouths.
Before Truths can be internalized, they must come from one's own realizations and
practices. Through a lifetime of personal practice, human beings are capable of
revealing all of the secrets of the cosmic essence.
You are your own best judge.
—Siddhartha, Buddhist philosopher

NAME YOURSELF AND YOUR POWERS

Okay, here are some questions for you. In your journal or sketchbook answer the following:
Which of the Muses do you identify with the most? Who else? (If you were representing a Muse, which one would your qualities best be able to match with?)

Which of the Muses would you choose to assist you in deepening your skills or overcoming your hurdles (you may even choose one of the ones you identified with, but now to go deeper in that realm...know there is always a new layer of excellence even in your strong areas.)

Can you imagine the presence of these Muses in your life, at your workstation, in the company of other mortals, when you are faced with a difficulty? Take a moment and close your eyes and visualize a difficulty, then picture one of the Muses there to help you. See yourself work through the problem together.

Is there another Muse that you think would be instrumental in augmenting your creativity or the creativity of other mortals?

YOU ARE A MUSE TOO

Monk, you and you alone are your refuge.
You and you alone are your pathway.
—The Buddha

Everyone has within him or her an inspiring quality, behavior, or set of beliefs. Think about what people have appreciated in you or about particularly with what you find self-pride. Christen these positive features about yourself as a Muse. This will deepen and strengthen your experience of yourself as the inspiring being you are. (Plus it's kind of fun.)

What would your Muse name be?

What are your powers?

Whom do you inspire?

When do mortals need to summon you?

What is your symbol?

What are your hobbies as this Muse?

As this Muse, what car do you drive?

What exercises would you have mortals do to learn more about you?

What is your motto or quote?

What is your meter range?

How would you take a walk?

What are your aspirations as a Muse?

How does this Muse make itself known in everyday life?

Depict your Muse in an art form; hang it, put it in a special book, send it to yourself.

Muse Song recommends that you do the same for a friend, parent, or mentor.

KEEP goiNg

Hide not your talents, they for use were made.
What's a sundial in the shade?
—Benjamin Franklin, statesman, diplomat, inventor, printer

Keep dreaming your dream,
stay true to yourself,
choose the path of trust over fear,
revise the journey as your intuition guides you,
cultivate love of yourself and others,
know that this life as you know it now
will come to an end,
ask "if not now, when?",
live creatively,
let go of worry, fear, judgment
dance until the morning glories dawn their smiles,
and do at least fifteen minutes of your creative
passion ...
every day that you can.

NEVER LET OTHER PEOPLE'S REALITY GET IN THE WAY OF YOUR DREAMS. -JILL BADONSKY

PART THREE
STUFF IN THE BACK

you can start
being just a little more
of your authentic self...

at any time

999

QUESTIONS TO MUSE
FROM THE MODERN DAY MUSES

1). **Aha-phrodite, the Muse of Paying Attention and Possibilities:**
What is working in terms of where I pay my attention? What ideas are presenting themselves to me and how can I remember them? Where is my body's energy and intuition leading me? When do I get my ideas? What small questions can prime my awareness for catching answers? What will be my inspiration today?

2). **Albert, the Muse of Imagination and Innovation:**
How can I think differently about my creative passion? How can I alter my past concepts about how to create? What can I list and go past the obvious? What attitude, genre, persona, can I come from to make it different? What creative rules can I change from someone else's to make my own? What thoughts entice my participation?

3). **Bea Silly, the Muse of Play, Laughter and Dance….**
What would it look like if I were more playful? How can I make my creative passion playful and fun? What if my idea wrote to me about what it wants to do next? How might movement help with ideas? How will it change my motivation to put "I get to .." in front of my to-do list? How can I remember to say "So what, I'll do it anyway" when my inner critic or anyone starts to discourage me?

4). **Muse Song, the Muse of Encouragement, Pampering and Good Company…**
How can I treat myself like the precious instrument of creativity? Who in my life is supportive or will it feel good to talk with this stuff about? Where can I give myself credit? To whom or what can I dedicate my creative actions? (e.g. I dedicate the creative passion of this to the people who believe in me, to my grandfather – this makes my action higher than myself).

5). **Spills, the Muse of Practice, Process and Imperfection:**
What's the easiest way to remember to experience the beauty of the process and surrender to possible discovery? What's it look like and feel like to give myself permission to begin small and deeply imperfectly? How can I remember that lowering my expectations gets me started when high expectations might immobilize me? With what quality do I want to season the process? Joy? Mischievousness? Effortlessness? Curiosity?

6). **Audacity, the Muse of Courage and Uninhibited Uniqueness:**
How will I stay true to myself during this process? What small, courageous step can I make? What if I imagine time traveling to the future and look back at how I solved problems? What small step can I take to honor my authenticity? How does it feel to stay true to one's vision despite what others say?

7). **Lull, the Muse of Pause, Diversion and Gratitude**
How will I let go of the process and take a pause every now and then? How will I incorporate gratitude into this process? How will I use diversional activities to inspire more fuel for creativity? What if I meditate, walk, daydream, and pause?

8). **Shadow Muse, the Muse of the Gifts of the Dark Side**
What are some shadow aspects of myself that may surface during the creative process? Can I accept these qualities with compassion? What truths can I admit in order to free the energy it took to suppress them? How can I use the energy of my emotions to propel my creativity forward? What can I channel into creativity?

9) **Marge, the Muse of Okay-Now-Let's-Get-Started ….**
How can I break the process way down or work on it in small increments of time? How can I practice a creative habit? Will that be small enough to entice me to begin? What structure, class, or partnership might help keep me easily involved with my creative passion? What would the delight of creative discipline look like? How can I remember to work even when I don't feel like it?

10. **The Bodyguard**
What anchor (or sentence of empowering self-talk) can strengthen me and cancel discouraging self messages? How can I feel stronger creatively, confidently, emotionally? How can I shift from victim to empowered individual or triumphant victor?

NEW ADDED EXTRA SPECIAL SECTIONS FOR THE THIRD EDITION...

O HAPPY DAY!

Take Some Time Today, Even if it is 5 Minutes,
To Fill Your Fountain of Youth.

THE MODERN DAY MUSES ZERO IN ON IMPORTANT LIFE AREAS

For the third edition, The Modern Day Muses wanted to add something new so they got together and brainstormed how their principles could be applied to areas where mortals want more creative brilliance and joy. For your magnificence and ease, they present you with the following.

This is an abbreviated version of what the Muses cooked up so visit: www.themuseisin.com and watch for the e-books that expand upon these areas with suggestions, prompts, and further instructions.

૭ Creative Agelessness
૭ Getting Through Perfectionism
૭ Muses and Marketing
૭ Yoga and The Muses

SMALL QUESTIONS:

In this section, the Muses want to clarify the tool of small questions. Small questions that you ask yourself may result in immediate answers. However, just asking them sets the subconscious into a percolating collection mode for your creativity.

When you do not expect an immediate answer your creative accessories of connection, association and eliciting more than one right answer emerge. Thinking you have THE answer can actually limit your resourcefulness. Leaving questions open for more answers expands your creative possibilities. So ask small questions over and over...all of a sudden your creative ideas and solutions will get oiled and be more fluid.

MODERN DAY MUSES FOR CREATIVE AGELESSNESS AND DREAM RECOVERY IN THE SECOND HALF OF LIFE:

My Bodyguard

Missions:
Guard Your Creative Self And Your Creative Time.
Guard and fortify your strong, resilient self making your strong self more accessible than the victim self.
Guard against complacency and giving up.
Rise and act - little tiny steps at a time.

Focus: Strength and power ... waxing invincible

Small Questions:
How can I guard against complacency?
How can I protect my creative time?
What "anchor" do I have to keep me strong?
What memory of passion, strength and will can I bring into the present moment to ignite those things again?
What inspires me to unleash my might?

Inspired Insight

"Strength does not come from physical capacity. It comes from an indomitable will."
—Mahatma Gandhi

"The block of granite, which was an obstacle in the path of the weak, becomes a stepping stone in the path of the strong." —Thomas Carlyle

"He who smiles rather than rages is always the stronger." —Japanese Proverb

"I was always looking outside myself for strength and confidence, but it comes from within. It is there all the time." —Anna Freud

Aha-phrodite

Mission: Power-up Your Focus on What Activates Joy and Creativity

Focus: Focus on what you want to be central in your life - you can choose from thoughts of possibility, gratitude and joy or thoughts of limitation. It's your choice. Focus on the freedom, pluses and possibility of this time in life versus aches and limitations. You get to indulge yourself.

Focus on cultivating spiritedness. Focus on the magnificence of who you already are, in this moment, as we speak.

Focus on your "soul-intention" - joy. Have anchors and comebacks for when you begin to stray.

Practice the focus: ask small questions ABOUT the focus.

Elevate the focus with art, obsession, celebration, parallel play.

Small Questions:

Where do I feel passion? Where did I feel passion in the past that might be something I can do now? How can I pay attention for new forms of passion?

What works for me?

Where am I getting it right? What's worked in the past?

Where have I been gifted with talent or a gift? How can I tap into this just a little more? What's the next tiny step I can take?

How can I readjust my focus off of detractors such as the Internet and TV and onto something that gives back in a more soul fulfilling, spirit enhancing way?

What would it feel like to pay attention to abundance, small delights, and the miracles?

Inspired Insight:

"Let your eyes transform what appears ordinary, commonplace, into what it is, a moment in time, an observed fragment of eternity." --Philip Levine

Albert:

Mission: Activate or cultivate the power of seeing differently. Break rules, invent new rules, and come up with agreements with your authentic self.

Ways to think differently about the second half of life...Ways to adopt thoughts that exalt your existence so they replace unhelpful ones.

Invent worlds of imagination that create inner strength, contentment, and connection to your higher self.

Play with Albert perspectives in attitude, art, writing,

Focus: Resourceful Thinking

Small Questions:

In what small way can I think different from any conventional thought that doesn't serve me?

What different thoughts can I think differently today to create an attitude of creativity, joy, or delight?

What perspective can I see through to feel more creative, resourceful, or vital?

What rules do I get to break today?

Inspired Insight:

"I have reached an age when, if someone tells me to wear socks, I don't have to."
Einstein

"Imagination grows by exercise, and contrary to common belief, is more powerful in the mature than in the young." - W. Somerset Maugham

"I think and think and think, I've thought myself out of happiness one million times, but never once into it." ~Jonathan Safran Foer

"I do not accept any absolute formulas for living. No preconceived code can see ahead to everything that can happen in a man's life. As we live, we grow and our beliefs change. They must change. So I think we should live with this constant discovery. We should be open to this adventure in heightened awareness of living. We should stake our whole existence on our willingness to explore and experience. " Martin Buber

"Now and then, hang a question mark on the things you have long taken for granted."
— Bertrand Russell

Bea Silly

Mission: Activate the child spirit, lighting humor wicks, playing, moving in order to celebrate life.

Focus: Humor, movement, making things fun, silliness in the interest of lightness and perspective, kidding around.

Small Questions:
How can I lighten up? What would it feel like to be playful?
How can I make my creative endeavor fun?
Who makes me feel more like a kid when I'm around them?
What did I used to like about myself as a kid?
Can I love me?
Where can I say "SO WHAT?" and feel liberated?

Inspired insight:

"We don't stop playing because we grow old; we grow old because we stop playing."
-George Bernard Shaw

"I like nonsense, it wakes up the brain cells." Dr. Seuss
Guess What? It's your turn to live. Make your goals sound fun. Jill

Muse Song:

Mission: The necessity of loving ourselves, good treatment, good company, inspiring role models in the interest of fueling ourselves for creative expression.

Focus: Nurturing thoughts and actions especially told to the self. It's your time to pamper and take care of you YOU. Make it big, or if you're unaccustomed to big gestures of self-care, and practice adding to that.

Your higher purpose is better able to unfold when you let go of the guilt that you may have paying attention to yourself.

Find and be fortified by the people who are excelling at staying young, keeping them in mind makes it more possible for you drift in that direction.

Find good company, and when needed reach out for help.

Gradual change negative messages you give yourself.

Small Questions:

What would it feel like to be on my own side?

How can I be kinder to myself in the next few moments?

Who are the people in my life who support me?

What can I give myself credit for?

Would a deep breath in and out leave me a little more relaxed afterward?

How good can I let it get?

What would it feel like to let go of the guilt that goes with self-indulgence?

Who is indulging themselves? Can they're expertise at it inspire my own?

Inspired Insight:

"If you let people into your life a little bit, they can be pretty damn amazing."
-Sherman Alexie

"Let love write on you for awhile." Jonathan Safran Foer

"You're the strangest person I ever met, she said & I said you too & we decided we'd know each other a long time." Brian Andreas

Spills:

Mission: Embrace the power without feeling the pressure of perfectionism, Elevate, embrace, yearn-to practice. Permission to lower standards in the interest of allowing the experience and the process to HAPPEN so we get better at whatever endeavor we are passionate about.
Starting with the freedom of beginner's mind.
Seasoning the process with intentions that feel good. Making the process fascinating...   Practicing EVERYTHING...thinking, feeling, PRACTICing... setting up practice opportunities.
Know when to say. "It's close enough!"

Focus: On being engaged in the process without pressure. Keep going without judgment. Give yourself permission to do things imperfectly.

Small Questions:
What would I feel like to give myself permission to engage in the process with lowered expectations?
What quality do I want to assign to the process? Peace? Lightness? Mischievousness?

Inspired Insight:
"I have done many things that I NEVER would have done if I had to do them perfectly. And they've opened an incredible number of doors." – That would be me.
"Life's not about staying on your feet. It's about getting up when you fall. Thank God!" – Jan Denise

"Supposing you have tried and failed again and again. You may have a fresh start any moment you choose, for this thing that we call "Failure" is not the falling down, but the staying down." – Mary Pickford

"A man knows when he has found his vocation when he stops thinking about how to live and begins to live." – Thomas Merton

Audacity:

Mission: Living your life and manifesting dreams with courage, trust, and sass.

Focus : Being authentic, jaunty, spirited, and confident. Embracing the freedom not to care what people think - are you capitalizing on it?

Small Questions:
How would it feel to be authentic?
What small courageous step can I take today?

What's one small way can I embrace the freedom that comes when we don't care what people think?

Inspired Insight:

"I am not a has-been. I am a will be."
-Lauren Bacall

"Spirit has fifty times the strength and staying-power of brawn and muscle"
- Mark Twain

"Oh Man! There is no planet, sun or star could hold you, if you but knew what you are." - RW Emerson

Moxy, freedom to be one's self, freedom to take a step toward courage. If not now...when? Staying true to the authentic self. Digging out.the authentic self out from under roles of wife, mother, employee, employer, survivor.
Question: what part of your authentic self was/is still evident even when you are fully engaged in your other role?

Lull

Mission: Let go of the striving, the hard work, even the efforts for self improvement every now and then. Refill with gratitude, joy, something new.
Take a break. Take an inventory of your abundance. Expose yourself to something different. Restore, restock, renew, reinvigorate.

Focus: Take a Break

Small Questions:
What would it feel like to let go of the intensity of my approach for awhile?
Can I give myself a pause and trust it will restore and deepen my inspiration?
Where can I refill and what small step will feel like refilling my reservoir of creativity?
What can I expose myself to for inspiration and refilling that is completely different from what I'm doing?

Inspired Insight:
"Woke up this morning with a terrific urge to lie in bed all day and read."
- Raymond Carver

Shadow Muse:

Mission: To encourage acceptance, comfort, and connection in the face of those things about ourselves we find undesirable.
Encouragement to channel the forces of our dark energy into art.

Focus: Acceptance, Sublimation, Compassion

Small Questions:
What would it feel like to accept the parts of me that I deem as undesirable?
What energy would I unleash if I didn't have to suppress my darkness?
Who would I light the way for if I was completely myself?
How can I channel my darkness into creativity?

Inspired Insight:
"Confront the dark parts of yourself, and work to banish them with illumination and forgiveness. Your willingness to wrestle with your demons will cause your angels to sing. Use the pain as fuel, as a reminder of your strength." - August Wilson

"We must laugh and cry, enjoy and suffer, in a word, vibrate to our full capacity... I think that's what being really human means." - Gustave Flaubert

"Art enables us to find ourselves and lose ourselves at the same time."
- Thomas Merton

Marge:

Mission: Defy complacency and inertia by taking little tiny steps toward adopting the habits you need to live your dream.

Focus:
Staying active in general.
Use the mind/creative expression.
Attitude and inner strength.
Meaningful connections with others.
Taking care of the body.

Small Questions:
What small step can I take in one of the five areas of creative agelessness?
What structure, classes, regular routines would reinforce small parts of one of the five areas?
How will I remember to do these things?
What small action can I repeat over and over, even if it's just for 5 minutes, that will help me create a habit? (Like showing up for my creativity or thinking a certain way)

Inspired Insight:

"In three words I can sum up everything I've learned about life: it goes on."
– Robert Frost

"We first make our habits, and then our habits make us." – John Dryden

"Start by doing what is necessary, then what is possible, and suddenly you are doing the impossible." – Francis of Assisi

I USED TO BE CHICKEN UNTIL I STARTED TAKING SMALL STEPS WHICH DIDN'T TRIGGER MY FEARS. ...OKAY., SO I'M STILL A CHICKEN BUT NOW I'M DOING CREATIVE WORK.. BE A CHICKEN AND DO IT ANYWAY.

no perfect people aloud

Embrace a mistake...
it might just result in an unexpected creative destination!

CURES FOR PERFECTIONISM
WITH THE MODERN DAY MUSES

Now that the book has been out several years, it is clear that one of the most debilitating blocks in the creative process is perfectionism. There are many successful perfectionists. Perfectionism becomes a problem when:

1. We work on something over and over trying to get it perfect but are never satisfied.
2. We have an inner tyrant that does not allow us to feel the joy of the creative process.
3. We do not even attempt anything creative because we do not want to encounter moments of ineptness.
4. We do not begin because we think we need all the right expertise, all the right equipment and the perfect time and space in order to begin.
5. We give up easily and early because we encounter difficulty or something we weren't expecting.

The kind of client that my heart goes out to the most is the one who is unable to feel the joy of what he or she has done or who tries to rigidly control the process instead of open to the possibility of discovery.

Here are some tools from the Muses to help you or your clients if you are a perfectionist:

Aha-phrodite:
Tool: Attention

Pay attention to your thinking: Perfectionists tend to torment themselves with unrealistic expectations and berate even the best efforts. They sadly need to practice feeling JOY in their body and choosing in many instances fun in the process versus pressure. Practice joy just 15 seconds at a time.
Pay attention to:

- Your thoughts and observe what you are saying to yourself (without judgment!)
- Practice lightening up when you are harassing yourself (without judging yourself for those thoughts or expecting yourself to be perfect about lightening up).
- Thoughts that edge toward joy - practice and acting "as if" you are edging toward joy.
- To Spills for practice and quality of process
- Giving yourself permission to lower expectations - chances are they are too high at least to get you started.
- Reminding yourself what works
- The use of gray areas and small moves toward your endeavor versus all or nothing at all thinking, Expect 5% more - practice 15 seconds at a time.

Albert:
Tools: Perspectives That Facilitate Uniqueness and Thinking Differently
Think differently about yourself, your worth is not based on what you do and don't do, you don't always have to be fixing things and striving, you can relax, you can lower your expectations and still do great things.
Make your own definition of perfection.
Make your own definition of being finished, of what's acceptable, of expectations.

Bea Silly:
Tools: Child-like Thinking, Humor and Play
Make it fun and play with it.
Ask yourself why you are so serious.
Ask yourself what it might feel and look like to equate joy with creativity.
Think of the uninhibited spirit of the child. Borrow permission from the liberated child to not care about being perfect.

Muse Song:
Tools: Pampering, Support and Encouragement from Self and Others
Be kind to yourself. If that's difficult, be 5% more kind or think kind thoughts just for the next 30 seconds.
Relax.
Come up with a comforting thought that you can pull out when needed. "I don't have to be perfect, I can be close enough."
Make a credit list.

Spills:
Tools: Permission to Be Imperfect, Embrace the Process, and Practice
Spills is the perfectionism-healer.
Give yourself permission to have lowered expectations.
Experiment with doing things at 40% below your expectations - see what happens.
Permission to make everything practice and to suspend judgment or practice suspending judgment even if it's 5% less judgment, or no judgment for 15 seconds).
Don't worry about not being perfect about not being perfect.
Think of places in your life where it's easy to feel joy and then apply that memory to the creative process in short increments.
Open to curiosity and discovery. Glide.

Audacity:
Tools: Build Confidence, Courage and Authenticity
Have the audacity to be comfortable with your imperfections.
Have the courage to start even if everything isn't "in place" or you don't think you know what you're doing.

Test your courage every once in awhile: What would you do if you didn't have to do it perfectly? What would you do if you knew you could do it perfectly and why not do it anyway?

Act as if you are fine with being imperfect even if it's for short periods of time.

Act as if you are courageous even if it's just 5% more.

To nay-sayings (including yourself) say, "So?"

Lull:

Tools: Taking a Break, Taking Stock, and Taking a Look at Something Different for Awhile

Take a break from: self-improvement, from any endeavor you're in.

Take stock of what's working in a way that's "close enough", of gratitude.

Make a list of all you've done today, what you're glad happened.

Shadow:

Tools: Embracing the Dark Side to Make the Light Stronger

Accept those parts of you that are not perfect, even if it's just 5% at a time more or for 15 seconds at a time.

Know that being imperfect is part of being human and you're human so it's okay.

Marge:

Tools: Small Steps, Repetition, Structure, Support

Our habit is thinking about ourselves and our environment as a jail or a paradise.
– Dr. Jay Dishman

Begin with small steps to make any of the tools above a habit.

Start very small on any endeavor in order to defy the paralysis that can come with being a perfectionist.

Take a class, pair up with a buddy, go to a workshop… LOWER your expectations of yourself…just enjoy.

Bodyguard:

Tool: Relentless protection of the idea, the time, of your creative self.

Have anchors to tell yourself when you find yourself: not enjoying the process because you're not feeling good enough, feeling pressured, working to get something perfect when you can let it go as "good enough" or "close enough."

Guard your precious creative spirit from the inner perfectionistic tyrant.

Note to Myself:
I Am Singular and Remarkable.
I Am Also Single and Marketable!

Dear Self,

Since each of the Modern Day Muses are creativity principles in disguise, you can apply them to marketing your business, your art, your writing, or yourself is filled with the magnetic forces only Muses can inspire.

They sincerely bring you the power to make marketing authentically YOU and convince you that if you are passionate about whatever it is you are trying to share with the world, and take small steps that feel like a blend of common sense and inspired intuition, you will attract all the business you need.

Aha-phrodite:
* What you focus on becomes stronger.
    Pay attention to:
    What you are passionate about. Share that passion in a genuine way.
    with joy, confidence and authenticity and people will flock to you.
    What worked in the past.
    What might work.
    What DOES work.
    Your strengths.
    What energizes you.
    Attitude and intuition and possibility.
    Your soul-intention with marketing and if you stray away from it, recalibrate:
    Do and think things that bring you back to it.
    When I trust my soul-intention and stay committed to it, I attract the customers who are perfect for me.

Albert: Tools to Be Unique and Think Different about Your Marketing-Self
* Thinking differently:
    How can I frame marketing so that it's funny, effortless and desirable?
    What makes you different? What rules are there for you to tweak to make them work for you? Or break?
    What personas can you see through in order to align your energy with effortlessness, originality, innovation and joy?

How can you treat the customer in a way that's distinctive and appreciated?

Time travel in your imagination into the future and look back to see what it is you did to successfully market your business.

Look at something unrelated to marketing to stretch the mind into a new way of thinking.

Use attitudes, personifications, points of view to think with originality.

- Attitudes

    There is enough business for everyone.   People WANT to give you money. Marketing and getting business keeps your higher purpose alive. Ask for enough money to keep you in business because we need people to share their higher purpose.

    If you stay true to your vision and your authenticity, your business will stand out from the others.

- Perceived value: Are you charging enough? Because when we ask enough, our services and products actually TAKE ON more value, energy, and motivation.

    Look at competition differently. As Marney Madridakis of Artella says, just imagine people are "running along side of you," not in front of you or instead of you. Run with them and look over and smile. The subconscious doesn't differentiate you from other people, so if you wish others well, the subconscious wishes you well. (and visa versa).

    List your marketing barriers: thoughts, attitudes, perceived limitations...

    then in your imagination, once again time travel to the future, look back and free write about how you broke through or made peace with these barriers.

- Ask questions differently:

    How will your customer find you?

    How will a client qualify for what you are offering?

Bea Silly: The Need for Child-like Thinking and Fun

- Ask: What would make this fun?
- Humor sells: how can you integrate humor into what you do and how you present yourself?
- Use your "I get to do" list instead of your "I have to do" list.
- Do kid-imagination exercises that break limitations.
- Say SO WHAT? to limiting thinking with willful inner-brat consciousness
- Make a list of absurd ideas about marketing... you'd be surprised at what brilliance is unearthed in the absurd.

Muse Song: The Essentials of Pampering, Support and Encouragement

- Who is your believing support team?
- What kind things can you say to yourself and what can you give yourself credit for?
- What compliments can you remember about yourself?
- How can you pamper yourself and treat yourself like a VIP customer of yourself?
- Who is your inspiration?
- Where are you getting it right?

Spills: Permission to Be Imperfect, Embrace the Process, and Practice

- Remind yourself you do not have to do this perfectly.
- You do not have to know everything about what you're doing in order to begin.
- Spice the process with an intention, have a soul-intention you are aiming for.
- Let it all be practice.
- Say "close enough" when you are trying to make something perfect.
- Lower your expectations at the beginning to lower the pressure trust the process will take you where you need to go.
- Lower unreasonable expectations.
- Permission to be imperfect and "close enough" To ready, fire, aim and then adjust.
- Get it out there in whatever form it's in.
- Attach intended qualities to the process.
- Let it all be practice.
- What would you do if you didn't have to worry about being perfect?

Audacity: Be Confident, Courageous and Authentic

- Dare to trust the process. When we turn from fear to trust, we also change our energy field from repelling to attracting, the catch is that you must trust that this is true.
- What strengths about yourself can you use to promote yourself? Talk about what you do well in an authentic, not ego-driven way- confidence is magnetic.
- What would it feel like to feel comfortable about asking for business, tooting your own horn, sharing your success stories?
- What testimonials, compliments, posts from happy clients or admirers, can you use to promote yourself?
- What tiny step toward audacious courage can you take today or this week?
- People gravitate to audacious, courageous people often times even when their style or talent is not as good as others. What if you had both?
- What outrageous step would just be fun to do?
- Who are you as a solution and how can you make that visible to others?
- Where was your success in the past.. How can you apply that now?

Lull: Take a Break, Take Stock, and Take a Look at Something Different for Awhile
- Let your marketing efforts go COMPLETELY every now and then.
- Take stock of gratitude and all you've done so far.
- Pause, daydream, clear, restore, renew.

Shadow: Embrace the Dark Side to Make the Light Stronger
- Write out on the page what it is you hate about marketing. Let that be okay and check with some of the other Muses to fuel your passion. How can you reframe them? See Albert for time traveling to the future and looking back to see how you overcame obstacles.
- Where can you let go of defensiveness and accept your humanness?

Marge: Get it Done Using Small Steps and Structure
- Understand the meaning of breaking it down. Small steps are especially helpful in this realm because marketing can be overwhelming. Break actions down to five minutes at a time, break steps down to minuscule expectations. You will get more done than if you overwhelm yourself and procrastinate.
    Subscribe to various methods of creating a container: partnering, coaching, mastermind groups, classes, workshops, deadlines.
    Plan events or deadlines that require action to move to the next steps.

The Bodyguard
- Protect your creative time and ideas. Believe in yourself and have affirmations and anchors that you plug in when you notice any discouraging thoughts.
- If you feel others are doing better or move than you, return to why you are passionate and what about you makes what you are doing different. Stay true to your vision.

Purpose: To use yoga to enhance the practice of creative thought and expression and to use creative thought and suggestions to enhance the practice of yoga.

Intentions of the Series:
Each Modern Day Muse lends itself to many yoga lessons. Choose quotes from each chapter to use as preludes or closing remarks before or after your practice. Use your intuition to select from the suggestions below. Keep your selections simple as not to dilute their power with too many. Yoga classes are about being present and unifying mind and body in the moment, so the suggestions below should be interspersed through-out the class lightly as not to interrupt with your or the student's union with their own inner messages.

Objectives:
- To allow the Nine Modern Day Muses to awaken your inner Muse or that of your students. To be present with the union of creativity and yoga with no attachment to results.
- To bring a creative question or questions to either the series or a particular class, and be open to the messages received

Instructions:
Here are a variety of ways you can introduce the Muses into yoga classes:

Essence of the Muse:
If you are doing a series of classes, you can begin each one by stating the essence of the Muse and asking yourself or student to embody that Muse during the practice.

Prelude and Closings:
> These are suggestions or questions meant to provide light inspiration at the beginning or end of class.

Mid-pose suggestions, questions and intentions:
> Short inspirational suggestion during yoga poses. Creative intentions can also be reminded gentle three or four times during class.
> Intentions such as from Muse Song: Let go of the struggle, embrace compassion.

Aha-phrodite
Essence:
Paying attention and Possibilities

Preludes and Closings
- Pay attention to the flow of possibilities in the mind and in the body.
- Be aware that inspiration, healing, possibility, creativity is in each and every moment. Pay attention to thoughts that court your highest purpose. Pay attention to moods that court your highest thoughts.
- Set your intention to being present.
- The seduction of an idea, the need to pay attention to the passion, the energy, the possibilities, thoughts and questions
- Paying attention to your intention, to what feels good, to the present moment, to the breath and the body moving together
- Paying attention to intuition
- What message will show up today in class or later, as a result of being present in class?
- Where will I find inspiration today?
- Anything done with focus, awareness or mindfulness is a meditation. ~ David Harp
- Don't go about here and there. Go inside and remain there. Author: Sage Yogaswami
- The source of all is abundance herself
- Be wholly present to the elsewheres of possibility.. and trust that the "how" will be made known.

Mid -pose Suggestions:
There is always a place of relaxation in each yoga pose...pay attention to where it is now.
Allow the breath to tether your attention to the present moment.
Allow the lengthening of your inhale to stretch what's available for you to receive, allow the exhale to help you release without attachment.

Albert:
The Essence:
Thinking Differently, Being Individual and Unique, Choosing thoughts that create a joy-filled existence and inner peace.
Preludes and Closings:
- I am a unique being and how I do things reflects the divine gifts I have been given.
- Rules are designed to be tweaked or broken; they give you a starting place.
- Characterize your practice today with a word and keep coming back to it (or have words on a card for people to choose from: kindness, acceptance, surrender, melting, release, compassion, joy, inner peace, love, possibility, unfolding, humor, play
- Stretch your mind and fly. ~ Whitney M. Young Jr.
- What you are thinking, what shape your mind is in, is what makes the biggest difference of all. ~ Willie Mays
- Tree Pose: When eating a fruit, think of the person who planted the tree.
  ~ Vietnamese Saying
- The unconscious is our best collaborator. ~ Mike Nichols
- "I never came upon any of my discoveries through the process of rational thinking."
  ~Albert Einstein
- "Do not exhaust yourself trying to change the world. Change yourself and your world will transform accordingly." ~ Sage Yogaswami
- "Let the beauty we love be what we do; there are hundreds of ways to kneel and kiss the ground." ~ Author: Rumi
- "People usually consider walking on water or in thin air a miracle. But I think the real miracle is not to walk either on water or in thin air,but to walk on earth. Every day we are engaged in a miracle which we don't even recognize: a blue sky, white clouds, green leaves, the black, curious eyes of a child -- our own two eyes. All is a miracle."
  ~ Thich Nhat Hanh

Mid-pose Suggestions
Twist: how can I see another angle? How can I twist and let go of the struggle.
What's something different I can discover or feel in this pose today?
You don't have to look like anyone else in yoga class.
"Mountain pose teaches us, literally, how to stand on our own two feet...teaching us to root ourselves into the earth...Our bodies become a connection between heaven and earth." ~ Carol Krucoff

Bea Silly
Essence:
The need to play with ideas, to lighten up, pairing moving with creative

Preludes and Closings

Where mentally, physically, spiritually can I lighten up?
"Don't think you have to be solemn to meditate. To meditate, well, you have to smile a lot." ~Thich Nhat Hanh
"A little foolishness, enough to enjoy life, and a little wisdom to avoid the errors, that will do." ~Osho
"Sometimes your joy is the source of your smile, but sometimes your smile can be the source of your joy." Thich Nhat Hanh

Mid-pose Suggestions
Child pose: Return to your child like innocence and feel yourself safe and taken care of.
Standing position: Swing your arms back and forth as your arms are limp like a kid who doesn't care.
Movement with the lightness of the child-like spirit.

Muse Song:
Essence: Nurturing and encouragement

Preludes and Closings:
- Touch the heart with both of your hands and feel yourself open to the great reservoirs of love you have inside.
- Surrender the struggle.
- Open to compassion and accepting.
- Allow your body to understand your breath, allow your breath to embrace your thoughts and soothe them.
- "The soul always knows what to do to heal itself. The challenge is to silence the mind." ~ Caroline Myss
- "Our listening creates a sanctuary for the homeless parts within another person." ~ Rachel Naomi Remen
- "Retire to the center of your being, which is calmness." ~Author: Paramahansa Yogananda
- "If you meditate, sooner or later you will come upon love. If you meditate deeply, sooner or later you will start feeling a tremendous love arising in you that you have never known before." ~ Osho

Mid-Pose suggestions:
The gentle head roll: allow the stretch to nurture and comfort each muscle in the neck, allow your gentle motion to allow nurture your mind and spirit in any way it needs it.
Feel where you are stretching and then melt the rest of body and mind.
If you're someone who pushes yourself too much, back off into gentle.
Think of something you love about yourself - amplify it. Make it something you would love about a child…think of yourself as a child, and send love to that part of yourself. Do this until your essence melts into that love.

Spills:

Essence: Let go of worry of perfection. Let go of attachment to the way things need to look. it's okay if you don't do it perfectly.

Preludes and Closings:
- "As long as our orientation is toward perfection or success, we will never learn about unconditional friendship with ourselves, nor will we find compassion. " ~ Pema Chödrön
- Focus on process - identify an intention for your process- joy, gentleness, discovery, present mindedness.
- Understand the practice of patience, go for close enough...open yourself 5% more toward a little more excellent.
- "Let this truth go as deep in you as possible: that life is already here, arrived. You are standing on the goal. Don't ask about the path." ~ Osho
- "Anyone who practices can obtain success in yoga but not one who is lazy. Constant practice alone is the secret of success." ~ Svatmarama, Hatha Yoga Pradipika

Mid-pose suggestions:
Remember the quality you are practicing.
Let go of the need to be perfect and enjoy what you are feeling.
It's okay to be "close enough."

Audacity:

Essence: Courage, authenticity, uninhibited uniqueness
Preludes and Closing:
- Get big during your practice today. Be expansive - mind and body. Invite in new ideas without judgment or attachment.
- Take the courage from today's practice with you the rest of today.
- Imagine testing the edges of your creative passion today.
- "When you can do the common things of life in an uncommon way, you will command the attention of the world." ~ George Washington Carver
- "Fear is a natural reaction to moving closer to the truth." ~ Pema Chödrön
- Stretching: "The personal life deeply lived always expands into truths beyond itself." ~ Anais Nin

Mid-pose suggestions:
Get big. Expand past your mental limitations.
Test the edge...experiment with moving just a little beyond what you believe your limitations to be, without forcing it.
Hero pose: Feel the power in your body merge with the power in your mind
Lion Breath: Express courage and believe that this courage is also available for your creative passion.

Big Ha!
Testing the edges

Lull:
Essence: Let go.

Preludes and Closings:
- Let go, let go of the struggle.

"Do you have patience to wait till your mud settles and the water is clear? Can you remain unmoving till the right action arises by itself?"
—Lao Tzu

"Sometimes the most important thing in a whole day is the rest we take between two deep breaths, or the turning inwards in prayer for five short minutes." "Etty Hillesum
"We too should make ourselves empty, that the great soul of the universe may fill us with its breath."
—Lawrence Binyon

Mid-pose suggestions:
"Observe the space between your thoughts, then observe the observer." ~Hamilton Boudreaux
As we breathe, pay attention to the breath in and then let go of the attention on the breath out. Allow the balance of attention and non-attention to be of less pressure.
In Savasana truly let go.
Feel the space between thoughts.
Let the body restore during the pause.

Shadow:
Essence: identity the struggle and then, let go

Preludes and Closings:
- Today practice acceptance, compassion and grace.

"Feelings come and go like clouds in a windy sky. Conscious breathing is my anchor."
~Thich Nhat Hanh

"Mindfulness is simply being aware of what is happening right now without wishing it were different; enjoying the pleasant without holding on when it changes (which it will); being with the unpleasant without fearing it will always be this way (which it won't)."
—James Baraz"

"Be creative, and the more creative you are, the more rejoicing, the more dancing, the more songful your aloneness becomes. Those periods of sadness, of grumpiness -- old habits -- will start falling like dead leaves falling from the trees. They also cling for a little while, but they have to fall." - Osho

"The more we witness our emotional reactions and understand how they work, the easier it is to refrain." - Pema Chödrön

"Yoga teaches us to cure what need not be endured and endure what cannot be cured." - B.K.S. Iyengar

"By embracing your mother wound as your yoga, you transform what has been a hindrance in your life into a teacher of the heart." - Phillip Moffitt

"Corpse pose restores life. Dead parts of your being fall away, the ghosts are released." - Terri Guillemets

Mid-pose Suggestions:
The struggle is optional… soften around the struggle.
Notice whether parts of your body not involved in the stretch are trying to help, if so just let them relax.
Remember compassion. Accept where you are and where you are not.

Marge:
Essence: gentle, small steps, developing a habit through repetition

Preludes and Closings:
"The little things? The little moments? They aren't little." - Jon Kabat-Zinn

"True happiness, we are told, consists in getting out of one's self; but the point is not only to get out - you must stay out; and to stay out you must have some absorbing errand." - Henry James

- Respond in some small way to every call that excites your spirit… even if it's just 17 seconds of appreciation for having that call.

Mid-pose suggestions:
Be gentle.
What small adjustment can you make that will change this experience mentally, physically or spiritually?

Bodyguard:

Essence: Protection of ideas, of creative time. Protection against discouragement and giving up.
Preludes and Closings

"Each time we face our fear, we gain strength, courage, and confidence in the doing.
To hold it together when everyone else would understand if you fell apart, that's true strength.
Strength comes from an indomitable will." -Mahatma Gandhi

Mid-pose Suggestions

Position the Body in a pose that evokes for you a sense of confidence and determination. Allow the posture to reflect confidence and strength. Then feel that strength both mentally and physically.

Once you have settled into the pose with breathe, attention and stillness, let the mind unify with the body's confidence and determination.

Warrior! - What idea in your life do you need to protect?

BIBLIOGRAPHY

Aha-phrodite
- *Wherever You Go, There You Are: Mindfulness Meditation in Everyday Life,*
- by Jon Kabat~Zinn (Hyperion)
- *Slowing Down in a Speeded Up World,* by Adair Lara (Conari Press)
- *The Artist's Way,* by Julia Cameron (Tarcher/Putnam)

Bea Silly
- Any Sark book: especially *A Creative Companion: How to Free Your Creative Spirit and*
- *Living Juicy: Daily Morsels for your Creative Soul* (Celestial Arts)
- *Go to Your Studio and Make Stuff* (Poster book), by Fred Babb (Workman Publishers)

Marge
- *One Small Step Can Change Your Life: The Kaizen Way,* by Robert Maurer

Shadow
- *The Dark Side of Light Chasers,* by Debra Ford (Riverhead Books)

Albert
- *How to Think like Albert Einstein,* by Scott Thorpe (SourceBooks Inc.)
- *How to Think like Leonardo da Vinci,* by Michael Gelb (Delacorte Press)

Audacity
- *The War of Art: Break Through the Blocks and Win Your Inner Creative Battles,*
  by Steven Pressfield
- *Ignore Everybody and 39 Other Keys to Creativity,* by Hugh MacLeod

Muse Song
- *The Woman's Comfort Book: A Self-Nurturing Guide for Restoring Balance in Your Life,*
- by Jennifer Louden (Harper San Francisco)
- *You Can Heal Your Life,* by Louise L. Hay (Hayhouse)

Lull
- *The Power of Now,* by Eckhart Tolle (New World Library)
- *Meditation Made Easy,* by Lorin Roche (Harper San Francisco)
- *Simple Abundance,* by Sarah Ban Breathnach (Warner Books)

Any book that is a festive diversion, or is of a style and subject you wouldn't normally read.

Excellent Books for Writers
- *Bird by Bird,* by Anne Lamott (Anchor Books, Doubleday)
- *A Writer's Book of Days,* by Judy Reeves (New World Library)
- *The Observation Deck,* by Naomi Epel (Chronicle)
- *If You Want to Write,* by Brenda Ueland (Graywolf Press)
- *How Much Joy Can You Stand: A Creative Guide to Facing Your Fears and Making Your Dreams Come True,* by Susanne Falter-Barns (Ballantine Wellspring)
- *Poemcrazy: Freeing Your Life with Words,* by Susan Wooldridge (Random House)
- *Fruitflesh: Seeds of Inspiration for Women Who Write,*
- by Gayle Brandeis (Harper San Francisco)

EXTRA PAGE TO CAPTURE INSIGHTS, EPIPHANIES, GROCERY LISTS, SCRIBBLES, MUSE ADVICE, OR TO GET STUBBORN PENS TO WORK

OTHER SOURCES OF MODERN DAY MUSE juju:

Jill Badonsky and the Muses also wrote the book:
The Awe-manac: A Daily Dose of Wonder Publisher: Running Press

For information on Creativity Coaching based on The Nine Modern Day Muses visit:
www.kaizenmuse.com

The Awe-manac Blog:
http://kaizentral.typepad.com/awemanac/

For regular Muse updates and a free monthly Muse Flash, visit:
www.themuseisin.com

Connect with The Awe-manac, Kaizen-Muse Creativity Coaching
and Jill Badonsky on Facebook